THE NEW YORK TIMES

BOOK
OF INDOOR &
OUTDOOR
GARDENING
QUESTIONS

Other books by Joan Lee Faust

The New York Times Book of House Plants
The New York Times Book of Vegetable Gardening
Around the Garden: Week by Week
Gardener's Diary

THE NEW YORK TIMES

BOOK OF INDOOR & OUTDOOR GARDENING QUESTIONS

edited by

**Joan Lee Faust and
Lisa Oldenburg**

Illustrated by Anne Koedt

Quadrangle / *The New York Times Book Co.*

To gardeners everywhere—the experts!

Library of Congress Catalog Card Number: 74-24293
International Standard Book Number: 0-8129-0538-5

DESIGN: BETTY BINNS

contents

trade
secrets

Gardeners soon find out that there are many ways of grow-ing plants—there is no one right way. Experience, trial-and-error, and an adventurous spirit are often the best teachers. Results may be rewarding or disastrous, but we all keep learning and we all become experts of a sort. It's part of the fun of gardening. Realizing that our readers were an un-tapped fount of expertise we began, as a trial balloon, *The New York Times* garden page Question and Answer column.

It was intended as a means of ferreting out all those expert tricks of the trade, growing and propagating know-how, or solutions for knotty garden problems that are never found in garden books. It was launched in hopes that gardeners, a friendly bunch wherever they are, would like the idea and would like to exchange ideas—ask and answer questions that were on their minds. The idea clicked, the response was enthusiastic, and the column has become a weekend reading habit with Sunday *Times* garden page followers.

The mail piles in. Letters average anywhere from 50 to 100 a week depending on the season and how fascinating the particular questions published. Questions selected for pub-lication are those most likely to generate reader response. Answers chosen are those written concisely and giving the best helpful information.

Questions not included are those common, general garden problems that can be answered from well-organized books and garden encyclopedias. Most frequently these are about culture. Plant growing is dependent on so many factors—climate, soil, care, region, variety, exposure, etc.—that only general answers can be given without on-site inspection. These questions are answered by return mail, however (if that stamped-return envelope is enclosed!). The answers usually suggest general helpful garden books and include a photocopy of the page referring to their problem.

Sometimes cultural questions are published, but these refer to specifically described problems: "Why do my geranium cuttings always turn black?" or "Why do my tomatoes have white spots?" or "What caused my squash plant to suddenly wilt?" These questions are published to bring out problems that may be happening in a specific season and the answers will provide quick remedies or explanations.

Sometimes questions are asked and published for which there appears to be no solution, but hopefully a reader somewhere may have found one. A case in point: A reader asked how to prevent birds from nesting in ivy growing on her brick walls. Although the family loved birds, the nests and litter were making their terrace an unsightly mess. The solution? A *Times* reader had it. He wrote that birds were afraid of snakes. Simply use a black hose to simulate a snake, attach it to the ivy in snakelike fashion, and the birds will depart.

Here's another: "How do I prevent my cats from eating all my house plants?" "Grow oats in pots," a reader suggested and the cats will leave the plants alone. This question-and-answer also provided some later amusement. A woman read the question and answer and followed the directions, but wrote to us that her planting was not as yet successful and she wondered why her Quaker oats were not sprouting. We explained to her that fresh oat seed, not rolled oats meant for breakfast cereal, was needed and that seed was available from grain suppliers or major garden centers.

Probably the most common topic is, "How do I get rid of ———" and the perpetrator could be anything from squirrels, raccoons, rabbits, neighborhood cats, muskrats or mice invading garden flower beds and vegetable plots to termites in the bark mulch. The most frequent nuisance apparently is the unleashed neighborhood dog and though the question has been published several times, the sum of the answers is, "Fencing and local leash laws."

Mystery plants are another popular topic. These are usually plants received as gifts or seen at a friend's home or on travels and the writer would like to know the name to grow a plant himself and learn its cultural needs. One mystery plant was described as "a hanging type with pale green beadlike leaves." Everyone seemed to know this plant's name and a record number of answers was received: 27! The mystery plant turned out to be none other than string of pearls (*Senecio herreianus*).

If a particularly tricky or technical answer is necessary, this information is sought and answered by the editor in italic type, just to keep the game score fair. Sometimes when an answer is published, one reader may not agree and send in a rebuttal or add some further helpful pointers. These letters are frequently included when space permits to keep the exchange of information flowing and to let everyone have his say.

Lisa Oldenburg, an avid gardener herself, has sorted through the maze of questions and answers published from 1970 up to December 15, 1974, and organized it into the splendid ready reference presented here. The book is divided into sections on indoor and outdoor gardening and within these sections, major category divisions have been made. Familiarize yourself with the table of contents. When you find your category, each question has been arranged alphabetically within it by subject so that you can run your (hopefully green) thumb down the column and find what you need. Occasionally questions stubbornly resisted the categories or seemed to fall equally well into several. A case in point is the wintering over of begonias from the garden. These can be brought into the house to bloom happily all winter and then replanted in spring outdoors. You will find this information in both the Flowers chapter and the last chapter, Other Hints. If the subject troubling you or that you are curious about is not where you might expect to find it, check the index for further help. But we hope the rationale of the book will soon become familiar enough so that you can easily locate what you need.

The puzzlements about growing will ever continue as long as there are gardeners to ask questions and gardeners to answer them. Those collected here are meant to reveal some of those secrets of the garden trade and to provide some practical commonsense solutions. If you have a question and don't see it answered here, mail it in to Garden News at *The Times*. After all, it's your column and you might as well try to stump the experts, your fellow gardeners!

indoor
and
city
gardening

plants
in pots

Q: Has anyone found a solution for African violet mite that works? I've tried sprays and soil compounds to no avail. Mrs. S. K., Paterson, N.J.

A: Marion Irizarry of Connecticut recommends, "Kelthane weekly for two to three weeks and then bi-weekly for another two or three sprays. Mites spread, so I recommend spraying other gesneriads that are close by."

Q: When my neighbor moved, I was given her collection of African violets, many of which are on long, leggy stems hanging out of the pots. What can I do to revive them? Mrs. K. L., Manhattan.

A: Mrs. James Craig of New Jersey writes that it is just a matter of shortening the plant stems. Cut off the plant from the stem, leaving about 1½ inches. Trim off lower leaves. Dip in hormone rooting powder. Obtain a clean pot and fresh soil. In the center make a core of perlite or vermiculite. Insert the plant. Water and cover with a plastic bag and new roots will form in a month. If the stems are not too leggy, merely shorten the root system and repot.

Marie Spiwak of Long Island suggests somewhat the same thing. However, she recommends cutting the stem off at soil level and rooting the plant in water before repotting.

Q: What is the secret for bloom on miniature African violets? Mrs. P. M. N., Orange, N.J.

A: Mrs. Tracy Sperley of Pennsylvania writes: "I don't know if this is a 'secret' or not but I find my miniatures are bloom-less through most of the hot summer. But when the heat

3

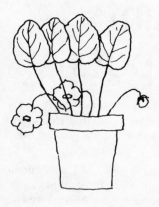

(**african violets**
continued)

goes back on in the den, where I have the plants in an east window, I start feeding with fish emulsion every two to three weeks and mist each morning. They always burst into bloom by late October and continue well into spring. Also, I repot any plants in plastic pots to clay pots as I like them better."

upright leaves

Q: My African violet leaves never spread wide and flat as they do on most of my friends' plants, but rather upright, prayer-fashion. Why? And their blooming is sparse, too, in spite of fertilizer every month or so. Mrs. O. I. G., New Jersey.

A: Mrs. R. C. Mannheimer of New York explains, "Her African violet leaves may be reaching up for more light, although the upright versus spreading out habit does depend somewhat on the variety. Sparse blooming may also be related to the light insufficiency. More frequent fertilizing with a weak solution every other watering or twice a month would help."

air fern

Q: My new plant is called an "air fern." Can anyone tell me something about it and how to take care of it? Mrs. N. H., Bronx, N.Y.

4

A: The "air fern" or miracle plant or neptune plant could be either of two filamentous aquatic animals which have been dried and dyed. Peter Puglia, a New Jersey reader, identified the "air fern" as a bryozoan, an ocean-dwelling moss animal. David Lane is a New Hampshire reader whose college zoology professor identified his "plant" as a hydroid, *Thuiaria thuja*.

air plant

Q: Years ago, my grandmother had a plant which she called an air plant. She would take leaves and hang them on her curtain and small plants would grow. Where can I buy such a plant today? Mrs. D. I., Connecticut.

A: Nina Tobier of Manhattan comes to the rescue to say that the plant referred to is *Kalanchoe pinnata*, a succulent from India, called air plant or magic leaf. New plants grow along the edges of the scalloped leaf if it is placed on some soil or on a window curtain. Most nurseries specializing in cacti and succulents will have the plant available.

aloe vera

Q: I purchased an *Aloe vera* plant to use on my skin. How do I propagate it so that I may give a plant to my sister? Mrs. A. J. K., Concord, Mass.

A: William Milau, a Long Island schoolteacher, writes, "I have had a plant in my class since September and it has propagated itself by sending up shoots around the parent plant. Just take a shoot out carefully and pot. The shoots are slow growing at first but eventually a new plant will take hold."

amaryllis
long stems

Q: Is there a way to keep amaryllis stems from becoming very tall before they bloom? Mine is almost three feet high and about to flower. C. D., Rochester, N.Y.

A: Mrs. Rita Gronwitz of Maryland writes, "It is the nature of the amaryllis bulb to shoot up a tall spindly stalk to support the flower. However, overwatering just after planting may encourage too rapid growth. I barely keep the soil moist until the flower stalk shoots up. My flower stems are about two feet high."

planting seeds

Q: I have pollinated my amaryllis bulb and now have seeds. How do I plant them to raise a new bulb? Mrs. P. H., Brooklyn.

A: Mrs. Carolyn Lipetz of Connecticut followed directions recommended by Molly Price: "The seed pod will ripen in a month to six weeks. Fresh seeds give a high percentage of

5

germination so plant immediately in a sterile mixture, an inch apart. Cover lightly. Set pan in tepid water until surface is moist. Cover with plastic and keep in a warm dim place. Keep moist. Feed lightly every two weeks. Repot individually in six months. Plants will bloom in two years."

amazon lily

Q: I have had an Amazon lily *(Eucharis)* bulb growing for about three years without blossoming. The foliage is plentiful and the soil is well drained. I feed every two months. Any suggestions? A. D. J., Provincetown, Mass.

A: Mrs. Paul Latimer of Pennsylvania writes, "Amazon lilies are content to stay in the same pot for years. They should never be allowed to go completely dormant and may be brought into bloom several times a year by alternately giving them a dry rest period followed by heavy watering and feeding. Feed every two weeks with soluble plant foot in spring, summer, and fall while blooming. Withhold during the rest period."

anemones

See Ranunculus, page 39.

azalea

Q: Last March I received a beautiful azalea which summered on the fire escape. It is healthy and looks luscious. What should I do now (November) to encourage it to bloom again? I have moved it indoors to a sunny window. Mrs. M.W.

A: Here is help from Mrs. Naomi Stein of New York. "I have had success with bringing indoor azaleas into bloom repeatedly over a period of several years. After the plant has bloomed in spring, keep it in a fairly sunny place and feed once a month with acid-type fertilizer. Water freely and spray foliage often, as azaleas require high humidity. By fall the plant should be budded. Discontinue fertilizer and keep the plant in a cool window (45–55 degrees). Continue to mist the foliage often; water the plant moderately. In early spring, move the plant to a warm, sunny location and water freely, keeping soil damp. Plant should bloom in three to four weeks."

bamboo

Q: What is the name of the bamboo that can be potted and how is it grown indoors? Mrs. M. B. M., Manhattan.

A: Maggie Doermore, also of Manhattan, writes "would a bamboo palm do? I have one that is a delight and growing well in north light. My local plant dealer gave me the botanical name *Chamaedorea errumpens.*"

Most of the true bamboos are too vigorous for pot culture. However the Oriental hedge bamboo (Bambusa multiplex)

6

can be grown in a pot where it spreads clump-type growth. Ed.

bay leaf

Q: How do I grow bay leaf plant? I have had a few failures. Clues, anyone? A. P., Brooklyn.

A: Mrs. Byram Plickett of Long Island has some suggestions. She writes, "I presume A. P. is referring to bay leaf (*Laurus nobilis*) which is the plant grown for leaves used as flavoring. I have had one for several years which I keep in a stone-floor plant room where the winter temperature is kept at about 50 degrees. Camellias and rosemary plants do well there also. All are moved outdoors to the patio in summer. The cool temperature and good light I am sure are important, as well as the moist climate provided by the stone floor."

The ancient Greeks and Romans used the leaves of this plant to weave crowns of victory for their heroes in sports and war. Ed.

begonias
rex begonias

Q: I have tried to obtain flowers on various Rex begonia plants without any success. The leaves are strong and beautiful with healthy stems. At various times I cut the tops to give cuttings to friends, and they get the most beautiful results. What am I doing wrong? M. C.

A: Mrs. E. Narr of New Jersey suggests that M. C. keep her begonias warm (75 during the daytime; 65 at night). High humidity is also helpful or try misting the leaves with a spray bottle daily. They need bright light but not sun, so a north window is fine. Keep the soil evenly moist.

rieger begonias

Q: I am having trouble with the new Rieger begonias and maybe someone knows the answer. The plants are growing well but have been totally devoid of blossoms since I bought them four months ago. They are growing in a north and east window and under lights. What is my solution? V. T. S., Clifton, N.J.

A: Frank B. Hanlon, a New Jersey greenhouse manager, writes, "If the begonias are healthy and not flowering, there are two remedies. One, begonias in general are light feeders. Regular fertilizing will cause dark, crisp foliage but inhibit flowers. Discontinue fertilizer if any has been added. Riegers are partially photoperiodic—that is they respond to day length as do poinsettias and chrysanthemums. Riegers will vegetate primarily during the summer months and flower more profusely in winter. Ideal temperature is 72 degrees with only 14 hours of daylight."

(begonias
continued)
rieger begonia mold

Q: Can anyone tell me what to do about a white mold that has developed on my Rieger begonia's leaves? Mrs. L. R. T., Manhattan.

A: *Riegers are subject to powdery mildew especially if there is poor air circulation around the plants or if their growing climate is too humid (hand misting). Diseased plants can be cut back and will resprout. Or, if the begonia can be safely isolated for a few days, Benlate or micro sulfur dust may control the problem. The variety Schwabenland Red is resistant to the disease. Ed.*

weak stems

Q: For years begonias have thrived on my kitchen window sill (southern exposure). Now the plants develop a stem weakness about one inch above soil line, wither and die. I have tried new pots, repotting, new plants, and it happens again. Help! Mrs. P. P., Manhattan.

A: Jessie Kemphill, a New York gardener, suggests that "in full sun, the begonias will grow rapidly. If pushed too much with fertilizer, weak stems could develop. Also, too much moisture or a too rich soil could cause this." She recommends potting in a mixture of equal parts of sand, soil, and humus.

wintering over

Q: Can the begonias I am now growing in the yard be grown indoors as house plants? How and when do I move them indoors? K. O., Manhattan.

A: Mary Tremble of New York writes, "Most bedding begonias make grand house plants. I select three or four of my favorite plants and pot them in four-inch pots in garden soil just after Labor Day. I cut them back a bit, keep them outdoors until mid-September, and then bring them inside to an east window. They last and bloom all year. In spring when they get too big, I cut them back again and root cuttings. The red- and pink-flowered plants carry over best for me. The whites have never been as successful."

See also Begonias, page 47.

bird of paradise

Q: Can anyone tell me how to grow a bird of paradise indoors? N. C. F.

A: Writing from Michigan, Mrs. Arthur C. German advises that she had a "bird" as a house plant brought from California and planted in a small redwood tub. Plants usually do not bloom until they are 8 to 10 years old. They require no special care except watering when soil is dry and general fertilizer, when actively growing, twice a month. Mrs. German's plant

8

bloomed several times and was kept outdoors in summer. Its demise came when it grew so large it had to be divided. The roots were "wrist size."

bloom

Q: My bird of paradise is 2 years old, beautiful and healthy, but it has never flowered. It grows in an eastern window with full sun in the morning and bright light all day. Does anyone know how to encourage flowers? G. K., Manhattan

A: Judy Morse of Connecticut suggests, "It is rare for a bird of paradise under 6 years of age to bloom. Try the following. Age 1–5: provide high light and moisture, feed with fish emulsion or seaweed fertilizer. Age 6: do not repot, give best light and adequate moisture and feed sparingly with low nitrogen. Mist daily to encourage blossom set. Patience: it may not bloom for 8 or 9 years."

Charles Clopper of Maryland writes, "It takes 12 leaves before bird of paradise will bloom. As the plant grows and forms new leaves, the outside leaves will die. When 12 leaves develop, it will split at the crown, and the next year it will bloom."

grown from seed

Q: For the past year I have been trying to start bird of paradise from seed with no success. Has anyone succeeded, and how? Mrs. K. B., Long Island.

A: Mrs. H. L. Edwards of Long Island writes, "Hang on! Several years ago I sowed a batch of Strelitzia seed and they germinated, off and on, for two years. Give them gentle bottom heat and constant humidity. Water the pot well after planting the seed, and encase it in a plastic bag kept tightly closed. The first seedling might appear in ten days or two months. Remove seedlings carefully for transplanting as they come up and reclose the bag to allow other seeds to germinate. It may take 8 to 10 years for the seedlings to flower."

Mrs. Charles Pitman of Connecticut adds, "Use a mixture of peat moss and vermiculite to germinate the seeds that are among the loveliest. If viable, they should be shiny black and the orange 'beard' should be fluffy and not appear wilted. Their roots are very long and they need deep pots."

bonsai
azalea

Q: I was given a 3-year-old azalea bonsai for Christmas. Although I have watered it faithfully, the shrub has done nothing but lose its leaves. How do I give a deciduous shrub "winter" care? Mrs. A. P. W.

A: Susan Resnick of New York writes, "Usually bonsai are kept outdoors during the winter, if you have the hardy type . . . or they are set in a coldframe. If your plant is grow-

9

(**bonsai**
continued)

ing in apartment conditions, find the coldest window in the apartment. Put your bonsai on the sill atop a metal tray filled with pebbles and water. Spray the leaves. Protect the tree from direct sunlight. Keep the soil moist but not drenched. I have heard that people in apartments keep their small bonsai in the refrigerator for a few months to simulate winter. There are numerous books and courses on bonsai and, in the New York area, information is available at the Brooklyn Botanical Garden."

suitable plants

Q: What house plants can I train for bonsai, if any? It might be interesting to try. Dr. L. K. K., Long Island.

A: Mrs. Marion R. Irizarry of Connecticut suggests the following: "Carissa is excellent, so is boxwood. Try hibiscus (keep pruning back the large leaves from the growing top), gardenia, lantana, English ivy, rosemary, malpighia. Always keep bonsai plants moist. Many do well if summered outdoors."

bromeliads
bloom

Q: My bromeliads seem to be growing well, but they have not bloomed in the two or three years I've had them. What's wrong? They were in bloom when I bought them. J. D. S., Long Island.

A: Kenneth Lazara of New York suggests, "Water thoroughly in the bromeliad's cup, then place the plant in a plastic bag with a ripe apple. Keep in bright light, but not sunlight, for one week and then remove the plant from bag and treat it normally. The apple releases ethylene gas which promotes blooming."

"I am of a different opinion concerning the answer to the original question on why bromeliads were not blooming," writes Amelia Isaacson of Connecticut. "J. D. S. asked how to make once blooming bromeliads bloom again and the apple-plastic bag treatment was suggested. These original plants that bloomed will not bloom again, but will sprout offshoots at the side which can be removed when they reach good size or when the original plant withers. The apple-plastic bag treatment mentioned by Kenneth Lazara can then be applied."

propagation

Q: I understand that the new shoots growing from the base of a bromeliad can be rooted and potted. How? Mrs. F. S. D., New Jersey.

A: Mrs. D. Meixner of Michigan writes, "The new shoots growing from the base of a bromeliad are removed when the base of the offshoot is hard and woody. To remove, break off shoots carefully but firmly from the main stem and plant in

10

small pots in bromeliad potting soil." *This mixture should be fibrous-peat, sphagnum moss, and leafmold plus some sand. Ed.*

cacti
cactus rot

Q: My friend and I have each lost three cacti recently. They appear to be thriving but suddenly become soft at the base and die. The plants were watered every six weeks. M. F., Bronx, N.Y.

A: Thomas Vallone, a Long Island reader, writes, "This appears to be the same problem I have experienced. Close inspection with a hand lens will reveal mites with a shiny spotted brown body and eight legs. They evidently feed at the base of the plant making it susceptible to rot. Either attempt to reestablish the plant by rooting cuttings taken from well above the rotted area or use a miticide such as Kelthane as a precautionary measure for new plants."

christmas cactus bloom

Q: How do I encourage a reluctant Christmas cactus to bloom? No blossoms in seven years. It is well fed, proper room temperature and watered properly. Mrs. H. K.

A: Many hints on Christmas cactus came in to help Mrs. H. K. Here are three. From Mrs. L. M. Bouchard of Pennsylvania, "My mother has beautiful blossoms on her Christmas cactus now. She does the following: After threat of frost is past in spring, she puts the potted plant on its side deep under the branches of a spruce tree and ignores it for the summer. In September, she takes the plant into her breezeway, feeds it every two weeks and waters it regularly. When too cool, she takes it indoors. The plant needs only natural hours of light in a bright room or window. No light before sunrise or after sunset. It should start setting buds about the time it's taken indoors. After blossoming, she puts the plant in a basement window, 65 degrees, with some light, but she waters it sparingly until spring."

From Mrs. J. L. Potter of New York, "In summer, I sink the pot in soil outdoors in light shade. A spell of cool weather— below 68 and above 42—is necessary to trigger flower bud set, so I do not bring the plant indoors too early. This year, it was the end of October and the plant is already covered with buds. I keep it in a fairly bright window. Be sure the plant is in complete darkness during natural hours of darkness. When I switch on the house lights, I put the plant in the basement."

From Mrs. Aron Pehr of New York, "Keep the plants cool from early October to mid-November. Keep them where they receive little or no artificial light during the fall. Don't overwater; I water once a week and have had prolific bloom."

11

If possible, put cactus on a stand outdoors or hang it from a tree. Ground contact invites the attentions of slugs. Ed.

christmas cactus bud drop

Q: Everytime my Christmas cactus *Zygocactus* gets a bud, the bud drops off. What am I doing wrong? H. S., Wayne, N.J.

A: Dr. Malcom H. Bremer of Texas writes, "I suspect that the plant is either in too warm a room or is being overwatered, or both. It prefers being a bit on the dry side at blooming time as opposed to many other flowering plants. The tendency to place it in a prominent setting when in bloom usually means a warmer room. Also, moist soil, short days, and cool nights from mid-September to mid-October promote bloom."

cochineal bugs

Q: Our desert Christmas cactus (*Cylindropuntia*) is plagued by persistent cochineal bugs. Sprays have failed. Now, I tediously use tweezers on both the bugs and my injured fingers. The cactus is a large one, and I cannot continue this indefinitely. Hopefully some reader has just the solution! R. A. L., Toledo, Ohio.

A: Although Ms. Elyse Christiansen, a Long Island reader, does not have a solution, she writes, "I would gladly trade the white fly on my avocado plant for R. A. L.'s cochineal bugs. Does R. A. L. know that these tropical scales yield a crimson dye used for wool? In Mexico and Central America, these scales are brushed from plants and killed in hot water or dry heat. Cochineal was once used to color the scarlet coats of the British soldiers."

Although R. A. L. noted sprays did not work, perhaps this reference may help. The Gardener's Bug Book by Dr. Cynthia Westcott suggests, "Summer-oil sprays have been advised for soft or unarmored scales . . . and some gardeners are using malathion or dimethoate. Sevin and diazinon are registered for control of many scale insects." Or use a cotton swab dipped in rubbing alcohol. Ed.

feeding

Q: Has anyone had experience with feeding a cactus water-soluble fertilizer? I have been told not to, but when I did feed some of mine by mistake, they seemed to respond. Mrs. O. N. P., Passaic, N.J.

A: Mrs. Eleanor Gaynor of New York does "not recommend feeding cacti during the winter months. However, when the plants are outdoors for the summer months, mine have responded favorably to feeding. Some sprouted new shoots, buds, and blossoms, too."

Cactus care depends a great deal on soil mixture fertility and the amount of sunlight plants receive. Overfeeding will produce soft, succulent stems. Ed.

grafting

Q: I am interested in grafting cacti. How is it done? L. M., New York.

A: Here are two ideas. From Ellen Pehek, a junior high school student in New Jersey, "I am doing a project on cactus grafting for school. Unrelated cacti can be grafted. Most times cleft grafting is used. A wedge is cut out of the stock or base plant. Then the scion or part to be grafted is cut off a cactus, leaving a wedge-shaped piece which will fit into the stock. This is placed in the stock and secured with soft string, such as raffia. Keep them bound until they have knit. Cacti are quite easy to graft as they knit more quickly than other plants. Ball-like or treelike cacti should be used for the stock with small cacti or branching cacti for the scion."

From Dr. Chester B. Allen of New Jersey, "Cactus grafting is easy. Both the stock and the scion should be actively growing. Two essential tools are a strong knife for the initial cut and a thin knife for the final cut. Be sure they are sterile by washing first with soap and water and soaking for five minutes in bleach solution. Secure the scion to the stock with spines from another plant and secure to the base firmly with rubber bands fastened around the pot and left in place for at least two months. Any uncovered cut edges may be dusted with flowers of sulfur."

mistletoe cactus

Q: Recently, while visiting friends in Georgia, I was taken by some hanging basket plants which were in their sunny den. My friends mentioned they were mistletoe plants. The leaves were pencil thin and looked rubbery and smooth. Does anyone know this plant and is it available up north? Ms. J. B., Manhattan.

A: Ms. Cynthia Isaacs of New York writes, "J. B. is speaking of the mistletoe cactus (*Rhipsalis cassutha*). It needs high humidity and protection from the summer sun. It grows slowly and stays small."

The plant is native to Tanganyika and derives its name from the white berries which form on this epiphytic, spineless cactus. Ed.

no growth

Q: I purchased the cactus *Cereus peruviana* more than a year ago. It was one and one-half feet high and I placed it in an eastern window. After one year, it has not grown one iota! What can I do? T. J. O., Princeton, N.J.

A: Mrs. Eleanor Gaynor of New York writes, "In early June, take cactus outdoors to a sunny south-side location, protected. Feed with house plant fertilizer, but be sure to bring the plant indoors before frost. It will grow."

caladium
carry over

Q: What do I do with my caladiums to save them for next year? M. M., Pennsylvania.

A: Marion Bakke of Long Island writes, "I have had great success with the following method. After the leaves fade in the fall, I place the plant's pot in a warm, dry, dimly lit furnace room. In spring, I take the pot outdoors as soon as the weather is warm and place it in an open, partly shaded place. The plant is fed every two weeks and watered and misted daily until the new leaves emerge."

leaves dying

Q: I have a caladium which I rest over the winter and start into growth in the spring. But each year the same thing happens: it grows three leaves and as soon as a fourth leaf appears, one dies off. Has anyone else found this and solved the problem? Mrs. S. G., Jamaica, N.Y.

A: J. T. Thompson, a Long Island reader, suggests that Mrs. S. G. probably needs to use a much more fertile soil mixture for her tubers. "One part peat moss, one part soil, and half that amount dried cow manure is what I use with great success. Or use sterilized potting soil, mix in more peat moss, and feed the tubers every other week with water soluble house plant fertilizers. Caladiums need cool shade to thrive."

camellia

Q: Our 4½-foot camellia has been growing in the living room for two years. The flower buds become plump and in February when they should open, they drop off. I mist it daily, and keep the soil moist. What am I doing wrong? Mrs. E. K., Lawrence, N.Y.

A: Mrs. A. B. Hart of New Jersey says, "Camellias need far colder temperatures than the average house can supply. I brought my camellia to bloom on a cold porch kept at 60 degrees maximum and 50 at night. But the blooms soon dropped off. A friend keeps her camellias on an enclosed porch with only enough heat to keep them from freezing. The plants bud and bloom when she moves them outdoors in spring."

Mrs. Dinah L. Foglia of Long Island suggests that it is "insufficient watering. After buds form in fall, I water copiously and fertilize generously. My plants are kept at 60 degrees in the greenhouse. And I have lost buds only when the plants became neglectfully dry. I mist only when I think spider mites are getting ahead of me."

citus plants
dwarf orange seed

Q: Is it worthwhile to save ripe seed from a dwarf orange and plant it? My children want to try it, but I don't want their hopes dashed if it doesn't work. What to do? Mrs. P. P., Madison, N.J.

A: Mrs. Rufus A. Fulton of Pennsylvania suggests, "I now have nine orange plants, started from seed. Allow the tiny oranges to ripen thoroughly, until squashy. Drop them into wet peat (they don't even have to be covered). The seeds will sprout in time. When seedlings are about two inches high, pot them separately and place where they get adequate sunlight. The seedlings grow very slowly. My plants are 24 inches tall now after two and one-half years of growth. So patience is the key. But isn't that what all types of gardening require? Every minute of it is fun."

In case there are impatient gardeners, two suggestions to speed things up: remove seeds from the dwarf orange plant, rinse away pulp and allow to dry before planting, or, cuttings can be rooted. Ed.

Pam Smyth, another New York reader, suggests, "My dwarf orange seedling finally flowered after about six years of waiting. Cuttings root quickly and flower faster."

grapefruit

Q: During the winter months, my 8-year-old started several grapefruit seeds which are now superb plants. He has asked me when he can expect grapefruit. Is it possible, and when? Mrs. W. C., Manhattan.

A: Leslie Kay Ehrlich of Connecticut writes, "The citrus plants seen fruiting in the home are the dwarf pot-type species grown from cuttings. Grapefruit grow only on large mature trees which, when full-sized, are 30 to 50 feet high. The dwarf pot citrus are widely available from house plant dealers."

lime

Q: I have a beautiful lime tree growing in a large tub. It blossoms and fruits well, but after a few weeks, the fruit falls off. Why? Mrs. E. J., Brooklyn.

A: Mrs. Mark Elias of New York had the same problem. This is how she solved it. "My miniature orange did the same thing, year after year, after I brought it indoors each fall. Lack of humidity is the cause and can be alleviated by misting the plant with water daily. These plants also require strong light and a regular feeding program with dilute fertilizer."

(citrus plants
continued)
no fruit

Q: About five years ago, I planted an orange plant in my home. The leaves have grown tall, but no oranges have appeared. The plant has plenty of sunshine and water. Why don't I have any oranges? A. A.

A: "A. A. probably did what I did," writes Mrs. Avery J. King of New Jersey. "I planted orange and grapefruit seeds for the children and thought hopefully we would have some oranges and grapefruits in a few years. No luck, but pretty plants! I have since learned that plants from seed are not fruitful. It is much more practical to buy the dwarf varieties, suited for pot culture."

orange blossom drop

Q: My dwarf orange tree is growing beautifully and flowers abundantly at this time of year (December). But the flowers soon fade, drop off, and no fruit forms. Why? J. K.

A: Harvey Jones of New Jersey suggests to J. K. that the blossoms of the orange tree should be hand pollinated. This assures development of fruit. He gently pulls the very ripe pollen (stamens) from the flowers and brushes them across the tops of the pistils of each flower. He always gets good fruit set. Or you can also use a dry, clean watercolor brush to dust pollen on the flowers.

orange drop

Q: I have an orange plant that produces many oranges which grow to the size of marbles and then fall off before ripening. What is the solution? Mrs. M. B., New York.

A: John Raider of New York suggests, "I may not have the full answer but less watering may help. The fruits may not need as wet a soil when developing or as frequent application of high nitrogen fertilizer which I know can cause leaf drop."

orange tree cuttings

Q: Can I root cuttings from my overgrown dwarf orange? When and how? D. L., Manhattan.

A: George Portmann of Long Island writes, "Orange trees are simple to root from cuttings. I put my plants outdoors June 1st, when they put on rapid growth. When this new growth begins to mature in early August, cut off four- or five-inch tips from outsized limbs. Trim off the bottom pair of leaves, and place in an azalea pan (filled with half sand and half peat mixed, or all vermiculite). Water well, cover with a plastic bag and put in a light north corner of the garden. By the end of September, the cuttings have rooted and I pot them up to use for Christmas gifts."

picking oranges

Q: How long can we leave the decorative oranges on our

miniature trees? Should they be picked off when ripe to encourage more fruit? They are so pretty! What should we do? Mrs. T. Y., Manhattan

A: Kathy Eismann of New Jersey writes, "I never pick the fruit, because it is so decorative. My tree is summered in a shady part of the garden where it blooms profusely, and in the winter it stays in a southerly window. I pollinate the flowers by hand."
For novelty, the fruits are edible, but rather sour. Ed.
However, Mrs. Margaret Brookover of Connecticut suggests another use. "I had a bumper crop of calamondin oranges in September (120 of them) and made them into the best tasting marmalade in the world. I use only the peel, thinly sliced, and two lemons and correct the amount of sugar. It takes very little cooking time and the flavor is distinctive, somewhat like tangerine."
Several whole calamondin oranges, mashed, can be used instead of orange peel in homemade cranberry sauce. Ed.

croton

Q: Is it possible to explain why a seemingly healthy, actively growing croton is only producing green leaves with none of the characteristic color? Mrs. J. A. R.

A: "My grandfather and I have experimented with croton over the past 15 years or so. I find that varieties purchased in the south tend to lose color rapidly even under greenhouse conditions. The natural sunlight in the Northeast is simply inadequate to produce colorations." Miss Elizabeth Buchanan, Connecticut.

crown of thorns

Q: I have a crown of thorns which is growing well, but I would like to encourage more branching. When and how should I prune it? Mrs. E. C.

A: To help Mrs. E. C. with crown of thorns, Mrs. Wallace Williams of Connecticut suggests her culture method: "My plant grows and blooms magnificently in a sunny cool window from late fall until spring. When the weather settles I put the plant outdoors under some trees where it gets minimum care and occasional watering. Then I prune scraggly ends back around Labor Day, bring it indoors, start feeding, and it blooms well."

cyclamen
carry-over

Q: The last blooms on my cyclamen from Christmas are just beginning to fade. Is it possible to keep it alive and have it bloom again next year? If so, how? Mrs. D. M., Lexington, Mass.

17

(cyclamen
continued)

A: Howard La Morder of Vermont suggests, "When the blossoms are gone, water the plants sparingly. By June 1, place the cyclamen outdoors in a cool, partially shaded location, preferably on the north side of the house. During the summer, keep it on the dry side. About September 1, repot the cyclamen in a well-balanced soil mixture and take it indoors to a window with good light, but not direct sun. Beginning October 1, feed once a month with liquid fertilizer. By December, the plants are in bloom again."

culture

Because of the unusual success with cyclamen, this Vermont reader's entire letter is reprinted as a help to all. Ed.

Q: I have had a cyclamen for 9 years and it has bloomed profusely twice and occasionally three times every year, with 24 to 30 blooms each time. It has produced a fruit the size of an acorn, which has matured and dried. How shall I plant it?

My plant thrives in the pot it came in; I have never disturbed it. It gets the most casual care in a cool northern windowsill. I keep the soil damp. Four years ago, I put a little dried rabbit manure on top of the soil. The corm is 4½ inches across. Several summers after it bloomed, I put it outdoors under the ferns on the north side of my house and retrieved it in the fall. I was surprised to learn that the plants are not usually kept successfully through the seasons. Mrs. John H. Howland.

A: William Fudge of Connecticut suggests, "If the seed pod does not open naturally she should cut it open for inspection and dry the seed before planting."

dieffenbachia

Q: Can anyone tell me why my dieffenbachia plants lose all but their top leaves? What can I do about it? P. R.

A: "Just do what I do," writes Margaret Fischer of New York. "Cut off the top of the dieffenbachia with a stem of about 10 inches. Put this in water for a few days; then pot it and it will root. The leftover stub of the mother plant should be cut short and it will send up a new sprout, sometimes two or three."

dizygotheca

Q: I'm about to give up with dizygotheca. I have tried sun, no sun, much water, no water, and have thus far "killed" three. Has anyone worked out the happy formula to keep this plant growing? Ms. J. K., Manhattan.

A: Here are several rescuers. Margaret Murdock, another city reader, has been growing her plant for a year and suggests, "Medium light (too much and it will scorch), medium

18

to light watering, protection from drafts and from cold in the winter, and feed in summer."

Elena Sorkin, a New Jersey reader, rescued her defoliated plant with misting.

Ida Myers writes, "All the leaves fell off my plant until it looked like a matchstick. I could not throw it out so I just let it stand and continued to water the stalk and kept it in north light. Soon a green shoot appeared. Now it's thriving."

dracaena
cuttings

Q: Is it ever possible to root tip cuttings from a Dragon tree dracaena? Ours is growing to the ceiling! Help. Mrs. S. K., Manhattan.

A: Here is a suggestion from Mrs. Joseph Sutton, a New Jersey reader. "Partially cut into the cane about two and one-half feet from the top. Insert a moistened matchstick dipped into rooting hormone. Moisten sphagnum or peat moss, wrap it around the cut and cover with clear plastic, fastened with string. When roots fill the plastic, cut the top portion from the plant and pot in soil. Cut the remaining cane into 1-inch pieces, dip in rooting hormone and place in a jar filled with moistened builder's sand. Cover jar with plastic bag and place in light, not sun. Pot the canes in soil after two leaves appear."

Edward Kurtzman, another New Jersey reader, easily roots his dracaena in water.

shoots

Q: Will the bottom bare stalks of my Dracaena marginata form new shoots if I cut off the leafy tops and root them? C. W. M., Forest Hills.

A: Mrs. F. A. Reinhart of Connecticut writes, "My dracaena was seven years old, four feet tall with a single stem and leaf cluster like a feather duster. I cut the top off, planted it in potting soil and it is growing. The original plant is sending out a shoot near the base. It is kept well watered and I think it will develop into a better looking plant."

19

Mrs. Lenore Grabowski of New Jersey adds, "I had a lovely two-foot dracaena until my toddler snapped the stalk leaving about six inches. Within a short time, two shoots appeared and are now nicely leafy although David still points to it and says, 'Broken.' "

Q: What can be done for a 13-year-old too-tall dracaena? It is one stalk and has virtually lost no leaves and is foliated, top to bottom. Two years ago it bloomed, and continued to grow upward. Air-layering midway on the stalk was not successful. It is a fine specimen (ceiling height now) and should not, I believe, be drastically cut. M. M. McL.

A: M. M. McL's query about too-tall dracaena indicates that she has an ideal environment for growing the plant. "Alas, if air-layering did not work and she does not want to cut it, the next best course is to find a larger home for the plant and start with a new 'youngster.' It's the nature of the plant to keep growing upward. She should see them in the tropics." Sandy MacQuire, New York.

Mrs. Ruth Puoti, also of New York, had a too-tall dracaena and S.O.S.'d to the local botanical garden for help. "I was told to cut it and water the plant even less than usual until new growth starts. I cut the stalk half way down and it has again reached the ceiling. The part I cut off I stuck in the earth of the same pot and it took root!"

Q: What is the correct Latin name for elephant ears? My mother once grew the plant and I would like to grow it, but none of the "elephant ears" in stores look like it. Mrs. G. T. O., Brooklyn

A: Roger W. Pease, Jr., G & C Merriam Company, New York, writes, "Based on the number of slips in the Merriam-Webster files of over 11 million citations, the commonest reference is to elephant ear, taro, or dasheen with the scientific name given as *Colocasia esculenta* or *Caladium esculentum*."

Alfred B. Graf's Exotica *lists several plants as elephant ear;* Philodendron hastatum; P. pertusum; Caladium; Colocasia esculenta; Enterolobium cyclocarpum; *and two elephant's ear ferns:* Elaphoglossum crinitum *and* Platycerium angolense. Ed.

Q: I have a large *Episcia dianthiflora* growing under lights, but it has never bloomed in four years. Why? Mrs. D. N.

A: In response to Mrs. D. N.'s non-blooming *Episcia dian-*

thiflora, Mrs. Mary Ann Zajulka of New York writes, "Episcia plants need a warm place, three to four hours of winter sun and humid atmosphere. Flowers appear in spring and summer. Water plants well and grow them in a well-drained mixture. Cut back straggly plants."

ferns
boston

Q: I have tried several times to raise Boston fern in indirect light, watering every other day to keep soil moist. But still the leaves turn brown and fall off. What am I doing wrong? M. G., Pennsylvania.

A: Sheila Gibbons of New York writes, "My two Boston ferns are thriving in a southern bay window with filtered light. I think M. G. is keeping the plants too wet and suggest soaking the pot until the root ball is well saturated about every six or seven days. I summer my plants outdoors on an open covered porch with western exposure. I feed them only in spring just before they go outdoors. These two ferns are five years old and about two feet across."

maidenhair

Q: Has anyone had success with maidenhair fern indoors? My plants wither in a few weeks time in spite of daily syringing, good strong light, and well-drained soil. Clues would be appreciated. Mrs. H. G. B.

A: Mrs. Joseph W. Ferrebee of New York has the solution: "Water every two to three days, never let them dry out and don't let them stand in water. Feed once a month with fish emulsion fertilizer and keep in light, not direct sunlight. The atmosphere should be moist, but not drafty. Repot in spring with new soil and cut off all the old fronds and save the newest. Once a month immerse pot and fern in tepid water for five or ten minutes and let drain. This is a good way to get rid of aphids."

spores

Q: What is the purpose of covering the soil mixture with tiny flower pot fragments (passed through a fine sieve) before sowing fern spores? This is advocated in several books. Dr. W. S. L., Brooklyn.

A: F. Gordon Foster of New Jersey writes, "The finely divided material is neutral and, when spread over the coarse soil, provides a smooth, flat surface for sowing the dustlike fern spores. This surface retains the dampness from the substrata and as soon as the fern spores start to grow, this barrier prevents fungal infection from direct contact with the soil."

yellowing fronds

Q: Will you please tell me what to do with a house fern that

21

has been doing well during the winter months but is beginning to yellow now (July)? I know that ferns like a shady place and I keep it out of direct sunlight. Mrs. S. M.

A: "I suggest she repot it in fresh soil enriched with compost. And then keep it outdoors in a cool shaded place for the rest of the summer." Mrs. Else Wyscksa, New Jersey.

fig plant

Q: Can anyone tell me how to raise a fig plant indoors? Mine produced two figs while outdoors last summer, but they shriveled up when the plant was brought indoors. C. H. Y., Troy, Ohio

A: Ulric Johnson of Connecticut writes, "The fig family has so many excellent indoor ornamental species—why doesn't C. H. Y. concentrate on them? My favorite is the tree species, *Ficus benjamina* or Indian laurel (*Ficus retusa nitida*). There is also the fiddle-leaf fig (*F. lyrata*) which resembles the edible fig species *F. carica*. The edible species is really more an outdoor plant in milder regions or at least a tub plant that can be summered outdoors. The edible fig must go through a dormant period after the leaves fall and is therefore not an attractive indoor display plant."

fuchsia

Q: What is the trick to making fuchsias bloom in summer? Our hanging planters are along the patio in a semi-sunny area. They bloom nicely at first in early summer, but soon wane and just produce a few leaves. Mrs. J. J. C.

A: Mrs. William Northdurft of Pennsylvania notes that early morning and/or late afternoon sun is the most fuchsias should get. Her plant receives no direct sun from 7 A.M. on and it is blooming for the fourth time this season. And remember to water well every other day at least.

Kathy Keating of Conn. offers her method: "Soil is half loam and half peat. Exposure is north. Water whenever dry and feed twice a month with fish emulsion fertilizer (if you can stand the smell)!"

wintering-over

Q: I have a beautiful large hanging fuchsia on my porch. Has anyone any practical suggestions for wintering it? Mrs. D. N. L., New Jersey

A: Two readers have suggestions. From J. Hull of New York, "In late September/early October, bring the fuchsia indoors. Start drying it out. After leaves have fallen, cut back to keep lower branches and trunk large. Place in the cellar or frost-free area and water every 10 days to two weeks. In March,

22

bring the plant into the east sunlight, then change to south and begin feeding and watering to promote growth. Do not put fuchsia outside until leaves are large and strong as they are susceptible to aphids and white fly."

From Mrs. Wilbur M. Young of New Jersey, "I wintered my fuchsia by bringing the plant indoors in late September along with other house plants left outside. It was trimmed back to within eight to 10 inches from the main root and put in a light, not bright spot. It was kept moist and fed every two weeks with liquid fertilizer. New shoots grew and, within a short time, the plant was full of new growth and ready to hang in a well-lighted place. I misted it frequently. In late May the basket was hung outdoors again, where it continued to grow and bloomed in June. I would also suggest repotting a pot-bound plant. Underwatering will cause the foliage to droop. Steady moisture is important. If new stems grow too much, trim them back to thicken the plant."

gardenia
dropping leaves

Q: In summer our gardenia is beautiful on the patio outdoors. Each fall we bring it in and then it starts to drop leaves continually all winter, never blooms, and just about lasts until May. Help! J. L., Staten Island.

A: Several readers came to the rescue. Mrs. E. B. Steffen of Connecticut writes, "I licked this problem when I began keeping my gardenia in a comparatively cool basement at a southwest window during the winter. The house is too warm for the plant. Before I bring mine in for the winter, I spray it to kill any garden bugs and feed it with acid-type fertilizer. After it is indoors, it sheds a few leaves, but then it really thrives. It blooms in January or February and again in summer. As soon as buds appear, I feed it again."

From New Jersey, Mrs. E. J. Foley writes, "I finally found the answer by having a local potter make a 20-inch dish in which I place gravel and set my plant on this. Keeping the gravel damp has kept the plant in great shape. It's 20 years old. Even the buds formed in summer continue to bloom in a light not sunny window. The original pot is set in a larger pot lined with peat moss which seems to help also."

And from Massachusetts, Mrs. Gerard Abeles writes, "Mist your gardenia (an empty Windex spray bottle works well) with warm water daily. Twice a day is even better. This is probably the most important factor in caring for gardenias indoors."

propagation

Q: I would like to know how to root cuttings from my very large gardenia plant. Mrs. M. A., New York

23

A: Here are four ideas. From Mrs. Kenneth Smeltz, "I have 100 percent success starting gardenia cuttings in a two and one-half gallon fish tank filled with a two-inch layer of pea gravel covered with a four- to five-inch layer of live sphagnum moss. The cuttings are six to seven inches long and inserted in the terrarium and covered. The terrarium was near (six inches) a fluorescent lamp kept on 14 hours daily. In three weeks, cuttings rooted in this boglike condition."

From Mrs. Robert W. Dixon, Connecticut, "I have rooted gardenias by planting them in moistened potting soil in the bottom of a tall jar, covering and keeping them in low-intensity fluorescent light for several weeks. Add water only if soil appears dry. This method worked for other moisture and acid-soil plants."

From Mrs. Sharon Stelzner, New Jersey, "The best time to root gardenias is in the spring. Use new growth that has not flowered. Strip off all but four or five leaves. Use rooting powder and put each in a premoistened peat-pot filled with damp sand/peat moss. Water each cutting and place an individual plastic bag over each. In a few weeks they will root."

From Chin-Hwa Wang, New York, "Cut a seven- or eight-inch branch with many healthy leaves. Put in water in a glass with a piece of charcoal and cover with a plastic bag. Leave it near a well-lighted window. Roots should develop in three to four weeks. Transplant into soil two to three weeks after roots start to develop."

too wet

Q: My gardenia has been thriving in a cool, sunny spot until recently—trouble! New shoots and some new leaves turn light brown, wither and drop off. I mist the plant daily and feed every month. Has anyone else solved this mystery? Mrs. T. U., Connecticut

A: Mrs. Franklin Meyer, Westwood, N.J., has some ideas. "The trouble sounds familiar. I kept pulling off browned leaves and pruning off bare branches until I almost had no gardenia plant. However, another gardenia near it was thriving—in a clay pot. (The troubled one was in a plastic pot.) I moved the plant into a clay pot and did not mist on cloudy days. Also, I let the soil dry out more before rewatering. The plant came back and is now thriving. I just think it was too wet all the time."

geraniums
bloom

Q: How do I get my geraniums to flower in winter? I have them in sun, keep them on the dry side and feed once a month. Only leaves. Clues anyone? Mrs. T. K., Bryn Mawr, Pa.

24

A: Here are two ideas. From Mrs. Jeanne Marie Adler, a New Jersey reader, "Contrary to popular belief, I keep my geraniums moist and feed with water soluble 15-15-15 fertilizer weekly. They are in south exposure and bloom all winter. The temperature should be 55 to 70 degrees, preferably with a 5 to 10 degree drop at night. I also grow dwarf and miniature geraniums under lights and on a south window sill."

From Mrs. Charles Wright, a Long Island reader, "Early in November I pot my geraniums in fresh potting soil and put them in a sunny window. I never fertilize, but water almost every day. They bloom all winter and in spring go back outside. My plants have been blooming continuously for three years."

bringing indoors

Q: How can I transplant geraniums from my city terrace into pots for use indoors? I am never successful and get only green foliage but no flowers. The indoor geraniums would have north light with about two hours of early morning sun. M. M. M., New York.

A: Mrs. Jacob Greenspan of New York writes, "Geraniums require more than two hours of sunlight in winter to flower. Overfeeding them will also prevent bloom and promote foliage growth only. I have had success with the miniature geraniums under artificial light. They flower nicely. Try those instead."

See also Geraniums, page 128 and Begonias, page 122.

ivy geranium bloom

Q: What is the "trick" for keeping ivy-leaved geraniums in bloom? Mine always stop blooming in mid-summer. Mrs. P. Y., Morristown, J.N.

A: Mrs. Thayer Morton, a Philadelphia gardener suggests the following. "Mrs. P. Y. didn't mention whether her ivy-leaved geraniums were in hanging baskets or not. Perhaps the system I have for my hanging-basket ivy-leaved geraniums may work. I find that feeding them every three weeks with fish emulsion keeps them blooming all summer. It is also important to pick off the faded flowers promptly so they do not form seed."

ivy geranium bud drop

Q: My healthy ivy geranium grows slowly but produces buds which drop off just as they are ready to open. This happened outdoors and now again in my kitchen where the plant is growing. Does anyone have a solution? Mrs. H. J. R., Manhattan.

A: J. Redington, a Connecticut reader, suggests, "Unlike

25

(**geraniums**
continued)

common geraniums, ivy geraniums do not like to dry out, nor can they withstand extremes of temperature. Mine have done well on a cool window sill with lots of sunlight. I suspect Mrs. R's kitchen is too warm."

*martha
washington*

Q: Can anyone share secrets of how to keep Martha Washington geraniums in bloom all summer? Mine bloom for about two weeks and then produce all foliage. Help! Mrs. H. G. A., Connecticut

A: Mrs. John Simpson of Virginia writes, "Martha Washington geraniums are cool weather plants. We moved here from California where they flourished in the Bay area. When I was unsuccessful to get them to bloom here in the East, local nurserymen told me that these geraniums will not set flower buds unless the temperatures are below 60 degrees. Friends in Maine grow them nicely, and that is another clue to their climatic preference."

propagation

Q: I would appreciate some help on rooting geranium cuttings. I have tried rooting them in water and in moist soil without much success. E. R. A., New Jersey

A: Here are many good ideas. From Mrs. John Boning of New Jersey: "Break off cuttings from original plant, remove all but three or four leaves and allow to rest three to five days to allow a callus to form. Dip ends in rooting hormone

26

and insert in damp sand or vermiculite. Cover with a plastic bag and if too much moisture forms, remove plastic at intervals. We have had complete success with this method and it's especially good for rooting scented geraniums."

Mrs. D. K. Z. of California suggests the same method but adds "Locally, we break off a piece from the geranium, stick it into the ground and water. Fifty percent of the time, they root."

Dr. David Greene, of upstate New York, has success rooting in water by "taking a healthy shoot, cutting it off about six inches from the tip and letting it dry out for 30 minutes. Remove the bottom leaves and put stem in water. Pot when roots form." Miss A. Gussow of New York also roots geraniums successfully in water, but adds, "It is important to keep the cuttings in full sun and to keep enough water in the containers so they do not dry out. I make a clean cut about ½-inch above the node."

Clemence Feihel, also of New York, has a trick for rooting them in soil. "The secret is to dip cuttings in hydrated lime first, then put them in sterilized soil. The lime keeps them from rotting."

rose geranium

Q: I have tried unsuccessfully to grow cuttings from a rose geranium, either in water or in soil. Can someone help please? Mrs. L. L., Manhattan.

A: Here are two ideas. From Mrs. E. L. B. of Connecticut: "After making rose geranium cuttings, let them dry for 4 to 5 hours (the leaves may wilt, but they will revive). This drying forms a hard dry scab. Then immerse in water and they will send out roots and can be potted."

From Eve Amir of New York: "I root cuttings in summer in rich garden potting soil kept moist but not wet. In winter, they will root in sharp wet sand or with less success in a mixture of sand and peat moss."

stem rot

Q: During the last four months, three of my geraniums have developed what I call stem rot. The new green growth topples over where the brown area and new green growth meet. Examination of the stem shows most of it has been eaten away by a black crud. What is this and how do I prevent it? E. W.

A: Steven A. Frowine, a graduate student at Cornell University writes, "The 'black crud' referred to by E. W. is commonly called blackleg. This is a disease usually caused by a fungus pythium and is found most commonly in soggy, poorly drained soils. This fungus can be controlled by raising

27

cuttings in sterilized soil or by dipping the ends of the cuttings in a fungicide such as Zineb or Captan. If the disease is found in a mature plant no control is effective. Discard it."

ginger root
culture

Q: Someone gave me a piece of ginger root which I planted and is now growing like a beanstalk. It is already three feet tall. Can it be pruned so other shoots will grow? Mrs. E. B. M., Manhattan.

A: Dr. David N. Teller of New York answered with this lengthy, but helpful, dissertation on ginger culture. "Most edible ginger root sold in Oriental or Latin American sections of the city is *Zingiber officinale*, the common ginger, originating in tropical India and the Pacific isles and now widely disseminated in the Caribbean and tropical America. It requires strong light and high humidity, normally growing 2 to 4 feet high from a shallow root system. It will tolerate temperatures from 50 to 95 degrees in moist, porous soil. The pot saucer may be kept filled with water as long as the rhizome does not rot. New shoots appear as small 'eyes' or buds on the rhizome. Their development can be stimulated by a 100-watt incandescent bulb shining one foot above the pot for six hours after the sun has stopped warming the soil. Feed with composted cow manure or sustained-release house plant fertilizers. Trimming the mature shoots does stimulate secondary eyes to break out, while staking the main shoot encourages flowering."

sprouting

Q: How can I sprout ginger root in an indoor garden? I understand it produces a lovely tree. We have tried keeping it in the dark, soaking or potting it and watering well. No luck so far. Clues anyone? Mrs. M. F. O., New Jersey.

A: Mrs. Robert Nelson of New York comes to her rescue. "I have often rooted ginger successfully by potting it in rather fluffy soil containing a good amount of perlite and either peat or sphagnum moss. Choose a piece of ginger which contains at least two eyes, shiny yellowish bluntly pointed areas on the same side of the root. They should be planted facing upward in the pot as the resulting plant comes from these areas. Keep it potbound to encourage growth. As more root develops, cut off bits with a sharp knife for cooking use."

gloxinias
under lights

Q: Can anyone tell me exactly how much light is needed, and how close to the top of the plant, to persuade gloxinias to bloom under fluorescents? If the light is too close, leaves burn; if the lamp is too high, the plant sends up lanky stems

28

which bud when the plant is two to three inches from the lamps. Mrs. H. L. E.

A: Mrs. Wendy M. Kessler of New York suggests the following: "I have successfully brought a white gloxinia to the blooming stage for three years by placing it 7½ inches from the tubes. I have also noted that different colored gloxinias react differently to the same intensity of light."

herbs

Q: How can I set up a means of growing herbs in my apartment? It would have to be a window box or tray as I do not have space for hanging plants. Do I start with seeds or plants? Mrs. F. B., Brooklyn.

I live in Manhattan and have tried to grow herbs in pots, especially mint, basil, and chives. But they only last a few weeks and fade away. If anyone has any special tricks, or favorites they grow with success, I'd appreciate some tips. Should I start with seeds or plants? Mrs. J. J. L.

A: Caryl Hudson, another city gardener, writes, "Many herbs can easily be grown in an apartment with any exposure except north. They will keep you supplied with fresh fragrant herbs, year-round. I have grown all of mine from seed in ordinary soil with a layer of stone beneath for drainage. The containers—clay, plastic, holes, no holes—it doesn't seem to matter. On a east-facing windowsill I grow chives, sage, anise, tarragon, thyme, parsley, and basil (a 5-year-old plant). Parsley is slow and a bit difficult. All herbs benefit from frequent use. When cutting, I do it to promote branching. They should not be allowed to flower."

From Mrs. Lydia Saiger of New York: "I grew chives, mint, and parsley from young plants in a Manhattan apartment with great success. I used commercial packaged soil, and placed the plants in a sunny windowsill with direct southern exposure. The plants required daily watering, frequent repotting (they grew rapidly and became root-bound), and trimming. I trimmed the plants when they needed it and stored the trimmings in plastic bags in the refrigerator.

And from Mrs. Adrienne Lind of New York: "Chive and basil can be grown from seed and mint can be purchased as plants. All three plants need adequate water, but not drenching, and I spray the leaves during the winter with water as the room heat dried the plants quickly. Use fertilizer at least once a month and keep mint out of direct sunlight."

hibiscus

Q: I have been growing an hibiscus plant indoors for eight months. Though it is thriving it never blooms. Clues anyone? E. L., Syracuse, N.Y.

A: Here are some ideas from Mrs. R. T. of Flynn, Long Island. "Pinch the soft cluster of new growth. I had three hibiscus in my garden room with the same problem and they responded so well to the pinching that they are always full of buds."

From Robert Randall of Pennsylvania: "Hibiscus grows indoors for a year or so before it will bloom. They need a lot of light, frequent watering, and some fertilizer."

hoya

Q: What is the trick to making hoyas bloom? I have a magnificent plant, about six years old, that forever puts out new lush growth and long graceful arching stems, but never a bloom. Hopefully, is there a solution? H. B. B.

A: Mrs. Eric W. Burgher of New York hopes that this will be of some help to H. B. B. "We have always read that hoyas need a fairly warm, 60–70 degree, moist temperature. But I am not sure that they are particular to culture. We have grown hoya with prolific bloom in a fairly cool northeast bay window for a number of years. We water it infrequently, but fertilize it with a weak 15-30-15 solution in the spring. Two important factors: The plant is pot bound and we never remove the flower clusters but let them drop from the plant. The new flowers develop from the same point, either in several weeks or the following year. Our success has been a case of benign neglect."

impatiens

Q: I have tried unsuccessfully to get impatiens to bloom indoors. I dig plants from the garden in fall and they produce numerous buds, but they always fall off before they open. Has anyone solved this curious problem? Mrs. D. D., Morristown, N.J.

A: Derek Van Dik of Vermont writes, "We have never had difficulty with impatiens indoors; they never stop flowering. We dig garden plants of medium size and pot them in sterile potting soil on Labor Day. They are kept in a sunny window and misted with water every morning. Leaves drop for a while, but new ones come on and by October flowering starts and continues through winter."

ivy

Q: All summer long my ivy plants have been beautiful in the house. I give them a lukewarm shower every few days, keep them in an east window, and the soil is watered when dry to the touch. Now, every so often, stems blacken near the nodes and whole bits of foliage and stems wither. What's wrong? Mrs. J. K.

30

I do not seem to have much luck rooting ivy in water or growing it in water. My grandmother did it all the time and I have had no results. Clues anyone? Mrs. M. McN.

A: Mrs. Jonathan David of New York suggests Mrs. J. K. may be overwatering and misting too much. "Perhaps if she allows the soil to dry out a bit in between waterings, this may help."

To help Mrs. M. McN. on rooting ivy, Mrs. H. C. Nelson of New Jersey suggests rainwater while Mrs. Douglas J. Grant of New York suggests putting ivy in a glass container so that light reaches the roots and keeping the container on or near a windowsill.

jade plant

Q: My jade plant (Crassula argentea) is 12 years old, growing in a southern window, and in fine condition. But it doesn't flower. Can anyone suggest a way to encourage blooms? Mrs. W. D. M., New Canaan, Conn.

A: Mrs. Philip Spigner of Long Island suggests, "Reduce water in the fall and do not water at all during the winter months. During these dormant months, keep the plant in a sunny location during the day, but cool spot at night (40 to 60 degrees). A southern exposure window without a storm panel is excellent. Start watering and feed the plant in March for summer bloom."

lichee plant

Q: Several months ago I was given some fresh lichee nuts from Hawaii and was told to save the seeds to grow a beautiful plant. I saved three seeds. Now what do I do? Mrs. E. H., Brooklyn.

A: Here are two helpful points. From Professor Carl Withner of Brooklyn College: "The seed must be planted fresh and not allowed to dry first. Many tropical plants can be grown from seed provided it does not dehydrate. The seed seems to lose its viability fast if dried."

From Dr. Stephen J. Danziger of Brooklyn, "I have been successful in growing them on two occasions. Fresh lychee can be bought in Chinatown in June and July. After enjoying the fruit, I plant the seed horizontally into potting soil and after several days the first shoot appears. Keep the soil moist and the plant in a light area, but not direct sunlight. About once a week, mist the leaves. The lovely almond shaped leaves are in pairs and are pale at first. Then the color deepens."

This fruit is known botanically as Littchi chinensis, particularly prized by the Chinese. Ed.

lily (easter)

See Lily (easter), page 131.

lily-of-the-valley

Q: I have tried without success to force lily-of-the-valley pips dug from the garden. I planted them in soil, peat moss and sand, and tried fluorescent light and a heating cable. They didn't grow. Why? R. J. B., Long Island.

A: The reason R. J. B.'s plants did not flower was his failure to pre-chill the pips. Pips sold commercially for forcing have been chilled at below freezing temperatures for at least three months before sale. Ed.

mango plant

Q: I understand that plants grown from seed of the mango fruit are attractive house plants. I have tried a number of times to grow the seed with no luck, both water sprouting as with avocado, or planting directly in soil. Clues anyone? R. P.

A: Many successful reports of growing mango from seed have come in to answer R. P.'s question. Here are a few replies. From Mrs. Charles Gager, a Long Island reader: "First remove the coarse outer husk of the mango seed with kitchen shears. Place the inner "bean" in an upright position in a mixture of garden soil and potting soil allowing the sprout portion of the seed to protrude one-quarter inch above the soil. Keep the pot in a sunny location and water it daily during the rooting period. Dark red leaves soon appear which change to shiny green as the mango plant matures. A handsome plant, fun to grow."

And from Mrs. Edward Levy of New York: "Clean the pod which contains the seed by rinsing in cold water and rubbing with a stiff bush. Let it dry for a few days, then find the softer end of the pod, cut open, and remove the seed. Plant it in a container with moist vermiculite and cover the whole pot with clear plastic wrap. When the seed sprouts in a few weeks, transplant to soil."

And from Louis Blume of Long Island: "I have had the same frustrating experience as R. P. with mango until I learned that you need really fresh mango as the seed loses its potency rather quickly. Using a seed from a barely ripe fruit in top condition, I planted it outdoors and it came up surprisingly fast. The tap root is long, so the plant must be dug up carefully and potted in time to bring it indoors."

From Josephine Morris, a New York reader: "Clean the husk of the seed by rubbing with a stiff brush. Let dry for a few days. Cut the pod open and remove the seed. Plant in moist vermiculite, allowing the sprout portion of the seed to

32

protrude one-quarter inch. Put the container in a closed plastic bag and keep out of the sun. When the seed sprouts in a few weeks, transplant to potting soil. Keep it in a sunny place and dark red leaves will soon appear. These will change to shiny green as the mango matures."

Mrs. Paul DeLuca, a Long Island gardener, has been experimenting with mango for several years and finally succeeded in this way. "Let the pod dry for a few days. Then open and remove the seed. Put two toothpicks into the slender end and suspend in water, wide end down, just as you would an avocado pit. In a few weeks, two purple shoots begin to form. My plant is about two months old and has three shoots with six leaves on each shoot. When the plant is about four or five inches tall, I will plant it in the soil. It receives morning light, and every time the water appears cloudy, I put in clean water."

narcissus

See Paperwhite narcissus, page 36.

norfolk island pine

Q: I was recently given a Norfolk Island pine, about four feet tall. What are the particulars about growing this beautiful tree? I should like to keep it out of doors while the weather is nice and bring it indoors for the winter. Mrs. K. N.

(norfolk island
pine continued)

A: To answer Mrs. K.N.'s question on growing Norfolk Island pine, E. King Graves of New York writes, "We have grown one of these lovely trees for about six years. It reaches six feet. During the winter it was kept in a pot and tray of pebbles in the living room, watered once or twice a week and fed monthly with dilute house plant fertilizer. Once or twice a winter, we gave it a shower bath in the bathtub. In May we sunk it into the ground by the bird bath where it thrived. But bright sun burned it one year, and we chose a more shaded spot. The plant is brought indoors mid-September."

too wide

Q: My Norfolk Island pine is three years old and growing wider on the top leaves, but not growing upward! What is the solution? B. H. L., Manhattan.

A: Mrs. Leo Waxman, a Westchester County reader, recommends, "I spray mine with water once a day at the top center of the stalk. I use an old-fashioned Windex bottle and it is growing steadily taller as it grows broader."

However, Mrs. Teddy McQuerry, a Rhode Island reader, found another solution. She writes, "My plant was doing the same thing. I knocked it out of the pot to see if it was rootbound and only a few tiny roots showed. So I put it back in the same pot and grew it for another year. Still no results. So once again, I knocked it out of the pot and fingered the soil a bit. What I found was a large heavy root balled up inside and covered by the soil. It was potbound and needed space to grow. So I immediately repotted the plant and in almost two weeks, a new shoot started to push up. Now it is doing gloriously."

olive trees

Q: Is it possible to grow olive trees indoors from a ripe olive? J. A. M., Riveredge, N.J.

A: If J. A. M. has access to tree ripened fresh olives that have not been processed, he might find the adventure of starting an olive tree from seed worth while. However, any olives, green or ripe, that have been pickled would not have viable seed. Fresh olives are intensely bitter, and they are soaked in lye before processing, washed, salted, and put through high temperatures for canning. Ed.

oxalis

Q: My *Oxalis bowiei* keeps growing and blooming and I am told that it must have a dormant rest period. When and how? F. O. D., Manhattan.

34

A: Mrs. Jennifer Tressman of Illinois suggests, "Oxalis are prolific during the winter months and into spring. They should be allowed to bloom as they will. My plants slow down in summer and leaves yellow. Then I let them rest by withholding water. Pots are kept in a cool corner of our garage. In September I knock the oxalis tubers out of the clay pots and find they have usually multiplied many times over. Repot in fresh soil and start growing again."

palms
germinating coconuts

Q: I have been told it is possible to grow a ripe coconut into a plant. If this is so, how? D. A., Brooklyn.

A: Gerald Evans of Long Island writes, "My experience might be of some help. During a recent trip to Florida, my wife and I happened upon a fallen coconut complete with shell and with two small roots extending from one end and a small sprouted leaf on the other. We carefully brought it back in some native sand and, after researching, planted it about ¾ under the earth in a 14-inch pot in a mixture of sandy soil, potting soil and peat moss. It is watered about twice a week not so much in the soil as right into the area where the shoot extends out of the coconut. (I must admit we do talk to it occasionally). We keep it near a huge window with natural light during the day. We must be doing something right since our Royal Palm is now almost 1½ feet tall and growing about an inch a week."

To germinate a mature coconut, the husk is removed and the seed is covered about half or more with soil and kept moist. Seeds need warmth (80 degrees) to germinate. Ed.

palm stones

Q: A friend recently brought me some palm tree seeds, like little coconuts, with husks on them. Now what do I do? Mrs. W. DeP., Parsippany, N.J.

A: Malcolm Muggeridge of Maryland writes, "There are so many kinds of palms that, without proper identification of the type of seed Mrs. W. DeP. has, I can just give her general clues. Most palm seeds (stones) are slow to germinate and should be soaked for a day in water. They require a deep sandy soil mixed well with rotted compost. The seeds can be placed in one clay pot—about five-inch size—to germinate. Keep the sandy mixture moist and put the pot where it will get good bottom heat, as on top of an old-fashioned radiator. Most palms are slow to sprout; when they do and reach a size large enough to handle, transplant the seedlings to individual pots, at least three-inch size. Keep them in a warm bright place to flourish."

35

paperwhite narcissus

Q: My paperwhite narcissus is just about to bloom. How can I take care of it until spring to plant it outdoors? J. P., Madison, N.J.

A: The paperwhite narcissus is not hardy in this region and would not survive the winter months. The bulbs are inexpensive and quick flowering and should be discarded once forced into flower indoors. They will not rebloom. Ed.

philodendron
split-leaf

Q: My beautiful split-leaf philodendron has new leaves, but none are split as are the older leaves. What am I doing wrong? Mrs. E. W., Brooklyn.

Rooted cuttings from my split-leaf philodendron have smooth leaves. None are split. Is the ability to split leaves left behind in the mother plant? P. G., Maine.

A: Maurice Reiger of Long Island writes, "The problem is common. In the natural tropical growing climate, this plant has abundant moisture and filtered light which promote good growth and the natural "split" in the leaf. Indoors in homes and apartments, the atmosphere is hot, dry, and warm and there is often too much or too little light. Cooler room temperatures and daily misting may help."

Mrs. Richard E. Kuehne of New York adds, "That may not be the whole answer. I have found that as long as the leaves receive direct support, they will split. I finally had to resort to a somewhat ungainly tree branch which I inserted in the pot behind the piece of bark, and fastened the leaves to it. To put it simply, no support, no split."

Another answer is simply lack of age. The older, more mature leaves of this plant will split if the humidity and light levels are sufficient. Ed.

pineapple plant

Q: Please tell me how to get a pineapple plant to produce fruit. Mrs. W. M. S., Melville, N.Y.

A: Mrs. William Knopfle of Maryland achieved fruit on a rooted pineapple top. She kept her rooted top outdoors on a sunny patio in summer. In the spring, she used the apple method for bromeliad bloom (placing an apple on the soil and enclosing the plant in a plastic bag for a week to 10 days.) Her plant soon developed a long shoot which bloomed and produced a small pineapple. Mrs. Knopfle cut off the small top plant which is now growing in water in a small jar.

The edible pineapple, Ananas comosus, bears a fruiting head on top of a straight stiff stem, and is field grown. The dwarf pineapple (Ananus) mimics the field species and can

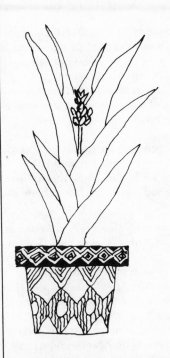

be grown in four-inch pots although the fruit is not edible. New fruits can be encouraged by planting suckers which form at the base of the mother plant after fruiting. Ed.

pineapple top

Q: How do you raise a plant from a pineapple top? M. B. K.

A: Here are two methods. From Mrs. Judith Quehl, Jr., of Connecticut, "Pick the nicest-looking pineapple from the grocer's bin; saw-toothed edge ones are preferred. Cut off the top and remove carefully all bits of pineapple pulp. Put pebbles or small stones in the bottom of an attractive bowl and place the pineapple top securely on these and fill with water to the bottom leaves. The pineapple will grow with no further attention. The plant prefers shade to sun. In summer, I move it outdoors under the shade of the apple tree. It's now about two years old and produces new leaves from the center. Bottom leaves may rot and are occasionally removed. Only once did I move a water-grown pineapple to soil, and it stopped growing. I've stuck to water."

And from *News and Views* of the American Horticultural Society: "Grab the pineapple top before it's thrown away,

37

making sure there's still an inch of the fruit attached. . . . Trim the flesh away to hard stringy tissue. . . . Dry for two to three days to promote formation of protective layer. . . . Insert the pineapple into African violet soil mix, placing the bases of the lowest leaves level with the soil surface and stake upright. Give plant sufficient light, not sunlight. . . . Let soil dry out before rewatering."

poinsettias

Q: I received two poinsettia plants last Christmas which thrived until April. I planted them outdoors and both are growing well. Can someone tell me about the dormant or light period needed to bring them into bloom for December? Mrs. J. R. H.

A: Poinsettias, like chrysanthemums, are short-day plants. That is, bloom sets when the days are shorter. This phenomenon is called photoperiodism. Poinsettias that have been outdoors all summer should be brought indoors by October 1, and trimmed back a bit to put them in shape. From then until the end of November they must have a short day. Keep them in a room that will be absolutely dark from 5 P.M. until 8 A.M. the next morning. This forces flower bud setting. If a light is turned on near the poinsettia for just a minute, it will not bloom. If there is no dark room, cover it or put the plant in a closet after 5 P.M. and don't forget to take it out at 8 A.M. in the morning. Ed.

pomegranate
grown from seed

Q: Will seeds saved from my pomegranate grow indoors, and how would I take care of the plants? L. B., Brooklyn

A: Robert Kurtz of New York writes, "Yes. Plant the darker brown seeds, but discard the white seeds which are not ripe. Eight years ago I planted some and I was amazed at the rapidity of germination. Mine were planted in ordinary garden soil around November and grown in a southeastern basement window. I grow mine for bonsai. They are dropping their leaves now (November) and I will water sparingly until new leaves appear in February or March."

wintering-over

Q: For the past three years, I have been coaxing a pomegranate raised from seed. It is kept outdoors in summer and brought in for the winter, when it sheds its leaves and puts out new ones in March. Can I keep this plant outdoors in winter in Michigan? Dr. D. N. S.

A: George Horne of Massachusetts writes, "The tree is strictly a southern tree and would not winter over above Maryland and possibly the Philadelphia–Jersey shore area. If he has a cool greenhouse, he might have success fruiting it there. Otherwise, keep it indoors in winter and prune it occasionally to keep it in bounds."

ranunculus

Q: Is it possible to grow ranunculus and/or anemones in Connecticut? I have planted them in spring and fall with winter protection. Results were poor. Is there a secret? Mrs. H. MacC., Connecticut.

A: Mrs. Wallace Briganne, another Connecticut gardener writes, "If she has a greenhouse or a large coldframe, yes. But these lovely flowers are 'temperamental' as far as temperatures go and they are not winter hardy, especially north of New York City."

However, Mrs. D. T. Moeller of New York says it can be done without a coldframe. She writes, "I would like to share my good experience with you. I first grew ranunculus in California and have been frustrated many times trying to grow them here. I tried one last time with success. Bulbs were ordered and arrived April 1 with complete instructions. They were planted, claws down, two inches apart and covered with one inch of fine soil. Six to eight bulbs were placed in a deep six-inch pot. They were watered moderately and placed in a cool place to root. In two weeks, they came up, and they were set out on the porch. On frosty nights, I brought them in. Directions said sunny place, temperatures no more than 50 degrees. Plenty of light, air, and water freely. Now they are coming into bloom. I suspect starting them early, and bringing them in on cool nights, watering well, and watching them on hot sunny days are the keys."

redwood burl

Q: I am growing a redwood burl that I bought in the Muir Woods, California. It has 12 or 14 fernlike sprouts, but no roots. Can I plant this in soil to keep it growing? Mrs. A. B.

A: Mrs. Cadwell Tyler of New York suggests to Mrs. A. B., "I have had several redwood burls which have lasted well over a year indoors. I have never been able to root them though I have tried various ploys. Do not give the burl direct sunlight and only keep it wet at the bottom. Sprinkle the foliage from time to time."

However, two successful reports of rooting redwood burl have come in to help. From New York, Mrs. Goddard Bauer writes that she planted her burl shallowly in a pot of well-drained soil when the leafy shoots showed signs of dying. The top of the burl should be exposed. Place the pot in a plastic bag to keep the moisture high; ventilate now and then

39

until rooted. After three years in a pot, Mrs. Bauer's tree was given to an estate where it would get good care.

Also from Manhattan, Mrs. Frederick Chance tells of her success. Her burl started to root in the bowl after she settled it in perlite. She misted the leaves frequently. She read that redwoods are shallow rooted and after limited success, she potted the rooted burl shallowly and covered it for some part of the day with a plastic bag to keep it moist. It is now lush and beautiful. She keeps the soil very moist and feeds occasionally with dried manure. This winter she will keep the redwood on a cool, glassed-in terrace.

roses, miniature
bloom

Q: What is the secret to get miniature roses to grow and bloom indoors? My plants last only a few weeks and die. Mrs. O. P. P., Delaware.

A: Mrs. B. A. O., New Rochelle, N.Y., has an answer: "Plant the rosebush in a mixture of two parts potting soil, one part peat moss, one part sharp sand. Just under the roots, sprinkle ½ to 1 teaspoon of steamed bonemeal instead of using liquid plant food. Prune back just enough to encourage new growth. Don't overwater and give full sun only in winter months. Don't allow the rosebush to grow too large and it will live longer. Prune it all the way back at least once a year."

Helen Humphreys of New Jersey adds, "I think the secret is a large deep pot. We repotted our miniature into a six-inch pot and it started to grow immediately. Soon blooms appeared and it has been blooming steadily since last spring."

Miniature roses also grow well under fluorescent lamps. Ed.

propagation

Q: Has anyone solved propagation of miniature roses? G. F., Mendham, N.J.

A: Joseph Schaefer of Long Island describes his method. "Cut off a three- to four-inch tip of a vigorous shoot, remove the lower leaves and dip in a rooting hormone. Set cutting on a tray of sand or peat moss/sand/perlite combination or in a jar of water to root. Mist once or twice a day so cutting does not dry out. Roots should develop in two to three weeks. Plant in two-inch pots in a mixture of equal parts perlite, peat moss, and potting soil. Pinch off tip growth to encourage branching."

rubber plant

Q: My rubber plant buds beautifully at the top, but the larger leaves toward the bottom fall off. Why? Mrs. E. H., Manhattan

A: Susan Umbarger of Massachusetts had the same problem and solved it by tossing out the old plant and growing a new plant from seed. She used seed of *Ficus macrophylla* and finds it closely resembles the common *Ficus elastica*.

As long as new leaves keep coming out, a large foliage plant is in good growing condition. Loss of lower leaves is caused by old age, adjustment from grower's greenhouse to home environment, or "pushing" of growth with too much fertilizer. Ed.

schefflera

Q: What can I do about a schefflera that has stopped growing? It's about three years old, under three feet tall, green and healthy. I transplanted it from a 6-inch plastic pot to an 8½-inch plastic pot because some of the healthy green leaves started falling off and I thought perhaps the pot was too small. Anything wrong? Mrs. I. D.

A: "I think I can tell her what is wrong," writes Mrs. Patty T. Smith of New York. "I did the same thing and my nurseryman told me I overpotted my plant. In other words, the schefflera likes to be a tiny bit potbound and I transferred my plant to too big a pot before it was necessary. After I repotted the schefflera, it stopped producing any new leaves for almost a year. It took patience, but now it is growing strongly. The plant spent a year growing roots in the pot, not leaves on the top."

shamrock

Q: I want to grow tiny pots of Irish shamrock for a children's party next year. None of my catalogs lists shamrock seed. Does anyone know where I can get it? Mrs. L. M. O., Dover, Del.

A: *Many seed companies sell "Shamrock" seed which would do fine for Mrs. L. M. O.'s party, either Burpee, Park, or Mellinger's. To be technically correct, no one really knows for sure what the true Irish shamrock is. According to Taylor's* Encyclopedia of Gardening *there are three choices: common white clover* (Trifolium repens), *wood sorrel* (Oxalis acetosella), *or a non-horticultural species of white clover* (T. dubium). *Ed.*

James A. Dougherty of Connecticut offers these tips on raising shamrock from seed. "Shamrocks are easy to grow but don't pour water on the soil or allow the top of the soil to become wet or muddy because the stems are very thin and if they get wet, collapse. To water, apply a little around the edge of the pot or water from the bottom and allow water to seep up into the soil through the drainage hole."

41

succulents
bloom

Q: I have two window greenhouses, southeast exposure, with a collection of succulents growing in them. Because of a roof overhang, these plants receive more sunlight in winter than in summer, but they bloom in spring. I would like them to bloom in the winter only. Is there any plan of watering/ feeding that could bring this about? Mrs. E. E. C., Syosset, Long Island

A: Mrs. B. Ortiz, a Westchester County gardener, writes, "Most succulents set their buds during the last part of their waterless period, which in nature is also a time of very short daylight hours. If they are not given winter rest, they usually refuse to bloom. Some winter-blooming succulents are: sedum, *Stapelia noblis*, *Neochilenia napina*, and the kalanchoes."

watering

Q: How often do you water succulents? If I don't water my plants for several weeks, they wither. Then when I do water them more often, their stems blacken and become squashy! I'm ready to give up! R. T., Bronx

A: Mrs. Phyllis Goldblatt of New York says, "He is subjecting his succulents to feast or famine. I water my succulents once a week, in the morning, with warm water . . . just enough so that the surface soil looks almost dry shortly afterwards. Most of my plants are at least 10 years old or cuttings from original plants. They are at east or west windows and are misted occasionally with warm water."

tulips

Q: What do we do to get bulbs such as tulips that we are forcing this winter to rebloom indoors next winter? L. D. Livingston, N.Y.

A: *The most practical solution for forced tulips is to discard them and buy fresh bulbs next year to force. Any forced bulbs are "tricky" to carry over for another year. Some gardeners do have good results keeping the soil moist, cutting off dead blooms, and growing the foliage until the bulbs can be planted outdoors. Sometimes forced bulbs will bloom the next spring outdoors. Often they do not. Bulbs kept in pots for the entire year cycle will not rebloom. Ed.*

**vegetables
indoors**

Q: Does anyone grow vegetables indoors? I would certainly appreciate knowing what and how. Our family's food budget needs help! Mrs. T. R. E., Newark, N.J.

A: Here are several ideas: From Karen Covitch, a city gardener, "I grew dwarf Pixie Hybrid tomato in my apartment in

42

a southern exposure. I fed the plants every two weeks and watered them thoroughly every other day. Problems: if plants are exposed to over 80-degree heat, the blossoms drop. For pollination, shake plants gently or use hormone sprays."

Edward Blas, another city gardener, suggests "sprouting mung beans which taste a lot like fresh green peas."

Dr. Marcia Frierdich, a Wisconsin reader, says, "Last year I raised endive and this year I am growing tomatoes, lettuce, a self-pollinating cucumber, and peppers."

E. S. of Washington, D.C., says, "I have had fantastic success with the cherry tomato, Small Fry. Five plants have kept us rich with tomatoes all summer. I start seed in a flat, transfer them to peat pots, and then a 4½-inch pot or put three in a 7½-inch pot. Water daily but feed once a week. Stake them, as they grow five feet tall."

Another Washington gardener, P. W., recommends, *Cucumbers in a Flower Pot* by Alice Skelsey, published by Workman Publishing Company, New York. "The book describes how to grow lettuce, green peppers, cucumbers, carrots, beets, spinach, and others."

Bonnie Love of New York writes, "The September 1972 issue of *Organic Gardening* has several pages devoted to growing lettuce and other vegetables under lights."

lettuce in pots

Q: Can I transplant garden lettuce to pots for indoor salads? Mrs. I. L., Bronx

A: Bob Saunders of Connecticut says, "Yes, but she would get larger, more productive plants if she started from seed. Keep the lettuce in shallow pots or flats near a cool exposure with morning sunlight. Break off bottom leaves so plant keeps reproducing foliage."

miniature tomato

Q: I am growing one of the miniature tomato plants in my sunny apartment. However, the plant is not thriving and every time blossoms form, they drop off. Has anyone a solution? D. B., Manhattan

A: The problem is essentially one of pollination. Ed.

Robert Martin, a Long Island reader, suggests, "I have successfully produced tomatoes during the winter in a sunny office window by using the commercially prepared tomato-flower hormone spray generally sold in garden centers."

Eric Schecter, a New York reader, adds, "The easiest way to pollinate tomatoes is to use a soft camel's hair brush and touch the pollen to the stigmas of the flowers (bee fashion)."

Q: Is there a successful way to transplant parsley from outside to grow in a pot inside? I have had two failures; the plants yellow in a few days and die. Mrs. B. S., Wayne, N.J.

A: Here are two ideas. From Mrs. G. P. Leyland of New York, "I have overwhelming success growing parsley on my windowsill. Here's what I do. Dig up the parsley, shake off the soil to bare root and soak it in cool water overnight. Next day, plant the parsley bare root in ordinary clay potting soil with good drainage. Water well and cut back all sprigs to about one inch. Set pot in a south window. Feed for a couple of weeks and, presto, thriving parsley. Cut back and use as needed."

From Mrs. Frank Stienfeldt, a Long Islander reader, "I plunge a six-inch clay pot in the garden row when seeding parsley in the spring. When cold weather approaches, I dig up the pot and the three or four healthy plants in it thrive all winter if well watered."

*strawberries
under lights*

Q: I live in a small apartment and am trying to grow vegetables under artificial light. Can I grow strawberries? M. G., New Paltz, N.Y.

A: Mrs. Jennie Cornwall of New Jersey writes, "It has been reported that strawberries started from seed will produce fruit under fluorescent lights, but in our experience it has never worked. We do very well with begonias, gloxinias, orchids, and assorted bulbs, but strawberries or leafy vegetables have never survived the seedling stage. The light is just not a substitute for sunshine."

venus fly traps

Q: Our children received Venus fly traps for Christmas. One plant has died and two others look as though they are headed in that direction. How do you keep these curious plants alive? Mrs. G. G.

A: To the rescue comes Steven A. Frowine, a graduate student at Cornell. He writes, "The following conditions are best for Venus fly traps: Temperature 75–85 degrees, 90 percent or more humidity, sunny window with a south exposure, and acid soil with a low pH, half sphagnum and half peat moss. The best way to maintain plants is to keep them in a brandy snifter with one to two inches of gravel in the bottom for drainage. Most fly traps die due to insufficient light."

J. Henry Jonquiere of New York makes similar recommendations but he adds that only distilled water should be used.

wood rose

Q: I have purchased wood rose flowers and tried unsuccessfully to germinate the seeds. Suggestions, anyone? D. H., Manhattan

A: Mrs. K. F. K, Christiansted, St. Croix, writes, "Wood rose seeds are very tough and will lie in the ground for years before sprouting. I sand one end lightly with fine sand paper and soak the seeds overnight. I hope that D. H. has room for a wood rose vine. In the tropics, they are rampant growers."

Ernest P. Lorfanfant, S.M., a New York reader, adds, "For wood rose seeds to germinate, bacterial action must take place. The seeds will exude a thick milky ooze before they fully germinate."

zebra plant

Q: I am trying to grow a zebra plant without success. One gift plant kept in the sun parlor dropped its leaves in a few days and died. A second I purchased was kept out of sunlight and quite moist. It has lost all but four new leaves and the blossom bud shriveled. Mrs. J. M.

45

A: "What plant does she have?" asks Marvin Cohen of New York. "Two entirely different plants can be called Zebra plant: *Calathea zebrina*, similar to the marantas, or *Aphelandra squarrosa*, with large oval leaves about eight inches long. Calathea requires a very moist, warm room. Spray the leaves often with water and give the plant good light. Don't overwater in the dormant winter season. Aphelandra requires evenly moist soil, but leaves drop if soil is too wet or too dry."

46

on the terrace, ground floor and high rise

begonias
bud drop

Q: I have been trying to grow tuberous begonias on my New York City terrace. The healthy plants are in six-inch pots, eastern exposure, with proper soil and fertilizer applications. But, the large flower buds drop off and never open. Any advice? A. H. B., Jackson Heights

A: Writing from Ontario, Canada, Mrs. Kathleen English says, "Tuberous begonias are a warm weather plant and cool weather is the reason for plants failing to bloom and for the drop of flower buds. The remedy is to remove them from drafts and, if possible, protect the plants if cold weather continues."

when to plant

Q: What is the proper time to start tuberous begonias for window boxes? Last year, we were too late and the blooms didn't appear until September. Or maybe we just did something wrong. Help, please. Mrs. R. G., Manhattan

A: Here are some tips from Mrs. R. C. Kline of New York. "In our zone, we put the tuberous begonias outdoors May 1, which means we start them about 4 to 6 weeks before that date. By the end of March, we plant them in a flat which holds about 12 tubers and keep it in a warm, not necessarily sunny place. When two to four good leaves show, they are planted in pots and we give them an application of fish emulsion fertilizer. When the weather is settled the plants are put outdoors. We continue with the fish emulsion feeding all summer and fall with the result: enormous blooms, heavy stems and good-sized tubers."

47

bulbs

Q: How late in the year can I plant bulbs on my penthouse? And do I need to mulch the boxes to keep them from freezing? My bulbs didn't bloom this spring and I think I did something wrong. Help! G. Y., Fort Lee, N.J.

A: Bulbs need a minimum 12 inches soil depth to winter through safely in a penthouse planter. Mulching should not be necessary, but watering a few times during winter dry spells (no snow or rain) is important. Planting is finished by mid-November. Ed.

care while away

Q: Has anyone a solution for keeping a penthouse garden going during vacation period? Is there a way to mulch or assure proper watering? We have had poor results with paid help to water and weed. R. R. B., Flushing, N.Y.

A: Heavy mulching on the planter boxes with straw or hay might help to keep the soil cool and reduce some water evaporation. However, the continual wind and exposure of a penthouse make daily attention necessary. There are no automatic systems for care. We know of no other solution than competent help or a reliable neighbor to look at the garden daily and water it. Ed.

compost in the city

Q: I'm trying to be an organic gardener on my city penthouse. I'm frustrated every time I read "put on the compost pile." Does anyone know how to build a penthouse compost pile? G. R., Manhattan

A: Several answers were received from quite distant states, and, curiously, not one was from Manhattan. Here is a practical solution from E. Urrows, Bermuda. "A redwood planter

half-filled with garden soil can be placed on the terrace. Each day place vegetable parings, tea and coffee grounds and leaves, left-over vegetables and anything without fat (no meats). Also add fallen leaves from plants. Work these into the soil base with an occasional addition of dried cow manure. This tuck-in composting works quite well. A separate garbage strainer in the kitchen for compost material will help, too."

Mrs. Ronald Lapinski, a Pennsylvania reader, writes, "I am surprised that no one recommended my simple method of composting. Puree in the blender any parings before adding them to the soil. This enables composting of practically anything such as grapefruit peels and even eggshells."

lantana

Q: I have a number of lantana trees growing in tubs on my terrace. They are about five feet tall. Does anyone know a way to protect them over the winter? J. H., Scarsdale, N.Y.

A: Mrs. J. C. Elsey, Westchester County reader, suggests, "For the last three years we have wintered our hanging basket lantanas on a porch off the living room which is screened in summer, but covered on the outside with sheets of plastic for the winter. The plants are kept damp, but not wet."

pollution

Q: It's happening again this year. My Manhattan penthouse tomato plants are yellowing, dropping leaves and not flowering. My white petunia plants have small leaves with tiny spots. What am I doing wrong? Mrs. G. H.

A: Thomas Zanoni of New Jersey writes that these plants are quite sensitive to air pollution. White petunias are being used at the College of Agriculture and Environmental Science at Rutgers University as indicators of air pollutants.

roses

Q: What is the key to success for roses in the city? We have tried two summers with hybrid teas and get foliage but no flowers on our twelfth floor terrace. H. D. McF., Manhattan

A: There is probably no one reason, but here are some suggestions that should provide clues. Floribundas do best in the city with climbers rating almost as "tough." Many hybrid teas will also flourish. The planting box should be deep—not less than 24 inches—to accommodate roots, and the planter must drain well. Soil should be fertile but also drain well, enriched with rotted compost or peat if available. Exposure is the key— at least four to six hours of sun where there is good air circulation but not high buffeting winds. Heat reflections from

49

other buildings can be damaging. Also, roses must be kept well watered and protected weekly from aphids and black spot with a general rose spray formula. Ed.

soils for a penthouse

Q: As new penthouse gardeners, we would like some guidance on a good basic soil recipe. We understand something lightweight is important for obvious reasons and drainage. Mrs. G. H., Manhattan

A: George Mitterman of New Jersey writes, "We mixed and messed sterilized soil, leafmold, sand and peat for our first terrace garden. But for our second one, we learned better. Most of the metropolitan garden shops will supply a premixed soil in 50 pound bags which is lightweight and much easier to use. A few phone calls will set things in motion."

strawberry jar
planting

Q: What is the proper way to plant and water the terra-cotta strawberry jar? The pockets always dry out and the plants die by midsummer. Mrs. T. Y., Connecticut

A: Mrs. Bailey Pratt of California writes, "Punch holes all over the side of one or two tin cans with both ends removed. Sink the can or cans, depending on the size of the jar, in the center of the jar and fill jar and pockets with soil. Plant the pockets with runnerless strawberries and water by filling the cans with water. Water will seep throughout the jar and after plants begin to spread, the top can is invisible. This method keeps the soil from drying out. Mist a few times as well."

Anne Cifu, New York, has a similar suggestion. Rather than cans she suggests making a cylinder of ¼-inch galvanized wire and filling it with gravel. Place two inches of shards in the bottom of the strawberry jar, then place the filled cylinder in the center. Fill around with soil and plant. Water through the gravel cylinder."

wintering over

Q: I have a strawberry jar filled with sturdy plants which I planted this spring. I don't want them to be killed by a frost. Where should I keep the jar this winter? Mrs. B. K., Little Neck, L.I.

A: Mrs. Isaac Feldman, another Long Island gardener, writes, "We have had two experiences with strawberry jars. First the bad news. One year we wrapped a terra-cotta jar in a plastic bag (from the cleaners) and put it in a sheltered north corner of the house. In spring, all plants were dead and the jar was cracked. Now, for the good news. Last October, we put our new jar filled with flourishing plants into a tool house attached to the garage but unheated. The temperature went

50

below freezing a few times, but the plants survived and the jar did not crack."

trees in the city

Q: What tree can you suggest for a small enclosed city garden that is sunny only in the morning? Mrs. W. L., Brooklyn

A: Here are two ideas from fellow city gardeners. From William Eier, "I have successfully planted a Chinese elm in an enclosed garden that is sunny in the morning. Not only is it disease resistant, but it is a winter hardy species, fast grower and not too fussy about soil conditions."

From Albert Glantz, "I have a small enclosed garden that has three hours of sun a day. Seven years ago, I planted two magnolias and one Japanese cherry. The magnolias started blooming three years ago, but no bloom yet has appeared on the Japanese cherry although I have seen them blooming in the neighborhood."

vines

Q: Has anyone found a vine suitable for a quick screen on a city terrace? We have tried morning glory and scarlet runner bean. Mrs. S. C., Manhattan

A: From Mrs. Thomas Smith, Manhattan, "My favorite is moonflower which blossoms in early evening. Although it is not fruitful, we also have a grapevine which thrives but must be cut back a few times each summer."

Prof. Doris G. White of New Jersey suggests "bittersweet, five-leaf akebia and fleece vine." She also lists actinidia, clematis, or honeysuckle.

weekend gardener

Q: I would like to grow vegetables in containers on my vacation property in northwest Connecticut. I will only be there on weekends. Is there a way to water the vegetables without being there? I. A. B.

A: Arthur F. Ulley of Pennsylvania suggests his method as follows. "I designed a watering system for my cuttings, a very simple arrangement with a poultry house timer and a solenoid electric valve. The valve is connected to the faucet by a section of washing machine hose, molded on the ends to resist friction. The timer must be selected carefully as it only needs 15 minutes 'on' a day and general house lighting timers do not have a short 'on' time. To complete the system, I use an ordinary length of garden hose and a spray head delivering about a gallon an hour. I have two hoses connected with galvanized pipe and a hose fitting hooked up to the basement faucet and run outside to the cutting bench. There is one difficulty, the automatic waterer works rain or shine. Total costs, under $15."

51

wintering over

Q: Is there anything special we should do to our penthouse garden to winter it over? This will be its first snow season. Mrs. M. L., Manhattan

A: Mrs. Frank Benkard of New York writes, "I have had a penthouse garden for nine years. A wind screen is essential. Be sure to keep the soil damp until nature takes over with rain and snow. After Christmas, collect discarded trees, prune off the branches and poke them into the soil to help break the wind on evergreens. I feed with a root feeder in April and in June."

chrysanthemums

Q: How can I winter over 'mums growing in terrace tubs for next summer? I tried last year and failed and would like to try again, if it's possible. J. K. P., Manhattan

A: Two things are essential to winter over 'mums: hardiness of the variety and sufficiently deep, moist soil to prevent the roots from drying out and/or freezing. Some pots of 'mums sold by neighborhood florists are tender and not winter hardy. Gardeners who want to carry over their 'mums to spring should buy from reputable sources who will verify a variety's hardiness. If hardy, 'mums will winter well in planters or tubs of eight to 10-inch depth. Cut back after flowering is over, and keep moist when there is no rain or snow. Ed.

dwarf peach

Q: I would appreciate some help on how to winter a dwarf Bonanza peach which has been growing in a redwood tub on the patio all summer. I have no basement and the garage is heated. Mrs. C. R. D., Pawling, N.Y.

A: The nursery which introduced Bonanza notes in its catalogue, "We do not recommend dwarf peach trees for areas with either extremely mild or extremely cold winters." The tub could be moved to a sheltered location away from high winds and winter sun and protected with straw around the base. A light straw mulch wrapped loosely around the tree when the weather turns cold might also help. Watering would also be important in case of a dry, snowless/rainless winter. The danger to peach trees is the late spring frosts which kills the tender flower buds. Ed.

roses

Q: I have two rosebushes on my terrace, each in a 12-inch pot. I am told that the extreme cold will kill the bushes. Is there a way to protect the rosebushes to survive the winter? J. M., Manhattan

52

A: Ms. Betty Feldman, another city gardener, writes, "He should have no trouble with his roses wintering through if he checks them during the winter months to be sure the soil is kept moist. My roses are in 12-inch redwood tubs and they winter through very well. But the soil must never dry out even in January, when there is often a thaw."

trees in pots

Q: I would like to have information on wintering young spruce, pine and willow trees growing in clay pots on a windy north terrace. Miss H. L.

A: To help Miss H. L. care for her trees on a city terrace, "I can offer what we have done successfully for several years," writes Max Goodman of New York. "About this time of year we soak thoroughly each wooden tub in which we have yews, hollies and a cherry tree. On top, we put wood chips as a thick mulch. Then every few weeks, but only on relatively warm (above freezing) sunny afternoons, I swish the evergreen foliage with the hose and let some moisture trickle into all the tubs. Winds dry out plants on terraces, even in winter, and it's important to check the plants frequently."

J. M. Charles of New York recommends, "Drive 6 to 8 1x1-inch stakes into the tub around the outside of the tree. Tops of the stakes should reach the top of the tree. Wrap burlap around the stakes and secure the burlap to the stakes. Leave the top open. Planter should be of adequate size to insulate roots. Water tree well before freezing weather. Pray!"

know it all

cats
and plants

Q: Is there anything I can grow for my indoor cat so she won't eat all my house plants? She doesn't like grass and the vet tells me catnip is not good for her. Ms. H. G. F., Fort Lee, N.J.

A: Mrs. Oliver W. Reese, Ohio, feeds her cats oats. "All four of my cats love it. I buy the seed at a rural feed and grain store."

Alice Cresap, New York, also feeds her cats oats and offered these growing tips. "Plant a goodly number of oat seeds in a four- to six-inch pot. Cover lightly with soil and keep moist, but don't overwater for they tend to mold. Allow 7 to 12 days of growth, or until they are about four inches high. Keep them out of reach of the cat or she'll devour the seedlings. I feed the cats blade by blade from my fingers. Keep three to four pots growing in rotation."

Ila Bossons of Canada feeds her cats wheat (grains are bought at health food stores) which she plants and grows in rotating pots.

Mrs. Helene Berg, Westchester County, feeds her cats cooked vegetables: string beans, broccoli, carrots, spinach and cauliflower, which she mashes or cuts finely. She writes, "Grass is not particularly good for cats as it is too stringy and catnip is a stimulant healthy cats can do without."

Nadine Miles, Ohio, doesn't grow anything to keep her cats from plants. She "puts a moth ball on the ground in each pot. It works out of doors, too. As the moth balls evaporate, put on fresh ones."

and poisonous plants

Q: I want to purchase plants for my apartment. However, I have two cats who will nibble on the greenery. Are any plants known to be poisonous to house pets if eaten? Can I grow geraniums, which are a favorite of mine? Mrs. F. M. V. Jr.

54

A: A helpful bulletin, Common Poisonous Plants, *by John M. Kingsbury, has been published by Cornell University. It is free to state residents and a nominal fee is charged nonresidents. Write Mailing Room, Cornell University, Research Park, N.Y. 14850. The bulletin lists the following house plants as poisonous: hyacinth, narcissus and daffodil bulbs, gloriosa lily, amaryllis, nerine, oleander, poinsettia, dumbcane, caladium, philodendron and mistletoe. Many other garden plants are listed and any pets should be kept away from these plants. Ed.*

Mrs. Edward J. Volkman of New York writes that "if a cat eats house plants it is because the animal needs greens such as grass. A good substitute is young oat sprouts. I plant a small dish every two or three weeks so there is a constant supply of succulent new green shoots for my cat to nibble on."

children's plants

Q: Has anyone found indoor plants that click with kindergarten ages? I would like to start a winter project to keep them interested. Clues please. J. L., Manhattan

A: Reams of replies arrived. Here are some highlights: From Hildegard Metzger of New York, "My class delights in observing the astounding growth of an amaryllis bulb."

From Mrs. Deena Linett of New Jersey, "My own children loved the Venus fly trap which I bought. Instructions come with it."

From Mrs. Frank Coyle of Connecticut, "Spider plant is hard to kill and has many plantlets. Grape ivy is indomitable and will grow up a string. Sensitive plant, all children love to touch. Lemon thyme, because it smells."

From Carolyn Dieselman, Connecticut, "Have each child plant two or three grapefruit seeds in a styrofoam cup filled with potting soil and holes punched in the bottom for drainage. Start a water garden and watch how plants root. For little folks who like to water, keep a baby's tears or a pick-a-back plant."

From Mrs. Barbra Freeman, New York, "Place lima beans, chick peas or pinto beans on wet paper toweling for a day or so. They will sprout and may be planted in soil. Suspend a sweet potato half in and half out of water to root and become an attractive plant. Purple velvet plant is quick growing, or try coleus."

cleaning pebbles

Q: My plants grow well under fluorescent lamps, but recently the pebbles in the plant trays have acquired a peculiar odor and white fungus. I have washed the pebbles many times and tried periods of drying them out but the problem persists. Clues would be appreciated. Mrs. J. K.

A: H. W. Penning, Jr., New York, writes that he had the same problem and this was his solution. "The addition of some liquid laundry bleach to the plant trays. The bleach also prevents the growth of algae. I added about one-fourth cup of bleach per tray. Be sure not to let the bleach–water solution touch the bottom of the pots."

Mrs. D. Lewis, New York, suggests adding charcoal to the pebbles to eliminate odor and fungus.

Or, when washing the pebbles, boil them for a few minutes in water to which a little detergent and bleach have been added. Rinse well and reuse. This method is particularly effective with marble chips, a very porous material. Ed.

cleaning plants
with milk

Q: True, or false? Milk is safe to use for cleaning indoor foliage plants to make them shiny. Mrs. M. K., Delaware

A: Mrs. Ernesta Drinker Ballard, President of the Pennsylvania Horticultural Society, Philadelphia, writes, "It is quite safe to use skimmed or very low fat milk to clean and shine the foliage of indoor plants. I have done it often. There is no danger of clogging the stomata (tiny pores in the leaves) provided the milk is not rich in butter fat. The very small amount of fat present in skimmed milk provides a short term shine."

with soap and water

Q: Has anyone solved the problem of keeping large foliage plants clean? Our figs, dracaenas, philodendrons, etc., get grimy with grease and soot, even indoors. Is it safe to scrub the leaves with soap and water? Mrs. J. K. L., Manhattan

A: Miss I. L. H. of Boonton, N.J., has found a formula. She suggests: "1 quart warm water; 1 teaspoon Ceda-Flora spray; 1 teaspoon Ivory Liquid. Spray it from an atomizer (an old

Windex bottle) and wipe each leaf with paper toweling. Soot and grime are removed."

compost indoors

Q: I don't have a yard, but would like to start compost indoors for my house plants. Can I use tea leaves, coffee grounds, lettuce trimmings, etc.? Has anyone tried? Mrs. B. D. D., Bronx

A: Robert L. Munhall of Connecticut writes that according to the December (1972) issue of *Organic Gardening,* a woman living in a New York City apartment tells of composting. She used a window box, obtained about an inch layer of soil from an area in front of her apartment building and added vegetable matter such as orange peels, coffee grounds, etc.— even cat manure. She recommends using very little water and stirring occasionally. The container is kept open and there is no odor.

Nouage Cassidy of New Jersey found a similar system described in *New York* magazine. Again, recommendations are for a window box, starting with a layer of garbage trimmings, egg shells, fruit rinds, etc. Then add a layer of potting soil and some agricultural lime. Follow layer system. Keep compost moist and turn occasionally.

fertilizer

Q: When shopping for house plant food, I am confused by the proportions in the fertilizer formula. Different manufacturers package quite different formulas for the same types of plants. Is there some rule to follow? Mrs. A. E.

A: "Here is my solution to buying house plant food which I hope will help Mrs. A. E. Recalling my early school days, we were told that N or nitrogen, the first letter in a fertilizer formula, is essential to produce green foliage and P or phosphorus, the second letter in a fertilizer formula, is to produce roots and buds. So I buy fertilizer for the results I want such as high nitrogen when I want to encourage foliage and high phosphorus when I want to encourage buds and roots." Mrs. Jamie Bergen, New York

fragrance

Q: Much is written and said about fragrant plants for the flower garden, but since I live in an apartment I would like to grow fragrant flowers indoors. Are there any plants with scented blooms that will thrive in a pot? Mrs. D. T., Manhattan

A: Joanne DeSimone of New York suggests, "For aroma from flowers I have had success with wax plant which trails and climbs with leathery oval leaves and pink-tinted flowers. Gardenia is more of a challenge since it requires more care but proves to be well worth the effort for its fragrant flowers. Orchid cactus has a penetrating sweet scent. Another is Persian lime with white flowers and citrus fruits. Three geraniums grown for fragrant foliage are peppermint, nutmeg and rose. All thrive in full or partial sun."

Another New York gardener, Mrs. Arthur E. Green, suggests *Clivia minata*. "It blooms only once a year but it is well worth waiting for the annual flowers—huge clusters of orange yellow blooms. It grows in an east window where it gets the morning sun. In afternoon sun it did not bloom. The plant is pot bound, watered minimally from June to February; more water the remaining months."

Maria Leyds, a Vermont gardener, also suggests growing hoya and the various jasmines.

home hybridizing

Q: Are there any indoor plants particularly easy to "breed" at home and raise from seed? I would like to try the hobby, now that I'm retired, but don't know where to begin. Clues please? Col. D. F. G., Maryland

A: Mrs. H. L. Edwards of New York offers, "I especially recommend pelargoniums, several genera of the gesneriads and sinningia, so-called gloxinias. If space permits, try amaryllis or begonias which are pleasant to work with. There are also cacti and orchids. I also suggest the Colonel join the plant society dealing with that genus, as hobbyists are generous helping beginners."

light
no direct sun

Q: I live in an apartment with no direct sunlight. The windows face north and overlook an alley and receive some reflected light. What plants will grow best in my Bronx apartment? D. R.

A: D. R. can grow many unusual plants besides the common philodendron writes Mrs. Wendy Kessler of New York. Here are some that she has grown and they have "done very well." Hoyas, bromeliads, prayer plant, pittosporum, podocarpus, Kafir lily, coffee plant, ferns, creeping fig and Norfolk Island pine. (*Add to this: Chinese evergreen, dracaenas, grape ivy and kangaroo vine. Ed.*)

tinted glass

Q: My sister, an experienced gardener, has moved into a high rise apartment building, facing south. The windows are bronze-tinted. She has had little luck so far raising plants

58

indoors. Does the bronze tinted glass have anything to do with this? Has anyone had similar experiences? M. J. L.

A: Dr. Henry M. Cathey, Leader of Ornamental Investigations for the U.S.D.A. Research Service, writes, "Tinted glass acts as a neutral filter and eliminates visible light. Plants act as if they were growing in the shade. The human eye adapts to the dim light and in time the light appears to be as bright as before without the glare. Plants in cities need as much light as possible without overheating of the leaves due to infrared rays." He suggests growing low-light level plants such as Chinese evergreen, Neantha bella palm, bamboo palm, dracaena, Kentia palm and philodendron, or joining the fluorescent light gardeners!

moving house plants

Q: We are moving to Florida. Has anyone transported house plants successfully for such a long distance? Mrs. R. C., Cambria Heights, N.Y.

A: Joyce Scofield, a Westchester County reader, has a simple idea. "Put plants in a sturdy box large enough to hold pots and stuff wadded-up newspapers in between to hold them in place. Protect the leaves from sun and wind by making a newspaper canopy over the plants and tape it. The finished box looks like a covered wagon. Our plants traveled 500 miles in the car back seat with no casualties."

When moving many, or large, plants professionally for any distance, consult the moving man in advance. Many moving companies make a specialty of handling your horticulture. Ed.

pests
earthworms in pots

Q: Neighbors keep earthworms in their potted plants and tell us it is good for the soil. Is this true? Mrs. Z. V., Manhattan

A: Arthur Wallkyl of New Jersey says, "No. Earthworms in the restricted area of a pot do more harm than good. Their tunneling in and around roots can break fine roots and weaken the root ball. Their castings on the surface are unsightly. Knock potted plants out of pots containing earthworms and poke around the rootball carefully and remove them."

house plant 'worms'

Q: I have a type of worm in the soil of my house plants. They are small, threadlike and appear to wiggle in the water after the plants have been watered. What are they and how do I get rid of them? C. K.

A: From Dorval, Quebec, Mrs. G. B. Brown writes, "The pests are called springtails. To get rid of them, try one teaspoon of washing ammonia to a little over a pint of water. Soak the soil until water runs out the bottom of the pot. As soon as the soil dries out, flush again. Or try two to three drops of nicotine sulfate (Black Leaf 40) to one-fourth cup of warm water.''

Mrs. J. L. Gardener of New York writes, ''I used the tea grounds from my used tea bags to get rid of the small thread-like worms in my house plants.''

C. K.'s pest might also be a tiny centipede-like creature called a symphylan, a ubiquitous pest feeding on organic material and fine root hairs. It can be eliminated by watering the house plant with lime water; repeat in 10 days. Lime water is available in drug stores. Ed.

soil pests

Q: My begonias are infested with hordes of curious creatures that appear only when the plant is watered. They rise up and scurry over the soil and look like minute thrips. What are they and how do I get rid of them? M. P. O., Pittsburgh, Pa.

Q: I am suddenly plagued with tiny black flying insects that look a little like fleas. They are hard to catch or swat and stay mostly on the soil of my house plants. Help! Does anyone know what they are and how to get rid of them? A. M. M., Manhattan

A: Dr. Cynthia Westcott replies, ''There are several species of small insects that act as scavengers in the soil, feeding on decaying leaves and other organic material. They are more of a nuisance than a menace, but they sometimes feed on fine roots and cause potted plants to lose vigor. M. P. O.'s problem may be elongate-bodied springtails, common in leaf litter and soil. A. M. M.'s problem is tiny black flies called fungus gnats or mushroom flies. They are often present in potting soil rich in humus. Such pests can be avoided by using commercial sterilized potting soil or by treating garden soil with malathion.''

Watering with limewater from the drugstore one or two times may also help. Ed.

pots
clay pot mold

Q: Practically all of my clay pots have thick ''beards'' of white mold! Has anyone else experienced this and how did you get rid of it? Ms. Y. McL., Dobbs Ferry, N.Y.

A: Mrs. Ann Androsky, a city gardener, writes, ''The thick beards of white mold are the accumulation of excess fertilizer salts in the soil. To clean empty pots soak them overnight in a solution of one cup of laundry bleach to two gallons of water. Scrub with a stiff brush. Neutralize the pots by soaking

60

overnight in a solution of one cup of vinegar and two gallons of water. Then wash pots with soap and water. The pots will look brand new."

Moss on pots is also an indication of overfeeding and should be removed by scrubbing with a stiff brush and plain water, or the plant should be repotted. In any case, reduce fertilizer applications. Ed.

old plastic pots

Q: We are accumulating piles of old plastic pots, all sizes. Is there any practical recycling use for them? O. D., New Jersey

A: Many readers suggested donating the old pots to schools, senior citizens clubs and Scout troops who might have uses for them. Ed.

painting pots

Q: I prefer clay pots to plastic pots and paint them antique white. However, I find that even with high gloss enamel the paint blisters away from the clay. What kind of paint should I use? Mrs. E. J. S., Brooklyn

A: Jay Dryer of Pennsylvania writes, "There is no way. The advantage of clay pots is their porousness; they breathe. Any moisture in the soil and root area seeps through the sidewalls of the pots and evaporates. Paint with undersurface moisture is always going to peel and blister. Enjoy the natural clay color."

Joseph A. Raphael, Belle Harbor, challenges this and writes that it is possible to paint clay pots in this way. If the original questioner is not interested in maintaining the porous quality of the clay pots, they can be sealed with an exterior sealer and stain killer which can be used on porous surfaces. Then the pots can be painted with any color paint desired. When perfectly dry, paint with another coat of the sealer and the paint will not peel. The sealer is sold in pint cans at paint stores.

sleep and plants

Q: Recently I was told by a friend that it is unhealthy to sleep in a room with plants and flowers because at night plants exude carbon dioxide and not oxygen. Is there any truth in this? Mrs. N. H., Manhattan

A: Dr. Max L. Resnick of Massachusetts writes, "Mrs. N. H. need not fear to sleep in a room with plants because of any carbon dioxide. Actually it is oxygen that is liberated; the carbon dioxide is utilized in the plant cells. Simultaneously, the plant is producing oxygen in excess of its needs and the excess is liberated to the environment."

61

Dr. Resnick's answer did not satisfy and resulted in many letters. The following tells why. From Arnold Grobman in Illinois, "Dr. Resnick tells only half the story. Plants like animals respire. That is they take in oxygen, which combines with stored sugars to release energy with an emission of carbon dioxide as a by-product. In the presence of light, most green plants would carry out both photosynthesis and respiration, the former releasing oxygen, and the latter carbon dioxide. At night, the plant would be respiring but would not be carrying on photosynthesis. In average-sized rooms with a reasonable amount of plants and taking into consideration the diffusion of gases that occur, it is highly unlikely that anyone need be concerned about an excess of carbon dioxide in the bedroom."

soil additives
coffee grounds

Q: Are used coffee grounds good to add to house plant soil mix? I understand they can be used safely as a mulch on garden plants, but are they safe for house plants? D. M.

A: Cathy Schonberg of New York advises D. M. that coffee grounds can be used safely on plants (as a mulch) but as for mixing them in house plant soil, they have little beneficial value. The grounds tend to be a bit acid, she cautions, and for house plant mixes either vermiculite or sand are safer to use.

Mrs. J. L. Gardner of New York writes, "I have used coffee grounds for several years and never had a failure yet. I used two tablespoonfuls to each six-inch pot."

sand substitutes

Q: We always have such difficulty finding sand for house plant soil mixes. Can anyone suggest an easily available substitute? V. S., Bronx

62

A: Mrs. K. K. K. of New York writes, "I have a parakeet and what could be simpler than parakeet gravel. It is clean, inexpensive, and has the correct fineness."

Try visiting a construction site with a plastic bag, trowel, and a smile. Builder's sand is ideal, and free in small quantities. Ed.

wood ashes

Q: I have always heard that wood ashes from the fireplace are good for plants. Please tell me on what plants I may use them? Mrs. A. J. E.

A: Mrs. G. H. Clawson of New York has information on the use of wood ashes. "They are a good source of potash when mixed with potting soils provided they have not been previously wetted, as the potash is soluble. Most textbooks recommend a proportion of two quarts of wood ashes to a bushel of soil."

See Eggshells, page 99.

soil mold

Q: A white funguslike mold has grown over the top of the soil on several of my house plants. What have I done wrong and how do I get rid of it? Mrs. G. H. L., Brooklyn

A: Mrs. Leah Isaacs, New York, suggests, "The plants may be kept too wet or are overfertilized. The simplest solution is to scrape the mold off, discard and replace with a small amount of fresh sterilized potting soil. In the future, do not overwater plants and cultivate the top soil lightly from time to time to keep it airy."

summering outdoors

Q: Every year when the weather warms, I put my house plants outside and sink them up to the rims of the pots. They thrive but, in the fall, I find that, no matter what I do to prevent it, the roots grow through the pot's drainage hole and digging up the plant causes a near fatal shock. What can be done to prevent this? Mrs. H. S. R.

A: Mrs. Philip Smith of Connecticut suggests a simple solution. "Place a three-inch layer or more of wood ashes saved from the fireplace under each pot before sinking it. If wood ashes are not available gravel, sand, or the like will do, but make the layer thick enough to be effective."

Or dig a trench, and place a wooden plank in the bottom. If the pots are of different sizes, adjust the soil height by raising the smaller pots on empty overturned pots. Ed.

terrariums
fungus growth

Q: The plants in my bottle garden seem to be thriving, but every so often I find fuzzy fungus growth at their base. I remove it carefully, but it keeps reappearing. What shall I do? K. D., Bronx.

63

(**terrariums**
continued)

A month ago, I started a terrarium. Recently, I noticed a fungus growth around the top of the old fish tank I used. What can I do? W. J. L.

A: "To get rid of it," John Goldman of New York suggests, "air the bottle gardens more frequently. In fact, I would keep it uncorked or uncovered for several hours as apparently the contents are too moist. Also, put the garden in strong light for a short period. This should clear up the fungus."

Mrs. Stanley M. Suchecki of Connecticut writes, "A terrarium bowl or fish tank should be cleaned thoroughly to remove any residual traces of former plant life. The glass must be kept clean and decaying foliage removed as it appears." She suggests removing the growth with a cotton swab or a damp cloth. "Poor drainage could cause the problem. A drainage layer of gravel should be in the bottom. Excessive moisture and warmth will hasten fungi growth. Ventilate the terrarium by removing the cover for an hour or so each day and provide a cool location with good light, but little or no sunlight."

moss growing

Q: Is there a way to "grow" moss for terrariums or must I always hunt for it when I can visit woodlands (which is not often)? J. B. B., Brooklyn

A: Judy Glattstein of Connecticut provides this help. "I read of this technique in a bonsai book but have not tried it myself. Fill a flat with loam. Place a layer of cheesecloth over the soil. Dry some moss and then crumble it evenly over the cheesecloth. Cover with another layer of cheesecloth. Keep damp and in a light, not sunny place. In six weeks or so, the moss will grow and the cheesecloth (both pieces together) can be lifted off and cut to size and placed where needed. The cheesecloth rots away. Also, moss does grow in the city on sour patches of ground and even in some damp outside cellar walls."

moss terrariums

Q: Is it possible to make small indoor terrariums of outdoor mosses? I'm intrigued, and would like to try, if someone could guide on when to gather the plants and transplant them. Mrs. P. P., New Jersey

A: Carla Golden of Westchester County, N.Y., writes, "I have transplanted moss in the dead of winter and in spring. Of course, in spring and summer, there will be a greater variety of mosses and small ferns in the woods. Use a glass container, place a layer of small pebbles on the bottom for drainage. Charcoal can also be added. Cover two inches with potting soil and begin transplanting. Lightly press the mosses into place and, for color, add small cuttings from a red leaved house plant. Mist water over the terrarium after planting to fully moisten the soil, and cover. Keep out of direct sunlight."

orchids in a terrarium

Q: Would it be possible to grow orchids in a terrarium? I'm not having much luck with them in my dry apartment and I thought the moister climate might work. Miss M. L. M., Kane, Pennsylvania

A: One negative response came from B. Ortiz, a Westchester County gardener. "I wouldn't advise it. Orchids couldn't stand the stagnant air. Fresh moving air, no drafts, is important. Spray the plants with a hand mister daily or place the pots on trays filled with pebbles kept damp."

But two people gave encouraging reports. John Kernan of Connecticut writes, "I have a large brandy snifter planted with two miniature orchids, *Oncidium barbatum* and *O. cheirophorum* in a mixture of firbark, silvabark, perlite, lime and fertilizers, with a half-inch of pebbles for drainage. The jar is in a south facing window and is misted once a week with no glass on top. So far so good."

Albert Bailey, also of Connecticut, writes, "I have produced beautiful cattleyas during the winter in a garage south window terrarium (20 cubic feet) with heating cables suspended below shelves to keep them at a temperature of 60 to 70 degrees. Orchids are potted in pinebark and given semimonthly feedings, otherwise they are watered only when potting mixture becomes dry, plus occasional misting. Plants are summered under a tree outdoors."

outdoors

Q: Is it safe to put terrariums outdoors for the summer? T. B., New Jersey

65

A: Since a terrarium or bottle garden is its own microclimate and self-contained, there is no advantage to placing it outdoors. These little gardens are particularly vulnerable to changes in temperature. Hazards of high winds and scorching sun outdoors make it too risky. Terrariums should stay indoors all year round. Ed.

woodland
gathering

Q: I would like to make some terrariums this spring and gather woodland wildlings but am not familiar with all the rules and regulations of protected ferns, wild flowers and mosses. Is there a general clearing house of information on what plants can be taken and what plants are protected? H. G.

when to dig

Q: When is it safe to dig wild plants from our own property to make some small woodland terrariums? We have heard spring/fall/winter. We are patient and want to do it properly! G. T., Connecticut

A: Mrs. Stanley M. Suchecki of Connecticut suggests contacting a local garden club or writing for New England lists from the New England Wild Flower Preservation Society, Inc., 300 Massachusetts Avenue, Boston, Mass. 02115. As for making terrariums in spring, she advises against it. "The plants are quite tender and difficult to transplant," she writes. "A much better time is in the fall, before frost."

From Mrs. Ellis Philips, Jr., of New York state, "I have dug mosses, etc., in the dead of winter with no ill effect . . . as long as the ground isn't too frozen to get a good grip on the roots."

And again from Mrs. Stanley Suchecki, "Fall season is the best, before frost. There is less shock to the plants when moving them indoors, and cuttings of wild plants will root more successfully. Even after frost and during the early part of winter, wild plants can be moved gradually into the warmth of the house. Spring is not recommended because the plants are tender after the winter months and woodland terrariums are difficult to maintain over the summer months."

topiary

Q: I have a small bay tree, *Lauris nobilis*, which I would like to train into a globe topiary. It has two branches, one 18 inches, the other, 12 inches, growing in a "v." Neither is straight. What do I do? K. S.

A: Preston Hiklon of New York suggests cutting the shorter branch of the "v" completely away. Then use a stake to support and gradually train the main stem upward. Keep the side

66

branches pruned off and gradually encourage only top growth. It takes patient persistence, but should work.

trees indoors

Q: I have a Kentucky coffee tree and a mimosa tree, each about six inches high, growing in pots indoors in a south window. With winter coming on, how should I care for them? Will they shed leaves naturally or do they need a period of dormancy? P. E.

A: Mrs. Eric Kocher, New York, writes "Last year I brought in a number of potted seedling mimosas from 3- to 8-inches high. All continued green and grew well in my sunroom. I repeated with the same plants this last month. They were re-potted from the garden. Several trees have already lost their leaves, but several new seedlings are thriving in a dish garden. I conclude that the young plants make good use of the growing conditions, in spite of shortening days, whereas the older plants respond to light and temperature changes."

watering
*in decorative
container*

Q: I have a large Kentia palm and have purchased a decorative 18-inch square planter. I would like to know the correct way to put the potted plant into the decorative container. There will be no drainage hole in the decorative container and I cannot lift the palm pot in and out to pour off excess water. How will I know that I am not underwatering or overwatering the palm since I will not be able to see inside the container? Clues anyone? Miss N. L. S.

A: M. K. Fishbein writes that if she cannot check whether there is excess water in the decorative pot in which the potted plant is placed, first she should place a layer of gravel or broken pot in the bottom of the decorative pot for drainage. Then use a flat stick between the two containers. The wet line will show if too much water has accumulated. A good thorough watering with tepid water every week to 10 days should suffice.

In East Hampton, Mrs. H. S. has four Kentia palms. She fills their inner clay pot to the brim about once a week. There is about 1¼ inches of water space in the pot. Once a week she mists the palms with a small plastic spray bottle, and every so often she gives them a shower bath. Brown leaf tips mean too much watering.

And from Manhattan, J. K. suggests measuring how much water is required to soak through dry soil in the palm's pot—until water runs out the drainage hole in the base. Then make a note of this and, about once every week to 10 days, add that specific amount of water to the palm. This will work for most

67

plants whether in a decorative tub or standing alone, and there will be no danger of over or underwatering.

*in hanging
planters*

Q: We would appreciate some ideas on how to water hanging plants easily. Our collection of about 15 takes almost a whole morning to water without damaging rugs and furniture. We take them down and to the sink to soak through. Is there a simpler way? B. L. DeP, Manhattan

A: "There is," writes Mrs. Emily Darmer, New Jersey. "Use ice cubes. They melt at room temperature and the water is absorbed easily."
Try not to let the ice cubes touch the plant. Ed.

hard water residue

Q: We have extremely hard water because of the presence of limestone. When I mist plants with this water, a white residue remains. Is this harmful? Also, is watering with this hard water harmful to house plants? C. B., Manlius, N.Y.

A: Robert L. Randall of New York writes, "Hard water does not harm plants but if the accumulation of salts is troubling, the water can be put through an ion-exchange demineralizer such as is used for steam irons. Do not use conventional water softeners as these replace the calcium and magnesium salts with sodium chloride which is harmful to plants."

while away

Q: I have plants growing under artificial light with an automatic timer. Next month I will be away on vacation for two weeks. Is there anything I can do to keep the plants watered while I'm away? M. P., Oceanside, N.Y.

A: Robert Medley of Pennsylvania recommends, "If there are just a few plants, they can be taken away from the lights, watered well, and inserted in plastic cleaner bags, and kept in north light. For a large plant stand with many plants, it is more practical to ask a neighbor to take care of them."
Or put them all in the bathtub and cover with a plastic canopy, sealed around the edges with tape. Ed.

outdoor gardening

nature's helpers and hinderers

ants
strawberry

Q: The everbearing strawberries planted in fall 1970 produced well the next year, but the berries were invaded by what appeared to be ants. Ant-Stix were of no help. What is the source of this pest and how do I get rid of it? Mrs. W. H.

A: To the rescue comes Mrs. M. F. Moore of New Jersey. "Try ant-traps sold in hardware stores. Punch holes in the sides, place them on the ground and cover with flower pots, inverted. A sticky syrup in trap attracts and kills ants; pot cover protects birds and animals from poisoning."

bats

Q: Is there a known repellent for bats? A group of them hang from the rafters of our unscreened porch and their droppings are most unpleasant. J. V. L., Wingdale, N.Y.

A: Here are three ideas. From Mrs. A. D. Onofria, a Westchester County reader, "We solved our problem by putting moth balls into small cloth bags and thumbtacking them up as high as possible in different spots."

From Mrs. James O'Hanlon, a Connecticut reader, "Moth balls did not work for us. This summer we installed two spotlights on the porch and we leave them burning from dawn to dusk. We haven't seen a bat dropping since. We hope once the bats have found a new nesting place we can turn the lights off and conserve electricity."

C. Laney of New York writes, "Bats will be discouraged if you hang strips of cloth dipped in turpentine around their roost. The cloths should be free to blow in the breeze. But remember bats are your friends and will eat flies and mosquitoes."

71

bees

Q: How can we prevent bumble bees from drilling holes in the redwood siding and overhang of our house? Mrs. J. H. E., North Carolina

A: Dr. Jon M. Wilson of New Jersey suggests, "I surmise that the problem is with carpenter bees, which drill neat round holes in various wooden objects and then proceed to live within the burrows. I have found Cyanogas works. I place it in a wad of putty and then push it up into the hole. Unfortunately, the holes are usually drilled upwards and the capsule is difficult to juggle. But the method usually works. Or as an alternate solution the holes can be sprayed with a wasp/hornet insecticide available in aerosols."

Honey bees occasionally swarm in houses, toolsheds, etc. When this happens, it is best to vacate the structure and call in a professional who will safely remove these valuable insects without killing them. Ed.

beekeeping

Q: Where can I find information and materials about bees and beekeeping? A. E. P., Manhattan

A: Asst. Professor Alphonse Avitabile, University of Connecticut, Waterbury, writes, "Two beekeeping magazines are *The American Bee Journal* and *Gleanings in Bee Culture.* Supplies can be obtained from: Dadant & Sons, Inc., Hamilton, Ill. 62341; Walter T. Kelly, Clarkson, Ky. 42726; A. I. Root, Medina, Ohio. Books on the subject are *ABC–XYZ of Beekeeping, Hive and the Honey Bee,* and *The Complete Guide to Beekeeping,* by Roger A. Morse. Also short courses are available from many universities as are correspondence courses."

Publications from the U.S. Department of Agriculture are Beekeeping For Beginners (15 cents) and Beekeeping Equipment (15 cents), both available from Superintendent of Documents, U.S. Government Printing Office, Washington, D.C. 20402. Ed.

bird feeding
bird feeders and cats

Q: We have a large bird feeder for our feathered friends, but there is a difficulty. One neighbor has three cats, the other has one. Is there some repellent to use that has an odor distasteful to cats? R. S. A.

A: Mrs. Charles Ganoe of Pennsylvania suggests a solution for R. S. A. "We fenced the bird feeders from our cats with a few tomato stakes and a turkey wire, leaving one area a little lower so you can step in to fill the feeders. This has discouraged the cats. Their occasional pounce over the fence gives the birds plenty of time to scatter."

in summer

Q: Now that spring is here, should I stop feeding the birds? My neighbor keeps it up all year round, but I should think the birds ought to learn to feed themselves! What is best for the birds? K.D.

A: Richard L. Plunkett, on the staff of the National Audubon Society, writes, "Summer feeding is probably unnecessary in most urban and suburban areas. It will often attract house sparrows and starlings which are considered nuisance birds. Few of the more attractive native birds will benefit from summer backyard feeding. Insect-eating birds rarely visit feeders. Winter feeding is important as it helps sustain many 'half hardy' birds that otherwise might not make it through winter. To help birds during the summer, a bird bath is a better solution."

thistle seed

Q: Is there a way we could grow our own thistle seed for bird feed during the winter months? It is expensive to buy and difficult to find. J. O. Y., Westchester County, N.Y.

73

A: The plant that produces the "thistle seed" sold for gold-finch feed is grown from imported seed of an annual herb of tropical Africa called niger (Guizotia). It belongs to the composite family and has large two-inch daisylike flowers. The seed also produces a fine vegetable oil and is widely grown for this use. Ethiopia, for example, exports 10,000 metric tons of niger seed annually. The thistle seed sold for goldfinch feed is usually sterilized so it will not germinate and cause weed problems in gardens from feeder spillage. Ed.

birds
bird houses

Q: Is there anything that should be done to bird houses in spring to make them suitable for new tenants? There are several on our grounds that were unoccupied last year and we would like to be better landlords this year. Mrs. L. P.

A: Mrs. Paul Whatten of Massachusetts writes, "There may be many reasons why the houses were unoccupied. They may be the wrong size for the local species or in the wrong location. An excellent chapter on bird houses is in the book, *Songbirds in Your Garden,* by John K. Terres (Crowell)."

bluebirds

Q: I have read many articles about bringing back the bluebird and have seen directions for making bluebird houses. We gallantly tried this year to bring them back, built a dandy pair of houses, but sparrows moved in and never did we see bluebirds. Has anyone had any luck? We live in farm country in suburban Philadelphia and there are a few bluebirds around. Some encouragement? J. J. J.

A: Carl E. Kleiber of New Jersey suggests the following. "Bluebirds are rather late nesting as compared to sparrows. Therefore I plug the entrance holes to my bluebird houses with corks until about mid-April, or a bit earlier if the blue-birds are in the vicinity. The bluebirds prefer boxes located on posts set in open fields or along fence rows. Very, very sel-dom will they nest in boxes supported on tree trunks or on woods edges. With about 20 bluebird houses that I maintain, I find that bluebirds will occupy but two to four of them. The rest end up filled with wrens and tree swallows or spar-rows. Also, I cork the cleaned boxes early in the fall to keep out field mice."

And from Hamilton, Bermuda, E. A. H. reports excellent success by following the recommendations given by the Bermuda Audubon Society. They store their bluebird houses in the basement until spring to keep the sparrows from taking over.

*blue jays in
the plums*

Q: I have a plum tree in my yard which fruits well every summer, but the blue jays peck into the plums ruining every one of them. We don't want to harm the birds but we do want to eat the fruit. What can we do? Mrs. L. R.

A: Here are several answers to the rescue. Both Mrs. John Costello and P. Crowley of New York suggest nylon bird netting available from mail-order houses.

John Benedict of Connecticut suggests fastening paper bags over the fruit just as it is about to ripen, making sure to insert a slit at the bottom for rainwater. When it is ripe remove the bag and fruit.

Ronald Lewis of New York used two long flexible wooden poles, 10 feet tall. He made owls of cardboard, covered them with aluminum foil and made eyes, beak and ears of colored plastic tape and attached them with wire to the poles. The poles extend out into the branches. Because the owls are flexible the wind makes them appear as dancing owls. With light reflecting off the foil, nuisance birds are frightened off without harm.

cardinals

Q: What can we use as feed this winter to lure the cardinals back? We miss them and they used to be regular customers. Ms. D. T. M., Mt. Kisco, N.Y.

A: Howard La Morder, a Vermont reader, offers this solution. "We find that cardinals, like many other song birds, prefer to eat under the protection of shubbery which serves as an

umbrella against winter storms and winged predators. The favorite menu is sunflower seed and watermelon seed but cardinals also dine on mixed bird seed. Whatever is supplied, scatter it on the ground generously. They seem to eat breakfast at sunrise and supper at sunset."

in the cherry tree

Q: This spring our cherry tree was loaded with cherries and before we could harvest one, the birds ate them all in spite of fish nets over the tree. Has anyone a solution? L. C. W., Indianapolis, Ind.

A: Here are two. From Mrs. Eugene V. B. Van Pelt of Virginia, "I can report my best success with scarecrows encircling the tree plus sound effects from a portable radio left playing fairly loudly under the tree from dawn to dusk. Only a brown thrasher was brave enough to rush in and grab one cherry at a time. When the radio was turned off, the birds flew into the tree and stayed to eat their fill."

From Mrs. Harry N. Cooperman, a Pennsylvania reader, "I tried covering the cherry tree with mesh, too. It was unsatisfactory. Then a lady from Holland told me what they do there and it works. Take a large spool of thread, hold one end and throw the spool over the top of the tree. Pick it up and throw it over again, back and forth, covering all angles until the thread is completely used up. The birds evidently don't like the thread and it interferes with their getting into the cherries. After a few attempts, they give up."

nesting in the ivy

Q: The English ivy covering the rear brick wall of our house is lush and attractive, but the profusion of sparrow's nests is an eyesore. Our patio and window sills are a mess unless cleared daily. Is there a way of preventing birds from nesting in the ivy? Mrs. L. P.

A: Here are two practical solutions to prevent birds from nesting in unwanted sites. Mrs. Hiram Brown of Maryland suggests to Mrs. L. P., "Take an old length of rubber hose— black—about three or four feet long. Point the ends and insert a long piece of heavy wire. Then just wrap the hose around some branches to stimulate a snake. That does it! Birds will not nest where a snake is apt to eat their eggs."

And, from Dr. W. P. L. McBride of Vermont comes this hint, "My wife had a problem with birds eating her raspberries. So she ran nylon thread in a crisscross pattern (with each strand about six inches apart) across the front and on top of each raspberry row. The birds' feet became entangled in the thread and, after a few attempts, they completely avoided the berries. The same method might work on ivy."

Q: How do you keep birds away from raspberries without covering them so heavily it takes "hours" to unwrap them to pick the fragile fruit? F. L. O., New Jersey

A: Mrs. Walter Beer, Vermont, has a solution. "We string a line above our raspberry bushes from one end of the row to the other. We dangle aluminum pie plates at intervals (one small, one large) tied loosely together so they jingle. They are tied every six inches or so apart. The breeze makes them flutter and give a cheerful jingle. For a large patch use several lines, one over every other row."

Ramon Rosswaag of New Jersey suggests "placing one or two crow decoys in the patch. These can be purchased in most any sporting goods store. Place them on a nearby fence or atop shubbery, not on the ground. It also works well for strawberries and cherries."

Mrs. Eleanor Maloney Gaynor of New York recommends dozens of strips of smooth, nontextured aluminum foil cut into strips measuring 9 × 2 inches. String them like baggage tags on the raspberry bushes to keep the birds away. The strips move with the slightest breeze and make a faint metallic sound as they swing from the branches.

Loeb Rhodes of New York suggests, "Grow mulberry trees nearby."

borers

Q: What can I do to protect my dogwood and rhododendron from borer? Mrs. H. J. S., Mineola, L.I.

A: Borers are the larval stage of moths which lay eggs on the trunks unseen. Eggs hatch into the borers and their presence usually goes undetected until branches suddenly yellow off and die. Holes in the stem, near the base, with protruding sawdust indicate borer invasion. Cut off and burn dead or dying branches below the point of injury. For borer prevention, tree trunks and lower branches are sprayed with malathion three times a season at three week intervals, beginning around May 15. Ed.

bulb eaters

Q: We love animals and tulips and crocus. But some kind of underground critter devours our bulbs each year. Has anyone solved this problem? We do not want to kill the animals, just stop their eating. Mrs. G. H. McF., Connecticut

A: From Maine, Cathy Kulka writes, "A foolproof solution is to make a topless cage out of wire hardware cloth. Sink it in the ground so that the top is level with the surface. The bulbs are planted within the cage and make normal growth since the roots penetrate freely into the mesh. Daffodils are left untouched by mice, etc., and therefore save a lot of trouble."

Mrs. William K. Brewster of Connecticut has still another idea. "I have had no trouble since I tried this experiment. Take an ordinary bottle, ginger ale size, and place the empty bottle in the mole run. Leave three or so inches of the bottle exposed. The wind blows in the empty bottle and makes a vibration that scares the moles away. I place the bottles about 15 inches apart."

chipmunks

Q: We have not been able to pick one ripe strawberry in two years because the chipmunks eat every single one. What can we do? We love strawberries. Dr. M. H., New York

A: Mrs. R. C. Kline of Westchester County suggests, "Having waged a losing battle with chipmunks for years, I placed coffee grounds on top of the soil where spring bulbs bloom. The bulbs grow and bloom freely now and the chipmunks are no longer seen. I do not know if it will work on strawberries, but it might be worth a try."

cutworms

Q: What can be done to eliminate cutworms? Last year they ate my petunias and I had to replace the plants three times. A. C.

A: To the rescue come several ideas. From Mrs. William L. Ransom of New York, "After planting petunias, tomatoes or anything else cutworms seem to like, I take a handful of fertilizer and let it run between my fingers to make a circle of fertilizer around each plant, about two inches beyond the outer leaves. The fertilizer burns the cutworm's bellies and provides nourishment for the plant."

James Jeffrey of New York writes that he "puts collars around each dahlia and tomato plant at the time of planting. Take a milk carton, cut it in half, remove the bottom or top and place half of it below the level of the ground so the cutworm cannot crawl under. The collars are left there and protect the plants from damage when cultivating too close."

earwigs

Q: Has anyone found a way to keep earwigs out of head lettuce without the use of insecticides? M. W., Amherst, Mass.

A: Ray Walker, a suburban Philadelphia gardener, writes, "Place rolled up newspaper near the plants upon which they feed. The papers should be rolled snugly and fastened with a rubber band. Put them out each evening and collect and burn them in the morning. The insects crawl into the papers

flea beetle

as they do plant leaves. This is slow and troublesome, but effective."

Q: Last summer soon after I put out pepper, eggplant and melons, the seedlings were peppered with tiny holes and I had to replace many plants. So this doesn't happen again, what is the problem and the solution? J. D., Darien, Conn.

A: Randy Harvest, a Long Island gardener, writes, "The flea beetle has been at work, a tiny creature that feeds on tender seedling leaves. If the seedlings' leaves are kept dusted (top and undersides, too) with such simple compounds as flour or sifted wood ash, they will not disturb the plants."

goats

Q: We are trying to restore a Maine garden and so far our pet goats have nibbled peonies, iris and a rosebush. Does anyone know what plants goats will not eat and any plants that would be harmful to them? It is not possible to keep them out of the garden. Mrs. I. F. L., Ellsworth, Maine

A: Mrs. Frances Houston of Ohio writes, "Both my experience in keeping goats and reading in goat manuals tell me that no plant is safe from goats. Keeping goats in your garden is like trusting your savings to Bonnie and Clyde. The only solution is to pen up the goats. They don't need very much space and are content with shelter, hay, some grain and attention. They supply much in return: milk, entertainment and unbounded affection. If Mrs. I. F. L. insists goats must be kept in the garden, she should know that wild cherry leaves, rhododendron and yew foliage are poisonous to goats."

ground hogs

Q: Can anyone tell me how to keep ground hogs out of the vegetable garden? I do not want to shoot or trap them. Mrs. L. T.

A: Here are three suggestions. From A. Curtis of Massachusetts, "I've done so on Cape Cod with unqualified success by installing an electric fence. One wire is three to four inches above the ground and the second one is 5 inches above the first. No animals enter the garden and no one has been shot or killed, just jolted a bit. Is there an easier way?"

From William Way of New Jersey, "An electric fence solved the problem for us. We used one charged wire at a height of about six inches and one bare ground wire at ground level. The animals soon learned to stay away whether or not the fence was turned on."

And from Mrs. Helen Tullar of New York, "Simply pour a generous dollop of gasoline down every woodchuck hole you find and plug it tightly. They are excellent diggers so plug the holes with rocks or anything that will make it tough for them to open up. There may be as many as four exits to a burrow, so it isn't likely you will plug them all. But the holes you find will be enough if you are willing to repeat the solution several times. The animals eventually give up and move away."

Another solution was received from Mrs. Robert Whitmer III, of Connecticut. "Ouch, Mrs. L. T.'s woodchucks are in for a shock if not worse. Instead of the electric fence, a good outer row of soybeans and an inner row of onions outlining the perimeter of the garden makes an effective natural barrier for woodchucks and rabbits. They just don't care for this combination and leave the garden alone. You just step over, no gate necessary!"

eating flowers

Q: Our property borders on a wooded area. Every spring the woodchucks eat my newly planted marigolds, zinnias, foxgloves, etc. Is there anyway I can prevent their visits next spring? C. B.

A: Many ideas came in for woodchuck control for C. B.'s property. Here are five. From Judith Nielson, New Jersey, "I live in a place practically surrounded by woods filled with woodchucks, rabbits and deer. For two years now I have had a good-sized organic vegetable garden with no fence. The animals do not get into it as I used dried blood. A towel-full shaken in a line around the garden about a foot out from the edge does the job. Repeat the application following rain."

From M. Janon of New Jersey, "I have gone through the

80

same frustration with woodchucks as C. B. This year I tried something different. I bought six pinwheels, the kind children play with, and placed them in my garden. Each had a little bell in the center. The breeze always kept them spinning and I haven't seen one nibbled plant this year."

From Mrs. John Wilbert of New Jersey, "We had woodchucks living across the road from us in northern Maryland, and they never bothered our flowers. Their woods were rich with raspberries, dewberries and nuts. Perhaps if C. B. supplied the woodchucks' woods with some of their own natural foods, they would not invade the garden."

From John Shaw of Connecticut, "The only and final answer is a trap which catches the woodchuck alive with an ear of corn or lettuce as bait. Then the woodchuck can be transported upcountry onto some open land."

And from Mrs. Elsie Cholet of New York, "We had woodchucks until our cairn terrier switched from chasing squirrels to woodchucks. We have had no further problems. And the woodchucks were safe, he never caught one."

through the fence

Q: Ground hogs get through and under the wire mesh fence on our vegetable garden, avoid traps and are impossible to keep out. Does anyone know how? Mrs. P. W., Croton-on-Hudson, N.Y.

A: George M. Haslerud, a New Hampshire reader, has this suggestion which he learned from a friend. He was told that while a woodchuck will dig down and under even a deep wire barrier, it will give up easily if the wire is bent to make an "L," its base covered with an inch or two of soil. "Use 30-inch wide, one-inch mesh chicken wire, bend it six inches outward and cover with an inch or so of soil. To keep it upright, every 10 feet I weave thin steel rods into the 24-inches and poke them into the ground (or use heavy stakes). At the corners, the wire is clipped to make the turn and the corners are pieced with wire so the barrier is continuous. In the fall, I pull out the wire support rods, straighten the bend and roll the wire up for storage. For two seasons now the woodchuck delicacies inside the fence have been untouched. Rabbits and grey squirrels stay out, too."

leaf miner

Q: Is there a systemic control for birch leaf miner rather than a spray-on pesticide? J. L. S.

A: Mrs. Paul Haston of Ohio writes that there is. The U.S. Forest Service Research Center located in her town recommended using Cygon 2-E, which contains dimethoate.

81

The first brood of leaf miner appears in mid-May and the first ground application should be made prior to this time. The second brood will appear in early July. A foliage spray of the systemic around July 1 would be absorbed quickly to control the second brood. Ed.

mayflies

Q: In Sullivan and Ulster Counties our problem in the summer months is mayflies. I am an organic gardener and don't spray, but what is the answer for these pests? J. J., Manhattan

A: John T. Meehan, Sr., New York, writes, "If J. J. is really an organic gardener with all that that infers he will leave the mayflies strictly alone. Mayflies swarm the streams and other waters in their mating and egg laying activities for only a short time during late spring and early summer. They do no harm, not having mouth parts with which to bite or feed. Their eggs go to the bottom of the streams or other waters and there develop into nymphs which for years to come can supply food to other water creatures, particularly trout."

mice

Q: My chief garden problem seems to be mice. All my tulip bulbs disappeared this last winter as they disappeared in previous winters. The bark around lilac trees was stripped clean at the base and a number of young dogwoods suffered a similar fate. I have tried moth balls around the tulip bulbs and have even dipped bulbs in castor oil before planting. Any advice will be welcome. Mrs. H. F.

A: M. B. R. of New York has offered some solutions. "A cat will help rid the garden of mice. Also, you can rid the garden of moles and beetle grubs. The beetle grubs are food for the moles, and mice travel through the mole's underground tunnels. Another solution, if none of these work, is a material used extensively by farmers, a chemically treated grain containing Warfarin, an anticoagulant. The material can be placed in the garden in below-ground "feeders" around the perimeter of bulb plantings. To do this, put the treated grain in plastic foam coffee cups, fill about half full. Place on the plastic cup top. Poke a few pencil holes in the top so that the grain can sift out. Then dig a hole, or several around the perimeter of the bulb planting, invert the plastic cup, and cover completely. The plastic cups are water resistant and will keep the poisoned grain dry. The mice will feed on the grain and not the bulbs."

millipedes

Q: How can we control millipedes which we find in great abundance this year around the foundation of our house? Mrs. E. W., Connecticut

82

A: *The insects should be eradicated by spraying with mala-thion, Baygon, Diazinon or Sevin in the areas they frequent near basement entrances and windows. Ed.*

moles

Q: Last summer my perennial, annual and rock garden were infested with moles. How can I get rid of them? Mrs. R. B., Long Island

A: Moles beware! Here is a battery of solutions: From Brig. Gen. F. P. Henderson of New Jersey, "Dig a shallow trench around the garden, two to three inches wide and three inches deep. In the bottom, put a generous layer of naphtha-lene flakes or mothballs. Refill and water well. The odor in the soil repels the moles and they will not enter the pro-tected area."

Ruth Jacobsen of New York just "pokes her fingers in the ridge of the moles' tunnels and drops in mothballs, about six to eight inches apart."

Katharine Shorthouse of Long Island "plants garlic around the garden since moles dislike their odor."

Mrs. Rodman Bouck of Connecticut "blends one pint castor oil, one quart of liquid detergent and one pint of water and puts it in a watering can and pokes a hole into the tunnel and pours a little amount in and repeats when new mounds appear, until eventually there are none."

Mrs. R. Lombardy of Long Island recommends planting *Euphorbia lathyrus,* an annual foliage plant which reseeds itself every year. Moles will not go within 50 feet of its roots. Seed is planted in spring.

Andrew R. Stevens of Connecticut suggests "grubproofing the lawn with grub-killer because moles will no longer have the food to eat that attracts them."

Commercial preparations of milky spore disease which is specific for Japanese beetle grubs and harmless to other life are widely distributed. Cats are also useful. Ed.

morning glories (bindweed)

Q: I have a pretty border of daylilies which is being choked with wild morning glories. How can I get rid of them without harming the perennials? Mrs. E. A. M., Vermont

A: Dr. Ira L. Schamberg of Pennsylvania writes, "I have gotten rid of it by dint of about five years of diligent persistent re-peated digging out of the long pulpy roots. It needs extensive excavation as some of the roots have measured about two feet in length. It can be done, but it takes persistence and elbow grease."

Wild morning glory or bindweed is difficult to control. Several applications of 2,4-D are effective, especially if a wax

bar applicator is available to keep the weedkiller away from the perennial. Or pull the weeds away from the daylilies and spray the plants on the grass. The weedkiller will travel systemically in the weed and reach the roots. Ed.

mosquitoes

Q: Does anyone have a practical solution to keep mosquitoes away? We have many pets (three dogs and kittens) and do not want to use sprays. Our outdoor patio is almost useless in summer because of the monsters! Help! Mrs. F. K. T., Mountain Lakes, N.J.

A: Mrs. Alice Grant, another New Jersey reader, suggests, "We use a 12-inch oscillating electric fan to make it difficult for mosquitoes to land. Not 100 percent effective, but it helps."

Chantal Strauss, another reader, writes, "If you do not mind the scent of basil you could try to plant some of it all around the patio. This is the custom of my country, Morocco, where almost every house has its own patio. It is also well known in Spain, especially Andalusia, that basil keeps the mosquitoes away."

mushrooms
deadly amanita

Q: Every summer, in August, the ground under a grove of young poplars at our New Hampshire home is dotted with deadly amanita mushrooms. I am told the best preventive is a pre-emergent chemical that will inhibit spore growth. Any advice? H. P. H.

A: Mrs. Theodore L. Stern of New York offers this point of view. "I'd like to say that there are many poisonous plants of all kinds, so many that we could never get rid of them. Since the amanita is a fairly easy mushroom to identify, why not just relax and enjoy its beauty? This could start H. P. H. on one of the most enjoyable pursuits I have ever undertaken—the study of wild mushrooms. An excellent course is given every fall at the New York Botanical Garden. Fungi can be fun!"

muskrats

Q: Could anyone tell us what to do about muskrats around our pond? How can we repel them or at least keep their number in bounds? We do not want to trap or kill them. Mrs. W. R.

A: Robert S. Jonas, Soil Conservation Service, New City, N.Y., offers this suggestion on the muskrat problem. "Since Mrs. W. R. does not want to harm the muskrats, cyanide gas, carbon monoxide and a rifle are out. The next best solution is to cover the ground in the critical area, usually around the dam, with coarse mesh, heavily galvanized hardware cloth or chicken wire and then add a six-inch layer of small stones or coarse gravel. The metal should extend from one foot above to three feet below the water level."

nettle

Q: We recently purchased a farm in Wisconsin and many areas near the house have nettles growing rampantly. Is there any way to eradicate them? F. M. C.

A: H. B. of Connecticut writes that nettles, particularly stinging nettles, are susceptible to 2,4-D. For big patches a sprayer can be used, but for spot treatment, try a common squirt oil can, or the handy aerosols, sold commercially.

**onion and
garlic grass**

Q: What is the best way to control wild onion–garlic grass without injuring the grass or plantings? I hesitate to use chemical sprays and pulling hasn't helped as the multiplying bulblets continue to develop. Mrs. S. F.

A: Here are two schemes for Mrs. S. F. to rid her property of these weeds. Grace C. Rapp of New Jersey suggests close cropping of the stems which seems to be an adequate way to reduce the spread of garlic grass almost to the point of extinction. By close cropping before the plant reaches maturity (November 15 to December) you prevent the formation of bulblets and seeds.

George Kelly of Pennsylvania suggests "mixing a small amount of weedkiller (2,4-D) in an old bucket. With both hands well protected with rubber gloves, dip the rubber gloves into the bucket and "pull" at the leaves of the pesky weeds several times, lightly. This seems to press the weedkiller onto the leaves well and in 10 days or so they start to brown off. Or for a large amount of the weeds, take a roast baster from your wife's kitchen and squirt the weedkiller from the bucket onto each weed. But be very careful when working with this material and throw away the gloves, bucket, and buy your wife a new roast baster when finished."

According to Home Lawns, Cornell University Extension bulletin #922, "Wild garlic or onion is hard to kill during most of the year. Treat with 2,4-D in very early spring and follow with a second treatment early the following spring. The two treatments are needed to kill both the plants of the current season and those that will grow in the autumn from hardy bulblets already in the soil." Ed.

pigeons

Q: We have pigeons nesting in the four-by-fours of our roof. We are tired of their cooing, littering and monopolizing the area around our bird feeder. How can we get rid of these unwanted birds? Mrs. P. R.

A: L. F., Washington, D.C., writes that her method is 100 percent effective. She hangs or stands two or three fake owls near where the pigeons roost. Owls are the enemies of pigeons. The fake owls may be purchased at country stores or through mail-order houses. The owls may be made of metal or wood; some are quaintly painted. Others are made of plastic.

Mrs. Vernon Hall of Connecticut concurs. The owl used at their home was suspended on aluminum wire from the roof. They chose a natural colored one and she suggests it can also be used in the flower or fruit garden.

George Stubbs of New York had good results with a no-roost product sold in aerosol cans for about $3. It leaves a sticky surface on the roosting site.

poison ivy

Q: Our property is rampant with poison ivy. How can we get rid of it without harming our two cats who like to roam in the dense woodsy area? Mrs. T. G. H.

A: *Poison ivy is controlled when in full leaf with amino-triazole sold as "Poison Ivy Killer" and other package names. Follow directions CAREFULLY. The herbicide is absorbed readily into the plants and is not toxic to the pets. The weeds will die down in about two to three weeks. Ed.*

pond weeds

Q: Can you recommend a weedkiller for a spring-fed lake? We do not want to use anything that would kill the fish. Mrs. G. J. K., Manhattan

What is, if any, a weedkiller for cattails? Mr. V. V., Manhattan

A: Since these two questions are related, the following information from Mrs. Elizabeth Biggart, New York state, may be of some help. "I found a product called Aquacide after looking for many months for a weedkiller that would not kill pond wildlife. The product information states that Aquacide is a herbicide in pellet form which effectively controls the growth of troublesome aquatic weeds in lakes and ponds. It contains 2,4-D which kills lily pads, arrowheads, cattails, etc. One 10-pound can will treat 4,000 square feet in any depth of water."

rabbits
in the garden

Q: I'm desperate! Has anyone worked out a solution to keep rabbits out of the garden? I'm not there during the week. Mr. R. V., Manhattan

A: George Kelsey of Connecticut writes "A fence. At least this is what we finally succumbed to after using dried blood, moth balls, aluminum "scare" plates tied on string and at-

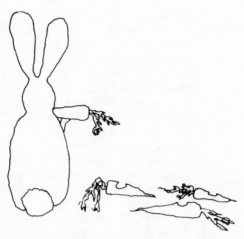

tached to poles. The rabbits outsmarted us every time and we found that rain quickly washed down the odor of dried blood so that it lost its effectiveness. Actually, a small chicken wire fence attached to poles at the four corners is not obtrusive. It is low enough to step over without need for a gate and the bunnies are, at last, on the outside looking in."

And Mrs. Richard Warren of Massachusetts writes, "Fill large green bottles half full of water (quart-size bottles are ideal) and half bury them at eight feet intervals in the border. There are two speculations why this is effective. The rabbits may be frightened by the glitter of water or the sound of wind over the top of a bottle may sound like an owl."

Mrs. George C. Buell, another Massachusetts gardener, also suggests the bottles, but her recommendation is to place the half-filled bottles upright on the ground without partially burying them.

Many of her neighbors use the same method and it works. So do old sneakers placed around the garden. Their odor drives off rabbits.

nibbling bulbs

Q: Every spring our bulbs come up very early and the tips are nibbled by rabbits. Is there something we can do in the fall to prevent this? Mrs. D. S. M., Rye, N.Y.

A: From Massachusetts, Mrs. David Squire writes, "Moth balls spread among the new shoots of spring bulbs will keep the rabbits away. They need to be replenished after a heavy rain and they may look a little odd, but rabbits hate them."

raccoons
in the corn

Q: How can I prevent the raccoons from harvesting the sweet corn? I. A. L., Bearsville, N.Y.

A: Here are several solutions. The first is offered hesitatingly for those in the suburbs; perhaps only wide-spaced country gardeners should try it. From Alvin Tresselt of Connecticut, "For the last three or four years I have kept raccoons out of the corn patch by playing a radio all night long, preferably a "talk" station. I also have a floodlight burning. I protect the radio from rain by placing it on a platform and covering it with a large upturned kettle."

R. P. Hunter, a Pennsylvania reader, uses "several farm kerosene lanterns between the rows, starting a few nights before the corn is ripe."

From Francis Baxendale of Long Island, "I have a dog run with two dogs. I carry the dog manure to the corn patch and place it not in the row but between the plants. My garden is exposed and open, and I suspect the raccoons are frightened by the scent of the dogs."

From Mrs. B. S. Ridgely, New Hampshire, "Sprinkle the corn tassels liberally with red pepper. If it rains, sprinkle again."

And from Russell Barbour, another Pennsylvania gardener, "We live in the woods and our only defense is the full chicken wire coverage—wall, and roof six feet high with the bottom edge wood-framed too."

See Squirrels in the corn, page 90.

and rosebuds

Q: Does anyone know how we can prevent raccoons from eating the buds on our rosebushes? We don't want to use any methods that could harm neighbors' pets. Mrs. J. D., New Jersey

A: Mrs. J. G. Balham of Vermont suggests what she does to save her corn. "Very lightly grease the tight buds with shortening and sprinkle on cayenne pepper. Once the rose starts to open, there will still be some pepper on the underside to protect it. My ears of corn were a bit greasy to pick, but at least I picked them and not the raccoons."

skunk

Q: Skunks are digging for grubs on my front lawn. I bought a quart of chlordane and applied the required treatment two nights running but they are still digging up the front lawn. I have tried moth balls and red pepper. What can I do? Mr. S. G., Fort Lee, N.J.

A: We hope that Mr. S. G. did not give a double dose of chlordane to his lawn. One should have been sufficient and more would cause serious problems to the grass and wildlife since chlordane is a potent pesticide labeled for restricted use. The far better solution for grubs is to use the biological control, milkyspore disease, which is sold commercially as Doom. One treatment should be sufficient for the future since the disease becomes established in the ground. Doom is harmful only to the grubs of Japanese beetles. Skunks as well as moles will disappear from lawns, once the grubs are controlled. Ed.

Readers have added some additional helps. Mrs. William Riley of New Jersey, writes, "There is another alternative, an excellent repellent called Tatgo, available in many retail outlets. It seems to repel anything from anything!"

From H. K. S.in the Virgin Islands, "The most interesting creatures we ever had in a lawn were skunks. They are magnificent little animals—gentle, slow-moving and very dignified and unless attacked, quite odorless. They are the most diligent and inexpensive yard workers we will ever have. Enjoy them!"

slugs

Q: What can be done to rid our garden of slugs? They come from between cracks and crevices in railroad ties. Baits and nightly raids have not worked. W. J. S.

A: From Mrs. Robert Karasiewicz of New Jersey, the answer, "A positive, yet simple way to rid a garden of slugs is to place saucers of beer in strategic locations around the garden each evening. The slugs are attracted to the beer, crawl in and drown. In the morning, empty the saucers and repeat for a few successive evenings."

snails

Q: Beer works fine as a control for slugs. Has anyone as practical a solution to get rid of snails? R. E. W., Long Island

A: Norman A. Foss of Connecticut writes, "I have used products containing metaldehyde for killing both slugs and snails. Usually supplied in pellet form, the product is sprinkled in the garden to attract them. The day following application, numerous dead snails and slugs are found in the garden."

Be cautious with these baits where pets and children are about. Ed.

snakes

Q: Our home in heavily wooded North Jersey is surrounded by rock walls. These walls are often homesites for a variety of snakes. Can anyone offer a suggestion on how to rid the walls of these pests (short of hiring a mongoose)? Mrs. J. L. V., Smoke Rise, N.J.

89

A: Mrs. Mary K. Muckenhoupt, a New Jersey reader, suggests, "Though Mrs. J. L. V. did not indicate whether her snakes were poisonous, I assume they are not, and recommend that she not attempt to get rid of them. The snakes eat small rodents and if she gets rid of the snakes, she may gain a rodent problem. On our five acres we encourage a wide variety of wild plants and animals, mostly by leaving them alone, and find our lives enriched by a growing knowledge of the plants, animals and birds we share the land with. We suggest a basic book about snakes, to learn a bit about the creatures."

Q: The squirrels are back in our attic. I want them out. Someone said plug the entrance with steel wool, or spun glass, but I understand this is not effective. I don't want to use rat poison. We have a dog, so a cat is out. Solutions? E. F. K.

A: Here are two ideas. From Thomas DeMartini of New York, "Use camphor balls or flakes thrown about the attic floor and between the floor beams where possible. I have found this method gives good and long-lasting results. Keep young children and pets out of the attic for the next month or two after the camphor is spread."

Albert Zulkowitz of Long Island suggests buying a live animal trap at sporting goods or Army and Navy stores. "The squirrels are trapped live, one at a time, then they can be released far, far away from the home. Then board up the entrance hole with a sound board, for squirrels will gnaw through rough wood."

Q: I had a great corn crop this year but the squirrels took quite a bit for themselves. How can I keep the squirrels away from my corn? I don't want to harm them but at the same time I'd like to eat my corn. Clues anyone? H. J. N., Jr.

A: In reply to H. J. N.'s query about controlling squirrels in corn, Otto Karst of New York writes that the following method has worked efficiently for him: "Purchase ¼-inch mesh hardware cloth and cut into 12x8-inch rectangles. Bend the rectangle into a cylinder which will be about 12-inches long and about 2½-inches in diameter. Jam this cylinder over the ear of corn when it is almost ripe and tie the top of the cylinder to the stalk of corn. This may sound like work, but it surely stops the squirrels, and even raccoons. The cylinders last for years. This year I also experimented with tin cans."

Q: Regardless of the quantity of acorns that developed this fall, the squirrels prefer to eat the buds on my dogwood trees. Is there a way I can discourage this so that I will have some dogwood bloom this spring? Mrs. D. D.

A: We have checked several cooperative extension and wild-life experts and none has been able to suggest a preventive. Live trapping has worked in some cases; dried blood in others. But at best, they are a gamble. If anyone has solved such a problem, we would all like to know how. Ed.

Here are two approaches. From Mrs. George W. Hart of New York, "We had squirrels who ate dogwood, tulip, willow, etc., buds. Then we fed the squirrels sunflower seeds and peanuts daily. After that, they never touched a bud or flower."

And from Mrs. William Riley of New Jersey, "Squirrels can be kept from eating dogwood flower buds by smearing the tree trunk with Tanglefoot or any of the other sticky substances designed primarily to keep insects from crawling up a tree trunk. There is also a product called "Squell" particularly distasteful to squirrels when they find it on their paws."

eating plums

Q: Is there anything I can paint on the trunk of my plum tree to stop the squirrels from eating the unripe fruit? Mrs. E. W. B., Larchmont, N.Y.

A: An Ulster County gardener, Mrs. William T. Golden, writes, "The best way we have found to keep squirrels and raccoons out of trees is to put a two-foot circle of aluminum (not foil) around the trunk as high as you can reach. This does not, however, prevent squirrels from jumping to the branches from neighboring trees."

eating tulips

Q: How can I keep the local squirrels from eating the flowers of the tulips in spring? The other flowers don't interest them, just the tulips. Mrs. W. I.

A: Josef Vecara of New York suggests, "I read of the same problem and the solution suggested by a London park gardener. Dried blood was used successfully on the park flower beds to keep squirrels away. We have also tried this with good results."

Mrs. Eleanor Gaynor of New York offers this scheme. "Squirrels completely wrecked our tulips and all suggestions of what to do failed until I placed bonemeal in a ring around the flower beds with a teaspoonful of bonemeal placed here and there within the bed. Now, our tulips are 100 percent squirrel proof."

91

termites

in bark mulch

Q: I had intended to put down bark chip mulch around the front of my house. But a neighbor tells me that these chips would attract colonies of termites. Is this possible? G. R.

in fireplace wood

Q: I have stored newly chopped wood for my fireplace in the basement. Do you recommend this or is there a chance of termites? J. L., Long Island

A: Termites are subterranean insects that eat wood or cellulose. They live in darkness and will make tunnels to travel through to keep them out of light to reach water and nesting sites. Wood stored in an enclosure would especially appeal to termites as well as carpenter ants which nest in wood. This (1972) is an unusually favorable year for insect pests because of the abundant soil moisture. Any mulch will help to conserve this. Gardeners are experiencing large slug and millipede populations and, in some cases, termites have been seen in wood chip mulches. In short, spread wood chip mulches to keep them from having direct contact with the house and always store fireplace wood outdoors, a good distance away from the foundation of the house. Ed.

ticks

Q: Could you help me? We have an acre of ground on the extreme eastern tip of Long Island, excellent virgin land, completely overgrown but infested with ticks. How do we get rid of the ticks? Mrs. H. S. W.

A: Writing from Long Island, Frank Spoerr suggests, "I have used Gardona 75 (wettable powder). It appears to do a good job but I limit its use to paths and most frequently used areas. Let's face it, as long as deer, rabbits, etc., rub against shrubs, high grass, etc., the ticks will reappear on one's property."

weeds

between bricks

Q: Does anyone know of a good way to destroy weeds between bricks? I have tried salt and even a flame gun but new weeds always appear. Mrs. C. J. C., Long Island

A: Mrs. C. Trendowski of New Jersey uses Borax for areas where she wants complete soil sterilization such as in cracks in the broken flagstone patio. "We pour it on before rain, if possible, approximately every six weeks or so. We avoid the plantings around the patio by about a foot."

in the drive

Q: We have a shell driveway on Cape Cod and for years have been fighting weeds that come up through it. Does anyone have a solution? A. K., Darien, Conn.

A: Here are several suggestions. From Dr. David D. Waugh of Connecticut, "Use Dacthal herbicide, a pre-emergent and seed killer. It is also used on the lawn against weeds, especially crabgrass."

From Mrs. A. F. M. van der Ven of New York, "Laundry Borax used dry as it comes from the box. Start early in the growing season and repeat applications as necessary."

From Catherine Phebe Lott of New York, "Rock salt sprinkled about in the spring." (*Caution here as there could be damage to near-by plant roots. Ed.*)

From Mrs. E. V. Ferguson II of Connecticut, "Calcium chloride, but sprinkle cautiously, in the spring at first sign of weeds. Do it again in June after spring rains and again in August if needed. But do not get it on skin or track it into the house." (*Caution as above. Ed.*)

in gravel

Q: How can I permanently end the weeds in a large gravel parking lot at my country home without using expensive commercial weedkillers? B. P. S., Bangor, Pa.

A: Charlene Costaris, a New Jersey gardener, suggests, "If there are no desirable plants nearby and none planned for the near future, most weeds can be killed by pouring salt (sodium chloride) on the ground around the weeds. Very few plants can grow in salty soil. Treatment might have to be repeated as salt leaches out."

violets as a weed

Q: My perennial bed is overrun with violets. I weed them out each year and sweeten the soil with lime, but they return. What to do? Mrs. J. A. K., Connecticut

A: Dinah L. Foglia of New York suggests, "The problem could be twofold. Cultivated violets nearby could be the source of seed which means removing the seed pods, a difficult task. The other possibility is that she may not be removing the roots in weeding. Violets have deep rhizomelike roots; any pieces left will continue to grow."

See Violets as weeds, page 111.

white fly
in greenhouse

Q: My cool greenhouse is infested with white fly. Is there any way of dealing with this pest other than pesticides? If spray is required, what do you suggest. Mrs. M. M.

A: In reply, Mrs. Marion Underhill of New York writes, "I, too, keep a cool greenhouse and my lantanas and fuchsias seemed to be the plants most infested with white flies. I bought two Vapona insect strips in the supermarket and

(**whitefly**
continued)

hung one at each end of the greenhouse. Voila! No more flies or any other insect." (*It is recommended that these strips not be used in children's rooms, sick rooms or where food is prepared. Ed.*)

on vegetables

Q: Many readers have written about troubles with white fly on assorted vegetable crops, particularly tomatoes. We are stumped. Has anyone been successful in eradicating this troublesome insect? We would all like to know. Ed.

A: George F. Stubbs of New York suggests, "First, start the program very early, using either Cygon or Diazinon. Then when nearing time to harvest use either Sevin or malathion. I have found it to be an excellent program."

Janet McMillan of New York claims her lack of a white fly problem is due to her practice of companion planting. She planted chives, parsley and marigolds between and among her tomatoes.

A check with Dr. Arthur Muka, extension entomologist for Cornell University, brought out some additional helps on the white fly problem. White fly does not overwinter outdoors but it can move indoors and overwinter in homes and commercial greenhouses. Many people often "buy" their white flies when they purchase bedding and vegetable seedlings for their garden. He recommends thorough inspection of seedlings before purchase next spring. The insect has three stages, any of which can be present on plants: egg (very difficult to detect), immature (an almost scalelike appearance), and adult. For control, he suggests malathion or Diazinon, used several times a week, if necessary, to reduce the population, then less frequently as necessary. Both pesticides could be used as close as one day before harvest because they are quickly biodegradable. A new synthetic pyrethrum, just appearing on the market, will also control white fly.

yellow jackets

Q: About this time of year, yellow jackets hover over the grass and barbecue area. Their sting is painful and long-lasting. I have been told they nest in the ground. How do you locate the nests and eradicate the insects? J. F. P., Westchester County, N.Y.

For many years we have been bothered by yellow jackets attacking our food as we eat on our open terrace. Can anyone suggest a solution? Mrs. H. S. C.

A: Writing from Connecticut, Mrs. E. V. Ferguson II suggests, "Locate the nests by watching where they go. There may be more than one hole in the ground, going to the same nest. Choose a dark, cool night and use carbon tet (if available locally) or something like Renuzit cleaning fluid. Pour some down the hole and plug it with a cotton ball that has been saturated."

Alta Indelman of New York offers another solution. "Give the yellow jackets a small share in the feast. Place a small dish of hamburger crumbs or other food scraps at one end of the table and the yellow jackets will accumulate there and will not touch the other food. If you can't beat them, let them join in!"

compost and mulch ideas

black plastic

Q: This past summer I used black plastic mulch on our vegetable garden. During the summer, the plastic disintegrated from the sun and storms. Tiny pieces have been incorporated into the soil. Does anyone know if these will harm next year's plantings? Mrs. V. S., Mexico City

A: Black plastic mulch is not biodegradable and should be removed from the soil at the end of the growing season. It can be saved and reused for several years. Mrs. V. S. notes that her mulch has already broken into pieces. It would be difficult to remove the plastic now. When replanting during the new growing season, any exposed pieces that turn up should be discarded. Ed.

chicken manure

Q: I have 40 egg laying hens. I have heard that chicken manure is good fertilizer. Can anyone tell me what I must do to make the best use of it? T. H. D., Ambler, Pa.

A: Alan J. Reff, who says he is an ex-resident of a central New Jersey chicken farm, writes, "Under no circumstances use fresh chicken manure on growing plants or vegetables as it will burn them. Either turn in fresh manure now (December) or used aged (weathered, at least 6 months) manure in spring. It is effective for corn and tomatoes."

The nutrient content of chicken manure is nitrogen, 5 percent; phosphorus, 1.9 percent; potash, 1.2 percent. Ed.

coffee grounds

Q: Are coffee grounds good for mulch and soil texture or are they too acid? Mrs. J. L. S., Freeport, N.Y.

A: Mrs. Anne Rudell, a Long Island gardener, suggests, "I prefer to add coffee grounds to the compost. They make the

resulting humus more friable and are more beneficial in a decayed state. Where I have used coffee grounds right from the pot, the results have not been good as the grounds are too acid."

Ralph E. Martin, a New Jersey engineer and gardener, concurs that coffee grounds for general garden and lawn use are too acid. He recommends small quantities for ericaceous (acid-loving) ornamentals.

compost
additives

Q: Can someone help us settle an over-the-backfence "argument." Is it or is it not necessary to use compost additives to aid rapid decay? Thank you! G. F., Connecticut

A: Bertram Waller, another Connecticut gardener, says, "Where additives are successful, there is something missing from the normal composting conditions. The necessary ingredients for rapid composting are moisture, air, fungi and bacteria which occur in normal soil, plus carbon and nitrogen in correct proportions. If all are present, additives will make no improvement. A small quantity of soil mixed in with other ingredients will inoculate the compost with microorganisms. If low nitrogen materials such as leaves, sawdust, twigs or brush are composted, add high nitrogen materials such as grass clippings, garden weeds, poultry manure, cottonseed meal, dried blood. If these cannot be found, add high nitrogen commercial fertilizers such as 10-6-4."

failure

Q: We used beech leaves and layered our compost pile last fall with woods soil and fertilizer. But when we turned it over last week (March), it was still a wet mass of leaves, not decayed compost. What did we do wrong? A. W., New Jersey

97

(**compost**
continued)

A: Here are two answers of encouragement: From Charles B. Stirhler of Long Island, "You did absolutely the right thing. Fall–winter is not weather for decaying. It takes heat and moisture. Also beech leaves will not decay as readily as some others. Patience. You will be rewarded."

And from Dr. Jon M. Wilson of New Jersey, "We have been making compost successfully for many years with the following routine. We buy 15 feet of two-foot-high chicken wire, joining the ends to make a circle of convenient diameter in which to work the compost. We then introduce our leaves, grass clippings, and vegetable kitchen scraps (we keep a separate kitchen container for these items, including egg shells and coffee grounds, which we add to the compost pile every few days). After eight inches of such material, we add a quart container of high-nitrogen fertilizer and garden limestone and a three-inch layer of soil, keeping the center of the pile low, to collect water. The pile should be watered during long dry spells. This layering is continued until the hoop is filled. A second hoop is then started alongside the first one, and the contents of the first hoop are transferred to the second hoop with a fork, breaking up the rotted leaves at the bottom of the pile, intermixing the soil and additives, and aerating the material, all for the purpose of accelerating decomposition. The first hoop is then reused, starting a new compost pile. We have found that it takes one year to fully compost a batch using this technique. Without additives and turning, it takes two or three years, and must still be limed before use in the garden."

liming

Q: Is it necessary to add lime to the compost pile? I have heard yes and no, and I'm confused. K. O. P., Pittsburgh, Pa.

A: No. Lime is calcium carbonate and does not improve the organic matter's ability to decompose more rapidly. In regions where soil tends to be extremely acid, some gardeners do add lime. Ed.

corn stalks

Q: Will corn stalks decompose in the compost by next spring or should I put something with them to hasten decay? Ms. G. T., Carmel, N.Y.

A: John G. Dreher, a New Jersey reader, writes, "Do not use corn stalks for compost as the European corn borer winters over in the old stalks. Discard or burn corn stalks with other residue."

If gardeners have access to a shredder/chipper, the corn stalks can be chopped up and composted. Ed.

98

egg shells

Q: Do egg shells enrich the soil of a flower or a vegetable garden? Are they good for compost? Mrs. J. U.

A: Mrs. James K. Landers of Connecticut writes, "Very definitely. They are a good source of calcium and have the same effect as lime. They are especially good to use where herbs are grown. The dried shells should be ground to a powder first in the blender before they are mixed with the soil."

George C. Whiteley, Jr. of Massachusetts, writes that egg shells are calcium carbonate chiefly and are good for soil and compost. But he asks why stop at egg shells for compost? He suggests orange skins, lemon rind and kitchen scraps dug in to avoid attracting flies.

M. H. C. White of New York has another use for eggshells. "Raw egg shells dropped into a covered quart jar of water (covered to avoid the odor) make an effective water for house plants. Recalcitrant plants, especially begonias, begin to bloom. After a week or two discard the egg shells and start over again."

fish fertilizer

Q: Is there any benefit to using fish heads and remains as fertilizer for vegetables as the Indians once taught the Pilgrims? J. R. D., Wilmington, Del.

A: Ray Walker of Pennsylvania writes, "Yes. Fish contribute calcium, sodium, phosphorus and potassium to the soil, and some iron for leafy vegetables. These nutrients are in water soluble form. The disadvantage of using fish remains is that cats will dig them up if allowed near the planting area. Try cat repellant sprays."

grass clippings

Q: Can anyone settle a neighborhood dispute? Are grass clippings to be raked up or left on the grass to recycle? M. L., White Plains, N.Y.

A: Tracy Scott of New Jersey, says, "Rake. We rake ours and then place them in a mulch pile where they decay and re-cycle. We have found that if the grass clippings are left on the ground, the grass does not get as much sun and yellows."

gypsum

Q: Does gypsum have any value as a clay soil conditioner; should it be used in preference to lime? R. P. R., Flushing, N.Y.

A: Gypsum is hydrous calcium sulfate while lime is calcium carbonate (or magnesium carbonate in the case of dolomitic limestone). Both are soil conditioners. However, gypsum is more effective and recommended generally for soils of high pH (alkaline) since it is more effective at higher pH levels. (These soils are more prevalent in the Southwest.) Gypsum will not alter soil pH as will ground limestone. Both sub-stances have the ability to flocculate clay particles in soil, that is combine the minute clay particles into small granules per-mitting better soil drainage. Gypsum does this more quickly than lime as it is more soluble. To answer R. P. R.'s question, gypsum is not a substitute for lime but can be used in con-junction with it. The local office of Cooperative Extension, located in the county seat, will test soil and make lime recom-mendation needs and can advise on use of gypsum as well. Ed.

horse manure

Q: My neighbor recently purchased a horse. There is enough manure to use on both our acre lots. Any suggestions on its use? J. M.

A: To J. M. and his neighbor who have the horse, Durban Wright of Delaware writes that the best use for the horse manure is as mulching material, after it has weathered. He mixes it well with rotted compost for mulch. He also digs it into his garden in spring when preparing the vegetable patch. To use it fresh on garden areas can be disastrous as the mate-rial can burn as easily as too much fertilizer.

with sawdust

Q: We have a lot of horse manure with sawdust. Can we use it as a fertilizer for the lawn? If so, when and how much? H. G. W., Pleasantville, N.Y.

A: Here is a suggestion from Mrs. Richard Rudell of Long Island. "The best time to use your organic gold is when the ground is frozen and snow-covered. Spread it evenly and thinly over the lawn, flower beds and vegetable garden. The manure combined with sawdust is more friable. Melting

100

snow and rains will seep the fertilizer into the ground without burning. Any manure left over is an excellent additive to the compost pile. We import this organic combination at high cost."

weathered

Q: What does well-rotted horse manure mean? How long should it be exposed to weathering before we can use it on the garden? J. J. K. Larchmont, N.Y.

A: The manure should be exposed long enough to reduce the high nitrogen content which has a burning quality if used fresh on plants. It is sufficiently weathered when crumbly and lighter in color. Ed.

iron

Q: If I were to shred up tin cans with a tinsnip and scatter them in my vegetable garden would this increase the iron content in my vegetables? F. S., Long Island

A: Peter Brown of Delaware writes, "F. S. must have many Band-Aids. I would hate to dig around in his back yard! There is a proper, efficient way to supply iron to the soil through the highly refined iron or chelated iron products manufactured for agricultural use and sold under trade names. Plants will take up only the iron they need, which is a relatively minor amount. You can't force a plant to absorb more iron than it would normally require. Maybe F. S. would rather try iron pills from the drugstore."

Plants most affected by iron deficiency are the ericaceous, acid-type soil plants such as rhododendrons, hollies, laurels. Fruit trees may also be troubled. Ed.

kitty litter

Q: Can the used kitty litter be added to the compost pile or serve as a mulch? A. L., Cortland, N.Y.

A: Gretchen Kreuter of Minnesota writes, "Don't do it. Most types of kitty litter are pelletized clay. The purpose of compost is to lighten the soil; clay has the opposite effect. I learned this only after dumping kitty litter on my compost pile for an entire winter. As an additional result, neighborhood cats were attracted to my compost pile."

Marion Cavanaugh of New Jersey writes, "I use kitty litter as a mulch on established plants—roses, peonies, lilacs, and shrubs."

Kitty litter is usually a refined and heated dried fuller's earth clay, ground to small porous particles. The material is extremely absorbent and does not break down and dissolve. It can be used as a salt substitute on icy sidewalks and to absorb grease on garage floors. Ed.

101

locust pods

Q: Is there a use for moraine locust pods in compost? Mrs. F. M. Z., Strasburg, Va.

A: Mrs. Mary K. Wheeler of Connecticut writes, "Since locust is a legume, the pods would have similar nutrient qualities to pea pods which we always toss on our compost pile. The locust pod is thick. Quantities of them will decompose faster if put through a chipper or shredder before adding them to compost."

Mrs. Gerald W. Johnson of Maryland writes, "I am horrified at the idea of consigning anything as beautiful as moraine locust pods to a compost pile. They can be used in dried arrangements as purple accents. Rub them gently with a flannel cloth moistened with lemon oil furniture polish. They will last for years. The pods also make charming mobiles and can be sprayed with gold or silver for arrangements or ornaments."

manure "tea"

Q: We know many good gardeners recommend manure "tea" fertilizer for vegetables and flowers. What is it and where do you buy it? B. R. T., New Rochelle, N.Y.

A: Marion Mackie, a New York gardener, suggests this recipe. "Put one cupful of packaged dried cow manure in a cheesecloth bag. Put the bag in a pail of water for two or three days, or until the color of weak tea, a pale amber. Now it is ready to 'serve.' I find that all perennials and vegetables respond well."

mulch
feeding through

Q: This may be very elementary, but I would like to know how to apply fertilizer to vegetable and flower areas where they are thickly mulched? Y. V., New Jersey

A: R. A. Uzar of New York suggests that Y. V. "use liquid fertilizer and leaf feed the leaves by spraying on the foliage. Also, water soluble fertilizers will soak through the mulch into the soil."

wind problem

Q: The wind on Long Beach Island keeps blowing away the mulch under my young pine trees. I've tried pine bark chips, large and small, behind a four-inch circular mound. There are 40 young trees involved. Any ideas? R. I. P.

A: Mrs. Emil Trautmann of Maryland tried several mulches and the only thing that remains where she puts it in her windy region is shredded bark which she obtains from a saw mill, a useless by-product, somewhat coarse but not objectionable. It has solved her problem of trying to establish creeping junipers on rather steep banks.

102

Raymond Willis of New Jersey suggests rock mulching which he has practiced successfully for some 20 years at a summer place on Lake Champlain. He suggests using stones of many shapes and sizes, slabs of slate or sandstone, cobble-shaped rocks, field stones or glacial pebbles.

newspapers

Q: I have read about mulching with newspaper and have done it successfully, but now I am concerned about lead from the inks leaching into the soil. Should I worry? Mrs. H. Z., Ancram, N.Y.

A: Work on the use of newspapers as mulch has been carried out by the Connecticut Agricultural Experiment Station, New Haven. A recent issue of their research report states, "Our results suggest that paper recycled from waste printed with lead type or with colored inks contains more lead than paper made from waste printed with black ink or by a lead-free process like offset. We also found that recycled newsprint is six-fold richer in lead than virgin newsprint. Since paper is often used to mulch vegetables, we experimented with lead-containing paper that might be used as a mulch.

"When we treated papers around vegetables with the equivalent of 8 weeks of the moderately acid rainfall that might be experienced in the Northeast, negligible amounts of lead leached from the papers. Thus, we concluded there seems little danger of lead contamination to plants from mulch." L. Hankin, G. Heichel, B. Botsford

oak leaves

Q: My Long Island property has many species of oak. The leaves are plentiful for the compost heap, but they don't break down in compost. I have one heap, three years old, and the bottom leaves are still yellow. Help, anyone? A. H.

A: Mrs. Alexander Berger of New York writes, "The secret of obtaining good compost is to chop oak leaves. If your power

mower does not have a mulching attachment, close off the discharge chute with wire mesh and wrap a piece of porous cloth over the air intake to screen out dust. This chopping reduces the bulk by 90 percent. My oak compost pit is a 12-inch deep trench, about 18 inches wide extending 20 to 30 feet along the rear fence. After the first lot of acorns, twigs, etc, are raked up, I chop the oak leaves and pile them into the trench. To it I add wood ashes from the fireplace. In lieu of ashes, use some lime and lawn fertilizer. If the summer is dry, soak the trench a few times. By September, you will have well rotted compost."

Stephen G. Belt of Maryland adds this help, "A compost pile that doesn't heat up very much or decay is usually low in nitrogen content." He suggests adding "nitrogen in some organic form, e.g., animal manure, cottonseed meal, dried blood or fish meal, since it is nitrogen which nourishes the microorganisms that break down the compost materials."

seaweed
nutrients

Q: I have over three hundred feet of Maine shoreline where from early July to late fall seaweed, called rockweed, comes ashore. Both local residents and myself use this as a mulch and fertilizer. They claim it is the best fertilizer in the world since it contains almost every trace element. Is there any definitive proof of this? E. W. R., South Harpswell, Maine

A: W. E. Teague, a New Jersey reader, subscribes to *Organic Gardening* magazine and quotes from a recent issue, "As fertilizer, seaweed compares very favorably with farmyard manures. It has a lower content of nitrogen and phosphorus but contains almost twice as much potassium. Most important, however, is its rich content of trace minerals such as iodine, iron, copper, manganese, boron and zinc."

and salt

Q: Is there a special treatment necessary before using beach seaweed as a mulch for our shore cottage plantings? Is the salt accumulation ever removed? D. S., Long Island

A: Here are two ideas. From Lou Hess of New York, "Fresh seaweed still wet with salt water I have used as a mulch without treatment for blueberries, Russian olive, pines, dusty miller, beach grass and other seashore plants. For other types of plants, I wash down the new seaweed by hosing it, turning the material frequently. After one to two hours, the water has run off and it can be used safely. Old seaweed which has been lying around for some time can be spread immediately, but I play it safe and use fresh seaweed and wash it."

From Mrs. David Domizi of Connecticut, "Treatment of seaweed is simple since the salt accumulation is external.

Place a 6- to 12-inch layer of the seaweed on a wood frame covered with chicken wire, and a good rain shower will rinse it and allow it to dry. Seaweed is rich in minerals and trace elements and is a marvelous soil conditioner and fertilizer."

stone mulch

Q: On some of my trees and shrubs I have a stone mulch approximately 3 to 5 inches deep, and I have great difficulty in feeding the trees. Any suggestions? D. M. E.

A: Mrs. L. J. Canale of New Jersey offers a solution. "A soluble fertilizer should be ideal for this problem. I feed my trees with plant food cartridges used with a root feeder attached to a hose. Directions for use are on the cartridge."

straw

Q: Our neighbor gave us some left-over baled straw which we dug into the soil before planting our vegetables. The plants are skinny, spindly and pale. What went wrong? F. H. H., Rye, N.Y.

A: Kate Showers, a graduate student in soil science, writes, "While adding organic matter to the soil is a good practice, it must be done with care. Organic matter is broken down, releasing nutrients to the soil system and providing valuable humus by the activity of various soil microorganisms. As they work, they require carbon and nitrogen. Straw, rotted hay and other dry vegetable matter (including newspaper) are very high in carbon and low in nitrogen. For the microorganisms to break these items down, they must have a source of nitrogen. If none is added to the soil, the microorganisms will compete with any growing plants for the nitrogen available in the soil system. The microorganisms are good competitors and plants growing in the area will be deficient in nitrogen. This deficiency is temporary (a few months), as nitrogen returns to the soil in an organic form. Fall is the best time to incorporate straw in the garden."

tea leaves

Q: Several months ago someone asked about the usefulness of coffee grounds in the garden. I would like to carry it one step further to used tea leaves. I have often heard that they are useful, especially around rose plants. Any truth to this? H. H.

A: James McAree of Pennsylvania writes that tea leaves can be used as a soil builder. Like coffee grounds, they are a source of acid in sweet soils. "I customarily use tea leaves and coffee grounds around acid-loving plants including low-growing evergreens such as rhododendron and yew." (He also uses them on roses.) "One should not expect dramatic change, but rather a slow build-up of the acid content; both are fine conditioners for the soil."

Tea leaves are from a species of camellia, an ericaceous plant and would have some acid quality. They can be used in moderation in soil or mixed with other plant materials and added to the compost pile. Ed.

wood ash
artificial logs

Q: We burn firewood and artificial logs from the supermarket in our fireplace. Are the ashes from these artificial logs beneficial or harmful if utilized in the garden? Miss B. S. J., Harrington Park, N.J.

A: Raymond R. Walker of Pennsylvania writes, "Most of the artificial logs use a plastic substance as a binder and some of these could leave residues that are toxic to some plants. Since the shortage of plastics may cause manufacturers to switch from one substance to another, one cannot be sure what the ash content would be. In short, do not use." He also notes that wood ashes are heavily alkaline and should be used sparingly.

nutrients

Q: What nutrients do wood ashes provide? Is it safe to use them for general garden purposes? W. M., Freehold, N.J.

A: Mrs. Marlene Spigner, a Long Island reader, suggests, "Wood ashes are a free source of potash and are generally safe to use, but since they are alkaline do not use near acid-loving plants such as holly, azalea and rhododendron."

Wood ash analysis is anywhere from 4 to 10 percent potash and 1 to 2 percent phosphorus. Ed.

spreading

Q: We have accumulated a considerable amount of wood ash from our fireplace. I am told that one should be careful in spreading it in the garden for flowers. What is the safe limit? A. E. V., New York.

A: *Wood ashes contain high amounts of potash, a soil nutrient and can be used on the garden safely. Since they are alkaline, they should not be placed directly on soil where new seedlings are growing. Mix the wood ashes with compost before applying in these areas. Or broadcast the ashes freely when preparing new soil for planting and rake in well. As much as 10 pounds can be spread in a 100 square-foot area. Ed.*

lawn tips

ajuga

Q: How do I get rid of ajuga that is growing into my lawn? R. E. B., New Jersey

A: Ajuga is sensitive to many herbicides. A wax bar of 2,4-D pulled over the lawn would be best. Ed.

brown grass

Q: We moved into our Long Island home last October and the grass looked like straw. It still does while our neighbor's lawn is now (April) greening up. What is wrong? J. L. K.

A: Nothing is wrong. J. L. K. has a zoysia grass lawn. This is a vigorous growing, warm weather grass that responds to summer temperatures. It greens up when the weather settles in May and becomes dormant and browns off with the first autumn frosts. Ed.

burnt lawns

So many gardeners make the mistake of burning their lawns with improper applications of fertilizer that we consulted the experts for a solution. Ed.

According to Walter Carpenter, Nassau County Cooperative Extension Agent, fertilizer-burned turf should come back with sufficient applications of water to flush it—at least one inch of water a week. However, it is possible to completely burn out tops and roots with too much fertilizer. In this case, the only solution, would be reseeding in late August or early September. Most lawns on Long Island brown off in midsummer from lack of water. They are merely in a period of dormancy and should come back green with the return of September rains and cooler temperatures.

chickweed

Q: How do we combat chickweed? We have tried various weedkillers, followed directions and killed the grass but not the weed. Mrs. T. A. H., Pittsburgh, Pa.

107

A: Dr. Arthur Bing, Cornell University, writes, "Chickweed can be controlled in lawns with Silvex (2,4,5-TP) by following the directions. Apply in late fall or in the spring before air temperatures reach over 80 degrees. At high temperatures, Silvex will injure grasses. Silvex is usually combined with 2,4-D and will also control dandelions and plantain. Do not use in non-lawn areas."

clover

Q: How do I get rid of clover in my lawn? J. T. L., Yonkers, N.Y.

A: Spring or fall applications of mecoprop, dicamba, or silvex may be applied according to the package directions. Use cautiously. Ed.

coarse fescue

Q: Part of my lawn is overgrown with coarse fescue. Is there any way of eliminating this short of digging it up and re-planting? J. W. W., New Jersey

A: James Gallagher of Michigan writes, "The only effective way to get rid of it is to dig it up with a sod cutter. Caco-dylicacid at double rate (enough to kill everything else in sight) will leave about one green shoot per square foot in an infected lawn. Sodium arsenite (withdrawn from the market) was the only weed-killer effective for this obnoxious grass. A sod cutter costs about $15 and is easy to use and effective."

crabgrass

Q: We were away when we should have put down the pre-emergent crabgrass killer. Is there anything we can do this late (June) to get it under control? J. O. D.

A: Young crabgrass can be eradicated with postemergent herbicides containing DSMA, MAMA or MSMA. They are sold under various trade names such as Clout, Crab-E-Rad, Dimet, etc. A second or third application may be needed in a week to 10 days. Ed.

dog damage

Q: We have a fenced yard for our dog. The yard has many circles of dead grass from dog excrement. We love our pooch but we also would like a nice green lawn. What is the solution? Mrs. E. T. G., Verona, N.J.

A: George Piper, another New Jersey gardener, says, "The only solution is to train the dog to use a particular area that is designated for its use."

dog-safe fertilizer

Q: What fertilizer would be safe to use on the lawn that would not affect our two dachshunds who are great grass eaters? T. S.

A: Barbara Axel of New York writes, "As an owner of dachshunds for 14 years and also a person who enjoys a garden, I recommend the use of 100 percent organic fertilizer on all plants and on the lawn. One of our dachshunds almost died after sampling a lawn which had been chemically fertilized almost a week before. After that unpleasant experience, we changed our methods and have had very good results, both plantwise and puppywise."

maple shade

Q: I have a great deal of shade from maple trees and in spite of three years effort, I still do not have a presentable lawn. Has anyone solved this problem? J. W. S., New York

A: The deep shade caused by the maple tree is the reason for the problem but here is how readers solved it: Thomas Callen of New Jersey recommends groundcovers such as English ivy, pachysandra and myrtle. Mrs. Andries Roodenburg of New York found that "violets are the only plants that propagate in my garden and even then they need frequent watering until they become established."

Gloria Dlugacz of New York writes, "After eight years of trying to grow a lawn with no success we replaced the remnants with a Japanese-type garden—pebbles, slates, evergreens and redwood constructions. Initially costly, but now maintenance free."

Two Connecticut gardeners, Sylvia S. Burton and Daniel Duarte were not discouraged. Both of them had tree surgeons open up and thin their maple trees and both have lawns.

Cortland Anderson of New York would like to add additional help to answer the problem of growing grass under the heavy shade of maple trees. He writes, "We live on a third of an acre plot with about 15 maples. There had never been an effective lawn since the house was built 18 years ago. I tried fruitlessly. Last year we had three trees moderately trimmed. Then we roughed up the soil and planted perennial ryegrass NK 100. We kept the seed well watered and moderately fed. We have a more than presentable lawn and I have been told it will improve during the second year."

moss

Q: Our yard is getting green moss all over it. The worst spot is around a maple tree. We have tried lime, fertilizer, etc. Nothing works. Now what? Mrs. E. S., Manhattan

A: Susanna E. Bedell of New York writes, "Chances are the soil pH (acidity level) is far below 7 (neutral). Moss often appears on acid soil. Lime would correct this. Or, there may be a drainage problem. Aerate the soil, work in some organic material such as compost or peat, or if these do not correct the situation, install drainage tiles."

Mrs. L. B. Borst, from upstate New York, writes, "We had a similar problem a few years ago with moss and decided to capitalize on what we had. We pulled up the remaining grass to make a moss garden with a variety of mosses, a winding flagstone path, rocks, ferns, Solomon's seal and shade trees. Given enough water, even on a hot day it is a cool, green reflective refuge."

salt and sand damage

Q: The lawn area between the street and sidewalk is damaged from road salt and sand. Has anyone found a grass variety that grows well under such circumstances? Mrs. G. P. W., Concord, Mass.

A: No grass or any plant would be durable. Perhaps an attractive bark mulch or pebble garden would be more practical. Ed.

school lawn

Q: What is the best kind of grass to grow on a lawn used by a nursery school? Little children will be running, falling, scuffing and jumping on it. Mrs. D. A. S.

A: For Long Island and southward into New Jersey probably one of the toughest aggressive lawns for hard wear would be zoysia grass but it does not green up until May and it requires two to three years to establish a tightly knit turf from plugs. Faster to establish and quite durable would be some of the newer perennial ryegrasses such as NK-100 and Pennfine. Ed.

seedheads

Q: About this time of year (July), some of the grass on my lawn goes to seed. The white seed heads give the lawn a burned look which spoils the green. What can I do? L. B., New Jersey

A: The white seed heads are of annual bluegrass (Poa annua), a weed that sets seed in early July. It dies off and leaves the

110

lawn filled with vacant holes, but often reseeds and appears again in fall and spring. To control the weed, some success is possible with betesan, applied in late spring. Ed.

soft water

Q: Would someone please tell me the effect of using soft water on lawns? Dr. S. T.

A: In a word, none. Hard water contains calcium, magnesium and iron carbonates and these can be removed by filtering the water through a salt resin. Mechanically softened water would be a needless expense for lawns, however, as the natural flushing of soils by rainfall would probably leach out any salt accumulations. Ed.

violets as weeds

Q: Is there anyone who has solved the problems of violets invading the lawn, short of digging them out? Mrs. R. B. McE., Lexington, Ky.

A: Violets are a problem, especially in shady areas, and there is no sure way to rout them. Try 2,4-D plus silvex as used for chickweed control. Ed.
See Violets as weeds, page 93.

weedkillers

Q: My lawn is peppered with dandelion, plantain and various other weeds. It is a problem for herbicides rather than me on my hands and knees. One neighbor says I should not apply weedkillers now in the heat of summer. Another says this is the only time to do it. I'm new at this sort of thing. Who's correct? J. J. McB.

A: D. Schechtman of New York writes that "most commercially available weedkillers can be used safely during the summertime if instructions are followed properly. Or, you can choose to wait until fall, when the weeds will die down naturally following the early morning frosts."

zoysia
patching

Q: Last year, I purchased zoysia strips to patch my zoysia lawn. I planted one in a bald area and the other I cut into pieces where needed. All through the summer, the lawn was green. This last winter, the strips I planted died and now I have bald spots again. How can I save the lawn? C. L.

A: John Weiner of New Jersey suggests to C. L. that zoysia is essentially a hot weather, summer lawn grass. It may be that he planted his fill-in strips too late in the season for them to take hold and the shallow roots froze during the winter months. Fertilizer application in the spring may boost growth for the established zoysia to fill in the bare spots.

111

Q: Three years ago I had my lawn rototilled to get rid of the zoysia grass. I find it coming through again. How do I get rid of it? J. K., Long Island

A: Dr. Arthur Bing, Cornell Ornamentals Research Laboratory, Farmingdale, N.Y., suggests either Paraquat or Erase. These materials will kill off the grass and other vegetation. There is little residue and grass can be planted at a later time according to the manufacturer's directions.

Q: Is there a way to get rid of a lawn of zoysia grass prior to sodding or seeding Merion bluegrass? D. B., Setauket, N.Y.

A: Mrs. Margaret Johnson of New Jersey has a solution. She writes, "After trying to pull up zoysia and using weedkillers, I was finally successful after renting a turf cutter and removing it in strips. I now have Merion bluegrass and after three years, I have not had any zoysia reappear. The rolls of zoysia removed have made wonderful compost."

Q: My zoysia lawn is now being crowded with weeds. Is there a weedkiller I can use safely without harming the grass? R. H. H., Manhattan

A: Weeds are not too much of a problem in a well-established zoysia lawn that has been fertilized and well watered. However, if the lawn is a new one, and the grass has not filled in completely, Dr. Arthur Bing, Cornell Ornamentals Research Laboratory, Farmingdale, N.Y., suggests 2,4-D can be used effectively to destroy the broadleafed weeds. For others, R. H. H. should send specimens to Cooperative Extension for proper identification and herbicide recommendations. Ed.

groundcover care

groundcover

Q: Pachysandra, myrtle and ivy are ubiquitous groundcovers in our neighborhood. Suggestions would be appreciated on something different for a semi-sunny, but damp area along our driveway. Mrs. S. C.

A: A number of good groundcover suggestions came in for Mrs. S. C.'s problem area. Miss Evelyn Campbell of New Jersey wishes more gardeners would discover the merits of epimedium, for a not too dry, or open location. Albert Skelding of New York recommends ajuga, especially the variety Bronze Beauty. Michael Johnson of New York suggests several, including creeping buttercup (*Ranunculus repens*) and wild ginger. Mrs. Adrienne Lind of New York likes the many kinds of thyme, for sun and well-drained soil.

growing near the sea

Q: What can I plant on an open, sunny bank, a few blocks from the beach, which is too steep to mow? M. N., New Jersey

A: Mrs. George Csabon of New York suggests bearberry, prostrate juniper, heather. Howard LaMorder of Vermont suggests crownvetch.

growing on a slope

Q: What is the trick to establishing vinca groundcover on a shady slope? Ours has been rain washed out twice and we are ready to give up. Clues anyone? G. T. B., Westchester County, N.Y.

A: Robert Jonas, District Soil Conservationist, Rockland County, N.Y., writes, "The problem is the slope. Water should be diverted away from the top of the slope. If the

113

slope is long, diversions across the slope may also be necessary in a pipe or paved channel."

Degradable matting used for highway bank planting might also be used to blanket the slope until plants take hold. Ed.

low growing

Q: Does anyone know of a good flat-to-the-ground groundcover that will thrive in acid soil on a steep slope, which is half sun and half shade? Mrs. G. R. W., Massachusetts

A: Here are several ideas. From Mrs. Reynolds Girdler of Connecticut, "I think the perfect answer is *Cotoneaster dammeri.* It hugs the ground, is evergreen and does well in sun or shade with white flowers in spring and red berries in fall." From Marshall Cluett of New Jersey, "Why not try some of the low-creeping junipers which hug the ground and establish themselves readily on slopes?" From C. Johnson of Massachusetts, "Try ajuga for a low dense groundcover that spreads easily."

ground pine

Q: How can I transplant ground pine to the small patch of woods behind my house? I have tried twice, once in May and once in late September with no success. B. R., Connecticut

A: Beverly Chase of New York suggests her method. She writes, "For deep running lycopodium (like the tree club moss) I have had good luck by digging three-inch squares around one plant, cutting it loose from the runner, leaving three inches of runner attached, and rooting it in a very damp moss enclosed in a plastic bag. Perhaps B. R. could root several cuttings of ground pine (*Lycopodium clavatum*) in a terrarium, winter them outdoors after established and transplant them permanently after frosts in the spring. I have had no luck transplanting to dry sunny areas, though in nature they sometimes thrive. My plants are on a shady stream bank, high above the water, where it's cool and humid."

ivy
removal

Q: A large ivy plant has rooted inside and under our stone wall. We have tried to remove it so that rock garden plants can grow on top of the wall, but the ivy returns. How can we kill the ivy short of dismantling the wall? Mrs. C. J. B., New Jersey

A: Harry Treplar of New Hampshire suggests, "Getting rid of some plants can easily be accomplished with simple home remedies such as kerosene or table salt. Perhaps kerosene could be applied to the ivy foliage without harming other plants or limited quantities of table salt might be drilled in under the wall where the ivy roots are. At least these simple products are worth a try and less hazardous than herbicides of unknown toxicity, and certainly cheaper than tearing out the wall."

rooting

Q: I have tried to root hardy English ivy in water, sand and various other combinations unsuccessfully. I would like to plant the rooted cuttings outside. Is there a time of year when this can be done more easily? W. G., New Jersey

A: Here are three approaches. Mrs. Richard Rudell of New York is successful by putting ivy cuttings on the ground, pressing leaf nodes into the soil and anchoring them with a pin or small twig without removing any of the leaves. Before long, roots form at the nodes.

Mrs. Neil Randall of Pennsylvania fills a used yogurt container punched with many holes on bottom and sides with a wetted mixture of half sand and half peat moss. Make cuttings about three leaves long, dip in rooting hormone powder and put in the container right through into the soil, about three cuttings to a container. Firm soil around the container and keep wet for six to 10 weeks and they will be rooted.

John Pike of New York uses several deep containers such as large coffee cans or gallon milk cartons, punches holes in the bottom, and fills them with vermiculite and waters thoroughly. Each container holds about 10 cuttings, about a foot long with leaves clipped off the lower 6 inches. Keep container in open shade where they receive normal rainfall but never direct sunlight. Cuttings taken in June or July will root in about two months.

on tree

Q: For the past three or four years, English ivy has been growing up the trunks of our black pines. We have been warned this will strangle the trees. Is this so? R. S. J., Babylon, Long Island

A: George Helmsley, another Long Island gardener, says, "The trees will not be 'strangled' by the ivy, but their growth will be hampered. As the vines grow, they become heavy and add additional weight for the trees to support. They also grow too thick and cut out the tree's light and air. Poison ivy and wisteria will also do the same thing. If they were my trees, I'd cut down the vines."

Bittersweet is dangerous as well. Ed.

on walls

Q: B. D. is interested in having additional ivy plants climbing on his brick-walled home and would like to know what par-

115

ticular varieties are best and what is the proper time for planting them.

A: E. H. F., Forked River, N.J., would like to discourage B. D. from planting ivy on his brick-walled home. "Many years ago, I started shoots of English ivy around the base of our brick house. It was at least five years before they began to climb. I wanted them just on the chimney, but they grew around to the north of the house and the birds began nesting in it. From then on we could never keep our back door-step clean of dead leaves and droppings. The ivy climbed to the top of the chimney and wound itself around the telephone wire. It did look beautiful—but I use the past tense. We had it all pulled off except on the chimney where we will try to confine it."

lichens

Q: Sometime ago I read an article about transplanting lichen. It involved scraping the lichen from rock, mixing it with something and spreading the "paste" on the new rock and protecting it from the weather. Can anyone help me? Mrs. W. D., Jr.

A: Norma Palmer of Ohio mentions that she has read about scraping the lichen and mixing it with cultured buttermilk. This is then spread on the new rock.

Mrs. Norman Kenyon of Rhode Island remembers reading something to the effect that buttermilk poured or painted on a rock will cause lichen to form. "It did for me," she writes. "A nice greenish color. I seem to remember reading that peanut butter will give good results, too."

moss

Q: How can I learn about moss? I have been transplanting wild moss from the woodlands to my property, but I cannot find much about it in books. Does anyone know of a source? M. D. W., Long Island

A: Mrs. William D. Gorman of New Jersey has a suggestion as follows, "There is an excellent little pocket book, *Non-Flowering Plants* by Shuttleworth and Zim, published by Golden Press. We keep this book and a similar one on wild flowers in the glove compartment of our car at all times."

Mrs. Percy Cashmore of Connecticut suggests still another source from the one given. She recommends *Forests of Liliput: The Realm of Moss and Lichens* by John Bland. Dr. Bland gives horticultural and botanical information that is practical and helpful.

pachysandra
blight

Q: My sizable pachysandra plot is more than 10 years old. Recently, the leaves shrivel, stems droop and the roots turn black. The plants are dying in an ever expanding circle. What is wrong and what is the solution? S. A. H., Summit, N.J.

A: Fred C. Lowenfels, a Westchester County reader, replied, "The blight was identified in my pachysandra by a local farm bureau and is evidently caused by surplus moisture of the past few years. Two applications, 10 days apart, of the fungicide captan, have helped. The stalks are green again and I think I caught it in time."

The pachysandra trouble is a fungus leaf and stem blight which often occurs in thick overcrowded plantings, especially where they accumulate excess leaf litter from shade trees. Infected plants should be removed and areas should be sprayed with any one of the standard fungicides such as captan, ferbam, etc. Follow package directions. Ed.

scale

Q: I have black specks on stems of my pachysandra which I suspect is scale. Is it scale and how do I get rid of it? J. W., New Jersey

A: George S. Geinrich of New Jersey agrees that J. W. probably does have euonymus scale on his pachysandra as the females are dark brown. During the early summer months, when the scales are out of their protective shells and crawling, apply malathion or diazinon making sure to get under the leaves and along the stems.

117

Norman Fine, New Jersey, also has an answer. He writes, "I was successful in ridding pachysandra of scale by using a dormant spray. The spray is used in March or April before the buds open, on a warm sunny morning. Use 6 tablespoons of dormant superior miscible oil per gallon of water."

yellowing

Q: We have pachysandra around the trees on our front lawn. During the fall and winter, it turns yellow. Most of the pachysandra in our neighborhood remains green. What's wrong? Mrs. E. G. G., Long Island

A: George Pratt of New York suggests, "The plants are probably 'hungry.' When the weather warms in the spring, apply a general-purpose fertilizer to the pachysandra, filtering it carefully down through the leaves. And sometime in summer, apply a foliar feeding with water-soluble fertilizer."

weeds in groundcovers
dodder

Q: Can someone please tell me what to do about dodder that invaded the bed of English ivy in front of our home? J. C. L., Jr., Washington, D.C.

A: Mortimer Furtsch of New York says that he found DCPA (Dacthal) effective and it will not damage English ivy. Follow directions and use as often as suggested.

grass

Q: What can be done to prevent grass from growing through ivy, pachysandra, sedum and other groundcovers? R. M., Westchester County, N.Y.

A: Mrs. Barbara van Achterberg of Connecticut solved the problem. "While transplanting myrtle along the front of our house, I threw grass clippings around the plants and kept replenishing the mulch with hay, sawdust, leaves, etc., to keep the soil covered. By the second summer, the myrtle had taken over, sending runners over and through the mulch. I do not mulch any more and my weeding is reduced to about five minutes, once a week."

Mulching before planting a groundcover is the most practical step for weed control and especially helpful to hold soil down to prevent erosion when establishing groundcover on a bank. Ed.

grass in vinca

Q: It is impossible to remove by hand the grasses that persist in growing through a dense vinca groundcover on my property. Is there an herbicide I can use on the grass without harming the vinca? This is my single most aggravating maintenance problem. R. W., Vermont

A: The ideal when planting any groundcover is to solve the weed problem first either by an herbicide application or heavy mulching material. However, an application of Dacthal used carefully according to the package directions may be helpful on established beds for some weeds. Or, a spring application of Eptam, raked into the soil if the planting is sparse and new.

A Westchester County reader has informed us that in his experience using Dacthal for weed control in vinca the planting was wiped out, not just the weeds. A check with the manufacturer concurs that plant damage has occurred with some use of Dacthal for weed control in vinca and the company notes that the product is not labeled for use with vinca. The Eptam recommendation stands. It is labeled for use with vinca as well as other groundcovers including ajuga, pachysandra, sedum and ornamental strawberry. Ed.

poison ivy

Q: How do we get rid of poison ivy in a bed of myrtle groundcover without damaging the groundcover? W. S., Longmeadow, Mass.

A: Several readers have since asked the same question. We consulted Dr. Arthur Bing, herbicide specialist, Cornell University. This is his recommendation. Amitrole (amino triazole) is the herbicide used for control of poison ivy. Mix the proper dilution according to package directions. Use an old bucket or watertight container. Wear rubber gloves. With an old paint brush, "paint" some of the herbicide on the poison ivy carefully. It will be absorbed down into the roots and kill the weed. There may be some yellow leaves on the groundcover foliage if touched, but amitrole should work well if applied carefully.

119

flower and vine wonderings

annuals
poor soil

Q: Are there any annuals that will thrive in a sunny area where the soil is poor along a drive and not worth the expense of adding fertilizer and compost? Mrs. T. U. V., Mt. Vernon, N.Y.

A: Here are some suggestions. From Heidi Granholm of New York, "I've had good luck with poppies, nasturtiums and zinnias in poor soil. The poppies and nasturtiums bloom profusely if the soil is not rich."

From Al Simpson, a Long Island gardener, "A few which we find work well are portulaca, petunia, zinnia, gomphrena and amaranthus. Hard pinching back and some water will do wonders."

transplanting

Q: Our gardener set out several flats of petunias, impatiens and other annuals, all in bloom, and immediately clipped the flowers off. He said it was good for the plants. We would like to know if this is standard practice and, if so, why? Mrs. G. F. V., Darien, Conn.

A: Jack C. Rossetter, an Illinois gardener, writes, "Mrs. G. F. V. should prune the salary of her gardener who whacks off the flowers of her transplants, unless the plants are spindly and not decently bushed out. Well protected and watered 'six-paks' with balls of soil do not need pinching, particularly impatiens."

Mrs. Williams Robbins, a Westchester County gardener, suggests, "We always cut back our annuals after transplanting, particularly single stemmed leggy ones such as petunias. Even if cut back quite hard, they branch and fill in the space splendidly. If we don't, we find we have skinny, spindly

120

plants all summer. Also, we find it helpful to feed with half-rate water soluble fertilizer at least once a week for several weeks to push them along."

tree roots

Q: In the past, we have planted annuals around the trunk of our maple tree, but recently the tree has grown thick surface roots. Has anyone found a way to plant annuals in such a situation? Mrs. B. T., Riverside, Conn.

A: Here are two approaches with variations. J. B. Milgram, a New York gardener, recommends, "Build up an earth platform around the trunk, five or six inches high and plant shallow-rooted flowers. For the past few years I have had a patch of petunias around a big Norway maple's roots."

And from Mrs. J. H. D. in Connecticut, "I built a low wall of rocks in a wide circle around the base of a maple tree, added topsoil to the rock level and then planted begonias and impatiens in pots. Although maple roots do creep to the surface of the soil, they do not interfere with the plants as long as they are in pots."

arbutus transplanting

Q: I have some arbutus growing in thick clumps in our woods that I would like to introduce to another woody section nearer the house. Neighbors tell me its impossible to transplant, but if there is a special trick for success, I'd like to try. G. G. McF., Dallas, Pa.

A: Mrs. Jean W. Graham of Pennsylvania passes along her suggestion. "Last fall, I gathered mosses, partridgeberries, wintergreen and cranberry to plant brandy snifters for Christmas gifts. They thrived quite well. In April, I found several patches of arbutus in bloom and very carefully clipped some blossoms with scissors to avoid uprooting the plants. After the flowers faded, I planted the tips in the brandy snifter with the other plants. The arbutus is thriving and sending forth new leaves. I intend to transplant it in the fall in a wooded area of my daughter's home in southern New Jersey near where I found the arbutus originally. I feel sure the arbutus will thrive with perhaps a mulch of oak leaves."

asters

Q: For many years I had beautiful asters. The past two years, the plants grew to several inches, withered and died. Both years, I replanted and the same thing happened. What can I do? Mrs. W. S., Connecticut

A: Dr. Doris G. White, William Paterson State College, writes, "Fusarium wilt, a soilborne disease, may be the problem. The disease often starts at the bases of stems and progresses upwards. Buy wilt-resistant asters. Collect and burn infected plants; do not compost them. Other aster diseases include verticillium wilt and bacterial wilt. Practice crop rotation with nonrelated crops."

begonias

Q: I have several unusual begonias and geraniums in my garden and I would like to carry these over for next year. Has anyone a special secret? Mrs. J. L. F., Woonsocket, R.I.

A: Here is an idea for begonias from Mrs. Dominick J. Fazio, a Long Island reader. "In the fall, around September 15, I pot up the begonias I want to keep and leave them outdoors in a protected spot. After one week, I cut them back severely, to three to four inches, take them indoors to a bright sunny window and in a short time, they develop into lovely bushy plants covered with flowers. In spring, I set them outdoors again. I have done this year after year."

For geraniums, Mrs. Doris Goldbloom, a New Jersey reader, suggests, "My method is probably most unscientific, but it works. At summer's end, I scoop up each geranium with enough soil so I do not disturb the roots, and set each in a flower pot. During the winter I keep them on a basement window sill where they receive some light. I water them once a month, thoroughly. In the spring, they are knocked out of the pot and replanted. Though a bit leggy at first, they are lovely later on."

And from Mrs. William Spackman, Jr., a Pennsylvania reader, "I make select cuttings of the choice begonias and geraniums in late summer. I choose a healthy full branch of four to five inches and cut it one-quarter inch below the bottom leaf. Strip off the bottom two leaves and dip each cutting in a hormone rooting powder and insert it into damp vermiculite. When a root system develops, pot the cuttings in soil. Geraniums require a more sandy soil than begonias. Geraniums do not bloom through the winter as my begonias do, but cuttings do ensure saving particular plants for the following summer."

See Geraniums, page 25 and Begonias, page 8.

bittersweet

Q: What is the trick in buying bittersweet plants which will produce the desirable orange-red berries so nice to cut and bring indoors for winter arrangements? When I purchased three nice-sized plants this spring, the nurseryman said all I could do was, "wait and see." Mrs. D. C. W.

A: Mrs. Harrison C. Coffin of New York writes of her experience. "I sowed seeds of bittersweet that were taken from dried branches in the living room. Nothing happened for a long time. Eventually the plants came up and, later, bloomed. They grew luxuriantly and had to be pruned to be kept under control." Mrs. Walter F. Cole, Jr., of Connecticut would like to discourage Mrs. D. C. W. from ever growing bittersweet. "This plant becomes a pernicious vine which is almost impossible to eradicate. It smothers shrubs, twines around trees and eventually kills them. It was brought to our area about 50 years ago and is inundating us. The only thing I've found to kill it is Ammate and it may take up to three applications."

Bittersweet (Celastrus) is polygamodioecious, a term describing species that can have perfect (male-female) flowers and unisexual flowers on the same plant. To be sure of fruiting plants, gardeners should buy from quality, reputable nurserymen. Sometimes a male form is grafted onto a female plant or a male and female plant are planted in the same hole. Judicious maintenance pruning will keep the plants under control. Ed.

bloom lull

Q: I have a perennial and annual flower garden which has a blossoming lull from mid-June to mid-July. What can I plant that will fill this bloom gap? Mrs. D. P. D., Connecticut

A: Many, many helpful responses were received. Here is a summary of some. Lawrence King of New York suggests "pink yarrow, platycodon, phlox, rudbeckia (both common black-eyed Susan and hybrid doubles), bergamot and a succession of daylilies." Mrs. Robert Ensher of Connecticut suggests "daylilies. Mid-July is the height of the season but there are many early and late varieties." Also, from Connecticut, Mrs. Gordon Malm suggests "English cottage carnations, Pacific Hybrid delphinium, floribunda rose, coreopsis, phlox, Miss Lingard, anthemis and platycodon." Mrs. Frank Coyle, still another Connecticut gardener, suggests what she calls "bridge plants" including daylilies, oenothera, gas plant, gypsophila and gaillardia.

bluebells

Q: Can someone identify the true bluebell of Scotland, and can I plant it in my garden? G. MacF., Connecticut

A: Richard Roblin of New Jersey writes, "The Bluebell of Scotland, or harebell, is *Campanula rotundifolia* and occurs in several varieties. It grows readily and can become a weed. Seed or plants are available in a blue or white form."

123

Q: This winter has been unusually warm and as a result all of our spring bulbs are starting to emerge (February). Will we lose our daffodils and tulips? Should we protect them in some way? Mrs. L. W.

A: *The unusually warm winter weather and abundant January rainfall kept ground temperature high. As a result, the tips of bulb foliage are poking above ground level in many regions. The flower buds remain safely tucked inside the bulbs, well below ground level. There is no cause for concern. Ed.*

Q: What is the proper way to transplant daffodils and tulips? We want to redesign the garden where bulbs are blooming now and want to save the flowers for next year. Mrs. G. K. W. Westchester County, N.Y.

A: Mrs. R. E. Rex of New Jersey writes, "I let the foliage ripen (yellow) then dig up the bulbs, sort them to size, dust with a fungicide and replant. I have had excellent success."

Q: Are any cactus species hardy on Long Island other than native prickly pear? I have a sheltered sunny seaside area where I'm hopeful of establishing a cactus garden for low upkeep. Am I foolish? D. G. G.

A: Prof. William J. Dress, Cornell University, lists many hardy cacti species. These include *Opuntia fragilis, polyacantha, rhodantha, imbricata, whipplei, compressa, basilaris, tortispina, phaeacantha* and *davisii.* Also, *Echinocereus baileyi, reichenbachii, viridiflorus* and *Echinocactus simpsonii.*

Pierre Artigues of upstate New York suggests many of the above and adds also *Sedum spinosum* which grows in a two to three-inch rosette. (This succulent looks like a cactus.) Sources: Sky-cleft Gardens, Camp Street Ext., Barre, Vt.; Prairie Gem Ranch, Smithwick, S.D. 57782.

For seed, Jill Hammel of New York suggests the hardy cacti packet from Park Seed Co., Greenwood, S.C. 29646.

Mrs. Maria Scher of New York writes, "Prickly pear is a hardy native cactus here in the East. Several thrived on my windy terrace all winter through freezing temperatures."

Sedums or stonecrops are hardy succulents that grow well in the open sunny exposure of the coastlands. Ed.

Q: We have Chinese lanterns (*Physalis*). The foliage is bright green but the lanterns are tan. What can we do to encourage the bright orange color? Miss R. K., Middletown, N.Y.

A: Mrs. Dwight Vanderle of Massachusetts suggests, "Although I may not have the answer, my guess would be that Miss R. K.'s plants are not in full sun and the orange pigments do not develop. Our plants are in a full sunny location and have excellent color. It helps when gathering the fruits to remove all foliage before drying. I place them in old quart jars, upright, and keep them in a cool extra bedroom until they are thoroughly dry. The pods can be sprayed with a laminating coating to make them last longer, but I find that keeping them out of sunlight when dry helps them to last for many years."

Ralph Kinter of Pennsylvania writes that the real answer is that R. K. "probably does not have Chinese lantern (*Physalis alkekengi*) but one of the species of tan colored *Physalis* which grow wild in New York State. Or she may have a related species, apple of Peru (*Nicandra physalodes*). The solution is in the flower itself. Tan-colored *Physalis* always seem to have yellow flowers while the Chinese lantern has a white flower. If the flower is blue, she may have apple of Peru."

christmas rose

Q: Our Christmas rose has not bloomed, in four years. What is the trick to flowering? Mrs. F. D. S., New Jersey

A: Jack S. Findley of Pennsylvania has a suggestion. "Perhaps our solution will help. We grew the Christmas roses (*Helleborus niger*) for several years with little bloom success. A neighbor suggested we transplant them by the side of the garage where they received just a few hours of morning sun. We did the following spring and that December they bloomed on New Year's Eve. Previously, they had been in too sunny a site and were burned by winter sun, we surmised."

chrysanthemum
protection

Q: I purchased some mums recently and planted them in my garden. Many catalogues do not recommend planting mums in fall, because they are not hardy. What should I do to protect my plants over winter? Mrs. R. J. S., New York

A: E. J. Collins of New York writes, "'Mums vary in their degrees of winter hardiness. Some of the newer fancy-flowered hybrids are not winter hardy and would be killed by severe frosts. It would be best if Mrs. R. J. S. could inquire from her nursery the name of the plants purchased and if they are a winter hardy variety. If this cannot be determined, then the plants should be left in place, and cut to three- or four-inch stubs after the first good hard frosts. When the

125

ground is frozen, mulch the plants well with evergreen boughs, clean straw, salt marsh hay or whatever. In spring, as growth begins remove the mulch. If the plants are hardy, they should survive winter in this way."

clematis pruning

Q: Can clematis be pruned severely each year? My Jackmani flowers every summer but all the growth and flowers are at the top one-third. Can anyone tell me how pruning might correct this, and when? Mrs. R. B. T., West Hempstead, N.Y.

A: Mrs. Edward Eschauzier, a Connecticut reader, suggests, "I have found pruning should be done early in February to the middle of March when the buds start to swell. I cut to the lowest pair of buds on each stem. One need not always stick to this rule but the snag is that the base of the plant will be left rather bare. On Jackmani, the flower is produced on the end of new shoots. Old manure put near the plant in winter, not around the base, is an excellent encouragement for growth."

columbine
blight

Q: Has anyone solved a columbine "blight" problem in which the leaves turn white, then brown, and the plant dies. Fungicides have not helped. Mrs. A. E. B., Westfield, N.J.

A: Barbara Twyeffort of Westchester County writes, "Her problem may be leaf miner which I solve easily with a systemic insecticide (absorbed inside the plant) sprinkled around the perimeter of each plant and lightly cultivated and watered in. My plants are fine this year after treatment last year."

from Colorado

Q: Friends in Colorado, knowing my fondness for the glorious Colorado columbine, sent me a few seeds they collected last year in a mountain patch. I would very much like to succeed in my southern Vermont wild garden, but I am also skeptical. Has anyone had any luck with these wild flowers in the East? Any special clues for sowing and locale for planting? G. C. W.

A: Success is reported from Mrs. H. Schindler of New York. "I grew seed in my wild garden in western Pennsylvania. The location: a moist, shady place with rather acid soil. I was equally successful on my penthouse terrace in Manhattan. Here the plants were raised in deep wooden boxes in full sun, not too rich a soil. This is the one thing to guard against. Plenty of watering is another requirement. The Colorado columbine is readily propagated by merely scratching the seed into the soil where the plants are to grow. I did this in

126

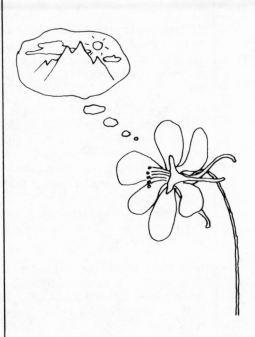

July. The flowering may occur the following spring, but it may take from two to three years."

daffodil
in the grass

Q: Our new home grounds surprised us this year with daffodils naturalized under two tall maples. How soon can we start to mow the lawn, it's almost a hay field now! Mrs. T. L.

A: Jacob Epstein of New York writes that Mrs. T. L. will have to wait until the bulb foliage becomes yellow and dies down naturally, usually by early July. This indicates that the flower bud for next year is initiated and the leaves have done their "work." To cut bulb foliage down to the ground before it yellows naturally greatly reduces the quality of future bulb flowers. Add some garden fertilizer to the area where bulb foliage is ripening.

seeds

Q: Can I plant the seed pod that forms on my daffodils to achieve new plants? Mrs. L. S.

A: Mrs. Whitney K. Smith of Ohio writes, "No, she should clip the seed pod off so strength goes into making new flowers next year Only hybridizers use seed pods, as four to five years are needed to achieve a bulb large enough to flower."

127

daylilies

Q: I had a bed of beautiful vari-colored daylilies. Now I seem to have a bed of ordinary orange roadside-type daylilies. Is it possible that over a period of years they reverted or have the common types taken over? What's to be done? C. E. C., New Jersey

A: Writing from Tuckahoe, N. Y., G. B. explains that "hybrid daylilies do not revert or change colors. The now-orange flower bed must have been interplanted with the sterile orange 'roadside' *Hemerocallis fulva* which compensates with strong vegetative growth. The hybrid daylilies are probably able only to send up foliage in the teeth of such competition. Sprinkle granular fertilizer in October and again in early April to induce the hybrids to bloom. Then weed out the 'invader'. Or dig up and compost the lot and plant some newer hybrids in its place."

delphinium pest

Q: Is there a sure way of getting rid of cyclamen mites on delphinium? I have tried Isotox and this year started a systemic but the plants still look quite infested. I'm about ready to dig up the whole lot and for a few years do without. Mrs. N. A. L.

A: Laura Davis of New York tells us that Kelthane "works fine."

geraniums
storing over winter

Q: What is the best way to preserve geraniums during the winter months? I have been told you can take them up and hang them in a cool place without soil or water, and keep them until planting time again in spring. Is there a better way? A. W. R.

A: Here are several schemes on preserving geraniums over winter. From Miss Ethel Vessiny of New York, "The best method is to take cuttings and put them in water or in pots of soil. I usually take cuttings about 4 to 5 inches for soil and a little longer for water. If put in a glass of water the cuttings will not only root, but also bloom in the water before spring. Both sets of cuttings transplant well in spring."

And from A. L. Wheeler of Massachusetts, "The only sure way is to dig up the plants from the garden or tip them out of the pots if potted. Water first. Then put each plant into a plastic bag and tie round the neck of the bag, leaving the greenery above. Pack them standing straight up in a bushel basket and put them in a cold cellar. Forget them until January, when they start to sprout again. Then you can repot them. I have done this for years."

128

And from Mrs. Caldwell Tyler of New York, "I semi-dry my geraniums and lift the whole plant in late October after cutting off all blossoms. They are dried in a cool shady place for several days, then put in large plastic bags, about four or five to a two-foot by three-foot bag. I poke 10 or so pencil holes in the bag and hang them in a cool, dark place where the plants will not freeze. I spray each bag monthly with about a tablespoon of water. In late April or May, plants are cut back to about three inches of the main stem and planted outdoors when hard frost is over."

See Begonias, page 122 and Geraniums, page 25.

geum

Q: In spite of separating and fertilizing geum, the plants have hardly bloomed in a sunny spot. Has anyone a solution? M. A. G., Croton, N.Y.

A: James McAree of Pennsylvania makes this recommendation: "Geum needs a light, high nitrogen growing medium. The soil is probably at fault. A pound of sphagnum moss and a quarter pound of sand per square foot of soil, spaded eight inches deep, plus a high nitrogen fertilizer worked into the soil prior to planting seeds or cuttings will assure full bloom."

gladiolus thrips

Q: How do I get rid of gladiolus thrips? Do they attack other bulbs such as begonias and ranunculus? Miss B. S., Goshen, N.Y.

A: Thrips are needlelike insects which scar foliage with white streaks. According to Dr. Cynthia Westcott's The Gardener's Bug Book, *after harvesting and curing, dust corms with malathion before storing. Some control has also been indicated by hanging Vapona strips in the storage area with the corm bags open. Also, soak corms before spring planting in a Lysol solution, 1½ teaspoons to one gallon of water. Don't store other tender tubers with the gladiolus. Ed.*

grapevine
blossom drop

Q: My grape blossoms fall off! I needed a vine to cover a fence and since I enjoy wild grape jelly, I rooted cuttings from a blossoming grapevine and transplanted them to the fence, three or four years ago. The vines grew very well and for the last two years have blossomed well. However, as the fuzzy blossoms turn to tiny green knobs, the whole cluster falls off, disjointing where it comes off the stem. This has happened both years to my great disappointment. Dr. E. F.

A: Joan A. Alder of Connecticut notes it is possible that the grape blossoms fall off due to lack of or improper pruning. If the vines aren't pruned every year, much set fruit will not ripen or will be a poor quality. Pruning is to limit fruit production so fruit yield and cane growth are in balance.

Grapes are borne on the one-year-old canes from the previous year. Proper pruning will maintain this balance. Bulletins on grape pruning are available from most Cooperative Extension offices in each state. Ed.

pruning

Q: Can anyone please suggest a simple, uncomplicated way to prune grapevines? Everything I have read has me completely confused. A. J.

A: To help A. J. prune his grapevines here are two simplified methods. From Julien Cornell of New York, "While the literature on the subject makes this look like a difficult art, the basic rule is childishly simple. Each spring the old, scaly shoots which are two years old must be cut back to the main trunk, leaving the smooth new shoots of the previous summer, which may then be shortened to a convenient length, leaving four or more shoots, each having from two to 10 buds, depending on the vigor of the vine. Suckers near the ground should be cut off and new suckers rubbed off as they appear. Only new wood bears fruit which explains the reason for cutting back the two year old wood."

From Jeffrey J. Wallach of New York, "Sometime in March, take each vine separately and tie it vertically to some support. Strip everything off except four shoots (of last year's growth, lighter colored wood). Leave two shoots on the right side, two on the left side of the main vine. Cut these back to about 8 buds each. Provide lateral wires for their support and seasonal growth."

lavender

Q: We were given some divisions of old lavender plants a few years ago which have flourished, but have never had much fragrance. Do only certain varieties have the strong fragrance or are we lacking something in our soil? Mrs. T. V., Connecticut

A: Jerry Petterden of Pennsylvania suggests the following, "Mrs. T. V. might do better with new plants that are known to bear fragrant flowers, or root cuttings from neighbors' fragrant plants. Cuttings can be rooted now (April) by clipping growth from last year. Many lavender plants lose their floral fragrance if they are grown in too fertile a soil or where the ground is cool and damp. Lavender does best on an open sunny site where a lime soil drains well and is not exceptionally fertile."

lily (easter)

Q: How do I care for my Easter lily now that it has stopped blooming? Mrs. R. G. B., Bucksport, Maine

A: If gardeners "go by the book," Easter lily (*Lilium longiflorum*) is a tender lily species hardy only to the Carolinas and eastern Virginia. However, Floyd Parliman, a Dutchess County gardener writes, "Gradually harden the Easter lily outdoors so it won't become sunburned. Remove the bulb from the pot, and plant it in a sheltered sunny spot about three inches deeper than it was. We planted ours eight years ago and it has bloomed every June."

And from Mark Sciarrillo of Connecticut, "When my lily stops blooming I cut off the foliage, take the bulb out of the pot and set it out in the garden in fall. This year, I find that the two bulbs I planted last year have now multiplied to five."

monkshood

Q: How do I germinate the seeds of monkshood? I have tried freezing, keeping them damp over heating cables, and other methods with no success. I have obtained seed from two different sources. Mrs. H. S.

A: Joseph Tomlinson of Virginia has come to the rescue. He writes, "The easiest method is to wait until there is a layer of snow on the ground where you wish to grow the monkshood. Select a site partially shaded during the summer months. Plant the seed in the ground, cover loosely with soil and then cover with the snow. Germination is slow and seedlings may not appear before the middle of May. Segregate monkshood as it spreads rapidly and the plants are believed to be toxic to handle." (*The plant is poisonous if ingested. Ed.*)

peony
few buds

Q: I have a peony which is about five years old and is healthy but never has more than two to three buds on it. Is there a solution for more bloom? Mrs. E. P. E., New Jersey

A: A Michigan gardener, Tom Schlegel, offers this solution, "Her problem sounds very similar to a problem we had with a transplanted peony. The solution turned out to be five or six tablespoonfuls of bonemeal worked into the soil around the edge of the plant in spring just as the shoots are breaking the surface. The results were spectacular the first year. With reapplication every year, our peonies have been growing and blooming for many years."

131

(**peony** continued)
no bloom

Q: In recent years my peony has budded but the buds have not matured into flowers. The plant produces plenty of foliage. Is there anything I can do? G. C. M.

A: The reason is probably botrytis blight, a fungus disease which rots the flower buds. From mid-May until the buds are nearly fully developed spray the peonies with either ferbam or zineb fungicide every 10 days. In fall, clean up carefully around plants and cut back old foliage and stalks. As soon as new growth tips appear the following spring, spray with either fungicide. Ed.

John P. Callahan of Ohio had the same problem, but his solution was cultural. He writes, "For two years my peonies budded but did not mature to flowering. This spring, the process repeated when, late in May, a gardener friend suggested that the roots were probably too deep and needed access to air. I removed soil from above the roots and loosened the ground around them with a spading fork, leaving penetrating air holes. Within a week, the buds matured properly into normal large peonies, one month after the neighbors'. This fall when the plants are dormant, I intend to remove the soil permanently or replant."

perennials in shade

Q: What pretty perennials will thrive in oak tree shade? I have daylilies and hostas. Anything else? Mrs. L. K., Long Island

A: Mrs. H. L. Edwards of New York suggests, "Iris tectorum, Iris cristata, plumy bleeding heart, Geranium maculatum, foxgloves, ajuga, and lily of the valley."

petunia
bloom

Q: My petunias have stopped flowering. Why? They are in a sunny site, not overfertilized and the soil is well drained. G. Y., New Jersey

A: Patience! All that is needed is more sunshine. If the plants have grown tall and leggy, prune them back and they should flower well in a few weeks. A wet spring in late May and early June encourages abundant leaf growth, but sunshine will bring on the flowers. Ed.

feeding

Q: Why did my petunias become yellow and scraggly only two to three weeks after I planted them? The soil was well enriched with fertilizer before planting. Only half of those planted remain. D. F. L.

A: D. F. L. revealed, I think, the problem why his petunias yellow a few weeks after planting, according to J. Pettersen,

132

Wisconsin. "He stated he well-enriched the ground with fertilizer before he set out the seedlings and my guess is that he burned the roots of the young plants with too much fertilizer."

poppy
seeds

Q: Is the seed on so-called poppy seed rolls really seed from the Oriental poppy? If so, isn't it a drug? Mrs. A. E. T.

A: The Oriental poppy is Papaver orientale, the large-flowered ornamental species. The opium poppy is P. somniferum which cannot be grown legally in this country. Poppy seeds do come from the opium poppy, but they contain no opium. Opium comes from the milky juice which oozes from cuts made in unripe fruits of P. somniferum. Ed.

winter sowing

Q: For some years I have tried unsuccessfully to plant hardy annual poppy seed on bare soil, on snow and even in early spring when the ground was still frozen. So far, only two small plants. Any ideas? Mrs. A. M. B., Massachusetts

A: G. Bowne of Pennsylvania suggests the following. "Hardy annual poppies are most successful as winter annuals on ground where poppies have grown before. The best time to sow the first crop is in July or August. Some plants may bloom, but most go into winter and bloom the next year. Thin to a foot apart. Winter-kill has been a problem only on heavy clay soil with high wind and no winter snow. A light mulch should help. Plants self sow once established."

primula
germination

Q: Can someone tell me how to germinate seeds of *Primula malacoides* and *P. polyanthus*? Mrs. H. S., New York

A: Julian Newcomb of Pennsylvania suggests, "Here are some keys to proper germination that should help—hardy primulas should be sown as soon as the seed is ripe—sow greenhouse types in spring—use a half-and-half mix of peat and sterilized potting soil—keep moist by putting seed pot in a plastic bag—transplant seedlings as soon as they are large enough to handle."

seed

Q: Does all primula seed need to be frozen first before it will germinate or will a period in the refrigerator do? Mrs. D. G. P., Kalamazoo, Mich.

A: Mrs. Fanny G. Henderson of Virginia writes, "My mother was always successful with her primroses and I can remember as a child little jars of primula seed tucked in the back of the refrigerator. Seed was planted in the late winter and kept

133

in her plant room and by early spring, there were ample seedlings to set out in our woods garden, where she mulched them with pine needles."

roses
aphids

Q: The aphids love our roses and we don't want to spray them as they border our vegetable garden. How can we keep them off, as we like to cut blooms but don't like aphids indoors? Mrs. I. F. G., Yonkers, N.Y.

A: Mrs. York A. France of Pennsylvania writes, "Plant marigolds among the roses. Aphids do not seem to care for their odor and stay away. This was successful for me last year."

From Pat McDonough of Long Island, "Aphids dislike the odor of onions and garlic and will avoid the area. Put a small onion or garlic clove in the blender and puree with two cups of water; strain and spray over the bushes. Do this two or three times a season and aphids will not return."

black spot

Q: Help! Most of my rosebushes are practically leafless from black spot. Shall I prune now (August), fertilize and hope or replant them all this fall? I have 20. J. K., New Jersey

A: *None of these. Black spot is a fungus disease which spreads rapidly in wet, damp weather. It is controlled by continual weekly spraying from bud break until late October with a good fungicide, such as Phaltan, Benlate, Fermate, captan, Manzate or Dithane. If this was not done, begin now to kill off infectious spores. Remove yellowed and disease marked foliage on plants and on the ground. Burn these. (It is too late*

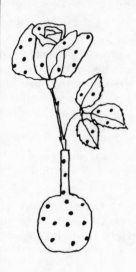

to feed roses now.) Spray weekly until late frost with one of the mentioned fungicides. The roses probably will put out some new foliage. Protect roses this fall with a six-inch soil mound from some other part of the garden and place it over the crown. Next spring, see what live wood is still on the plants, prune to it, feed and start spraying as buds break. Ed.

borers

Q: In spite of spraying, dusting and the use of systemic pesticides, my roses have central cavities in about half the main canes which necessitates cutting them to the ground. What can be done to prevent this borer infestation? V. F. G., Rye, N.Y.

A: Here are several solutions. From Stuart C. Dobson, Westchester County Rose Society, "Seal the ends of the canes promptly after pruning to discourage infestations of borer larvae. Among the materials that can be used: commercial tree sealing compounds, linoleum cement, white glue, nail polish, shellac."
From Melissa B. Levi of Rockland County, "I put a dab of floral clay on the cut. It is not unsightly and is weatherproof, lasting through several winters."
And from Mrs. A. Criswell of New York, "I use thumbtacks or large carpet tacks and push them into the ends of all large canes when cut. They end the borer problem and are much easier than painting them with another substance."
The rose borer is a rare insect pest on roses and attacks mainly the species. They cause a cigar-shaped swelling on the cane and are controlled by cutting out and burning these canes in early spring. Ed.

cuttings

Q: Please tell me if there is any way to root a slip from a rose bush? Do you root it in water? J. M. W., New Jersey

A: *If the rose is a patented variety, propagation is illegal. Patented roses are protected by law and rooting of cuttings from such varieties is an infringement of the U.S. Patent law. The label on a patented rose states this. If the rose is an old-fashioned variety or one on which the patent has expired, the rose may be propagated. However, most modern roses are grafted on a rootstock to give them a stronger root system and ensure a sturdy, hardier plant. A rose growing on its own roots may be less vigorous and less winter hardy. Ed.*
With this preamble, here is a recommendation from Martin Smolin of New York on how to root a rose. He writes, "Here is a method taught to me by a little old man with a green thumb. Prepare a hole about a foot deep in a sunny spot.

135

Water it well and add a mixture of peat moss, soil and leaf-mold. Take a strong branch from the rosebush early in the day before it is weakened by the heat. Trim the branch to the healthiest nine inches, remove lower leaves and sink the bottom half into the wet bed. This should be covered with a wide-mouthed gallon jar and a trench dug around it. The trench gets a gallon of water daily until the first frost. The jar is not removed until Memorial Day the following spring. This has always worked. My own innovation is a little rootone dusted on the bottom of the slip. I have not had success with roses started after mid-August. The following summer the rose bush will be puny; the third year will bring it to normal."

dwarf

Q: Several species of dwarf roses have flourished in my Connecticut climate, but the two- and three-year-old plants have grown immeasurably tall now and are no longer dwarf in size. Clues anyone? A. J. T.

A: Since A. J. T. does not specify how tall his roses have grown we can assume they have just been growing vigorously. All true dwarf roses are closely related to the species Rosa chinensis which are anywhere from 6 to 18 inches tall. Hybrids with mixed species may grow a bit taller. Ed.

mulch

Q: Has anyone had a successful mulch for roses? Peat moss cakes, compost blows away in dry weather and I don't like the look of straw or salt hay. Any suggestions? Dr. K. L.

A: Many mulch ideas were received. The letter from Frederick Rosenthal, a member of the Potomac Rose Society, summed them up. He writes as follows: "In level areas, buckwheat hulls and cocoa bean hulls are pleasant looking. Small-sized pine needles are fine but have an acidifying effect, so ground limestone should be added at the same time to counteract this. Sawdust is cheap and effective but uses up nitrogen in decomposition and some nitrogen fertilizer should be added to make up the loss. Other good mulches are seaweed, tobacco stems, vermiculite and woodchips. Possibly the best-looking are tanbark mulch and ground or shredded tree bark, especially from hardwoods."

pruning

Q: I want to prune my rosebushes now (November) to prevent them being ripped in winter winds. My neighbor says it's wrong and to wait until spring. Can someone tell us who's correct? G. P. O., Metuchen, N.J.

A: George Musselman, another New Jersey gardener, says, "In spring. There is an old gardener's rule, prune rosebushes when forsythia blooms. There is a reason. Some new wood could be winterkilled, especially if winter is open, windy and snowless. Spring pruning permits the cutting away of this winterkill and proper shaping of the plant. Fall pruning is needless. The only time pruning shears are used on rosebushes in fall is to cut back long unwieldy canes on climbers that might be damaged or whipped in high winds."

pruning climbers

Q: How hard should you prune climbers on a split rail fence to promote bloom? Our plants are thick with leaves but few blooms. Why? Mrs. E. J. L., Long Island

A: George Kretchmer, another Long Island gardener, writes, "If the plants have not been pruned well in a number of years, they can be brought back to good bloom with hard pruning. Cut back the thick heavy canes and allow the youngest new canes to remain. The plants can be reduced as much as one half. This renewal pruning may encourage a little fall bloom, and certainly better bloom next year. Then each year, always cut out about one-quarter to one-third of the oldest thickest canes and retie and reset the branches on the fence. Also, I use rose fertilizer once in spring and again the first of June. My plants are 10 years old and a constant display of blossoms all summer long."

rootstock

Q: Why do our tea roses become "floribundas" after a few years? Mrs. P. H. H.

A: "Mrs. P. H. H.'s question is puzzling, suggesting that tea roses revert to floribundas," writes C. George Chamberlain of Ohio. "Modern hybrid tea roses—either tea, grandiflora or floribunda—are budded onto a standard rootstock. Uniform growth characteristics and blooms will grow from this budded stock. Could it be that the inquirer's roses were improperly planted and undergrowth from the rootstock is coming up through the ground and taking over? If so, prune this unwanted growth out now and encourage the budded top to grow. If the roses were planted too high, it may be necessary to replant them in late fall or early spring."

rosa rugosa

Q: How do you grow Rosa rugosa from seed? J. F., Bronx, N.Y.

A: Mrs. John L. Lewine of Massachusetts writes, "In 1959, I brought Rosa rugosa hips (fruits) back from Maine, smashed the pulp, took out the seed, planted them in an out-of-the-way place and forgot about them. Next spring, small seedlings appeared. I left them in place for a year then trans-

(**roses** *continued*)

planted them. In nine years they bloomed, and are now flourishing. I suggest planting Rugosas where they can spread for they do send out long roots.''

Some members of the Rose family require two years to germinate from seed. Ed.

in shade

Q: Is it true that there are some varieties of roses that will endure slight shade and bloom? Can anyone tell us their names? I. V., New Jersey

A: George Weir of Ohio writes, ''I. V. did not say how much shade. Some roses will endure midafternoon shade. Preferably roses should have six hours of sun. Mine get four hours of morning sun and again some in late afternoon but none at high noon. By process of elimination, I have found the floribundas do best. Also I have one old rose that was on the property when we bought it, a bush type that blooms well.''

Additional answers have been received which may be helpful. Mrs. Eleanor Perenyi of Connecticut suggests the bedding rose, Gruss an Aachen. Mrs. Roberta Hale of Pennsylvania writes, ''I have had good success with the polyantha rose, The Fairy which grows on the north side of my house in deep shade and flowers abundantly from June to November.''

tree rose grafting

Q: A tree rose ''top'' displeases and we would like to know if it would be possible to remove this graft and bud another variety on top. If so, when and how? Mrs. L. H., New York

A: Budding of tree roses is a highly skilled art best left to professional grafters. We would suggest donating the unliked tree rose to a neighbor or municipal rose garden and buying a desired plant. Ed.

winter protection

Q: Should I give my beautiful tree roses any special winter protection? They are new this year and very sturdy. J. L., Bronx

A: J. D. McDwyer of New York writes, ''I have found success by wrapping tree roses in this way. After Thanksgiving, I prune back the long unwieldy branches. I pack dry sphagnum moss around the crown. Tie the branches together loosely around it and then wrap the entire top in burlap. Tie it securely. Then I wrap the burlap covering with a plastic bag saved from the cleaners to keep the bundle dry all winter. I unwrap in spring, when the buds on my hybrid teas are breaking.''

winter protection

Q: We live in a very cold ''pocket'' in southern Vermont and have had mixed success with roses. Most of them are winter-

138

killed. Has anyone devised a good means of winter protection that really works for cold winters? D. D. H.

A: Miss Margaret de Schweinitz of Vermont writes, "Apply dormant oil spray to the bushes and prune them back to 10 to 12 inches. Before the ground freezes mound up over each bush with fresh soil to a depth of 8 to 10 inches; after ground freezes, surround entire bush with salt hay and then make a tent of pine boughs and anchor well."

Mrs. William P. White of New York suggests, "Install posts at least three feet high at the corners of the rose bed, attach chicken wire and enclose completely. Fill the fencing with dry leaves and lash on more chicken wire on top. Bank earth and bales of straw around the outside. Or, he can plant the old-fashioned roses, which need no attention as winter draws in other than mounding up the crowns with fresh soil to a foot or more. He can also plant the Sub-Zero roses from the Brownell Company which has gone out of business, but their stock is available from Stern's Nurseries, Geneva, N.Y.

yellow lines

Q: What causes traces of yellow lines on apparently vigorous rose foliage? Mrs. I. P. B., Mt. Kisco, N.Y.

A: Dr. Cynthia Westcott, the noted rose expert, writes, "The lines are probably symptoms of a virus disease. The most common virus on rose is prunus ringspot. The rose strain is not carried in seed or pollen and is not spread by insects. Affected plants usually have normal vigor and bloom and may be safely left in the garden, but do not take cuttings from such a bush. Much of the foundation rose stock in this country carries this virus and research is being done on heat treatment to provide healthy sources."

tulip
blossom

Q: I planted over 100 tulip bulbs, correctly spaced and six inches deep. Why would one tulip develop a lovely tall flower and many others no flower, not even a bud? Mrs. J. R. S.

A: George Kertesz of New York suggests that inferior quality bargain bulbs may have been purchased. Cheap bulbs often are not fully matured to flowering stage. It really is worth it to buy quality, full-size bulbs in the fall. Or, he adds, "Did she plant them upside down? The pointed end or nose is the top."

blossom rot

Q: Can you tell me the cause of rot which appears in the inside of the tulip blossoms? This is the third year they have been planted in my Vermont garden and I have never had the problem before. Should the bulbs be dug up and destroyed? B. S. G.

139

A: Mrs. J. Becker of Connecticut wrote, "I have a thought which may help B. S. G. with the problem of rot in the tulip blossoms. Could it be tulip fire, a fungus problem that usually affects the foliage? Though the problem is usually not very serious, and most prevalent in wet springs, it might be helpful to rotate the garden area this fall and not plant tulips in the same place again."

wild flowers

Q: We want to start establishing a wild flower corner in a shady part of the garden with nursery plants. When is the best time of year to do this? F. E., Greenwich, Conn.

A: Another Connecticut gardener, Mrs. Amedee J. Cole, writes, "Right now (late June–early July). I began such a garden two years ago in July. Make sure the soil is moist before planting, then water as necessary during the hot months. Plants competing with tree roots need more water sometimes than one realizes."

winter seeding

Q: We have read with fascination of many kinds of annual seeds that can be sown on snow but we have always hesitated to try as we suspect the plants might come up in a rather weedy, unkempt pattern. Can anyone give us their secret of winter seeding with attractive blooming results? Mrs. J. D.

A: To help Mrs. J. D. with winter sowing of annuals, here are some hints from Mrs. Edward Eschauzier of Connecticut. "The trick is sowing seed late enough to discourage germina-

140

tion. Give the seedlings light airy protection against sudden changes in weather. In October or November, sow alyssum, cornflower, gypsophila, pansy, snapdragon, larkspur, poppy, sunflower, calliopsis, dianthus, nigella, portulaca. In November or December when there is likely to be snow on the ground sow cosmos, sweet peas, calendula, candytuft, petunia.''

wisteria
bloom

Q: What can we do to force our beautiful wisteria to bloom? It has flourished for several years without a blossom. Mr. D. K., Connecticut

A: Nelva Weber, landscape architect, made this recommendation in *The Times* last year. ''Wisteria flowering is encouraged by pruning the young succulent growth. In mid-June, cut back the top and the new shoots, leaving only four leaves on each shoot. By August, there will be more new growth. Cut this back, leaving only two leaves. The following March, shoots that were originally cut back to four leaves are now reduced to two buds. Keep the top of the plant cut back or it will develop into a bushy non-blooming mass of foliage.''

removal

Q: Can anyone help me get rid of an old wisteria vine? I have just finished having the vine removed from the back of my house where it was pulling down the drain pipe and tangling with the telephone wire. The vine has been sawed off at the root and I have tried stump removers but little sprouts persist in coming up from below ground level. Mrs. N. K.

A: Sumner B. Irish of New Jersey wrote, ''My final solution to rid my property of an unwanted wisteria was to dip the young sprouts that came up in a solution of Triox, a weedkiller product of the Ortho Division, California Chemical Co., The Triox evidently worked down into the root system.''
   This "dipping method" is sometimes used to rid grounds of noxious plants but it should be done with great caution, wear rubber gloves, and read thoroughly the package label directions. Ed.

seed

Q: My wisteria tree has seed pods on it. Has anyone successfully grown plants from the seed? H. F. W., Rockville Centre, N.Y.

A: Mrs. Joseph Star, another Long Island gardener, describes how she grew a plant from seed. ''Remove the wisteria seeds from the pod, place them on damp cotton and cover with another layer of damp cotton to cover. Keep cotton damp and in a week or more, the seed will begin to germinate. Plant seeds outside. Our wisteria did not bloom for five years or so, but now it is covered with blossoms."

The question was asked about a wisteria tree and it is important to realize that the seedlings germinated will produce a wisteria vine. The tree form or standard, as it is called, is the result of staking a strong vine and pruning it heavily for many years to develop a crown and trunk. Ed.

shrub solutions

Q: For a space planted with azaleas, rhododendron and dogwood, I would like to plant a shrub that is compact, acid-loving, shallow rooted and blooms in August. Is there such a shrub? D. E., Brooklyn

A: Frank Menzinger of New York writes, "Abelia would be ideal. It is a handsome, glossy-leaved shrub that has delightful pink flowers in August. It doesn't grow too tall and requires little care. Pruning back of some winter twigkill may be necessary each spring."

Q: I understand that there are evergreen azaleas hardy for the New York metropolitan region. Has anyone had success with them and what varieties were grown? M. K. D., Connecticut

A: Writing from Massachusetts, Dr. Max L. Resnick says, "Yes. For a start, I recommend the Gable Hybrids, about 50 of them, many readily available and especially developed for the Northeast. Big Joe and Mildred Mae (purple), Rosebud (rose) and Stewartsonian (brilliant red) are generally accepted to be the best varieties. Azalea Whilhelmina Vuyk, while not a Gable, is floriferous white. However, one should realize that temperature hardiness is but one factor. Proper soil and culture are paramount: acid soil and well mulched. Plant where drainage is good and protect from exposure to wind and excess sun."

Q: The early flowering pink shrub which blooms with forsythia is *Rhododendron mucronulatum*. My nurseryman

143

insists it's an azalea and calls it Korean azalea. Who's correct? T. T. T.

A: George Morris of New Jersey writes that the rhododendron "bible," *Rhododendrons of the World* by David G. Leach, settles the azalea/rhododendron question for the species *R. mucronulatum.* According to Dr. Leach, "The gardener will regard this species as midway between a Rhododendron and an Azalea and the botanists will agree. . . . It is a deciduous Rhododendron with a mature height of about eight feet."

bamboo
hardy

Q: Since moving to northern New Jersey from Maryland we have been looking for an outdoor species of bamboo which would be fast growing, tall and hardy. What is the name of this bamboo and where can we buy it? A. W.

A: Writing from Virginia, Mrs. Robert Alexander notes, "We are in the same hardiness zone as New Jersey. Ten years ago we planted the Golden Japanese bamboo (*Phyllosatchys aurea*) as a hedge and windbreak. In 3 years it was 15 feet high and now seems stabilized at 20 feet. It is evergreen and survived 8 years of severe drought. It is confined from root running by surrounding it with plastic lawn edging. We bought our bamboo at Gardens of the Blue Ridge, Ashford, McDowell County, N.C. 28603."

nuisance

Q: My property is plagued with hardy bamboo which spreads from one year to the next. How do we get rid of it? We have tried burning, cutting, pulling it out! Mrs. M. R., New York.

A: Many readers have shared the same problem and sent in their solutions. Here they are: From Leonard C. Richmeyer of New York, "After many years of trying everyone's product we finally did find Tordon (Dow Chemical Company) has conquered Mexican Bamboo. The root system can go six feet deep." He suggests using caution with the product which is in the form of herbicide beads and is a highly potent product.

Miss A. Bowman of New Jersey writes, "I have finally had success at the end of five years destroying a 50x70 foot growth. It required digging up the roots; any piece left was a source of new growth. Heavy black strips of plastic were laid down over the area and the bamboo that worked its way through was allowed to leaf out and sprayed with dicamba which must go on the leaves to be effective. Last year only two plants came up."

Mrs. S. P. R. of Washington, D.C., conquered bamboo this

way: "I cut down bamboo cane last spring, shredding the waste. Then during the spring and summer, I clipped off each new shoot which appeared. Gradually, the roots died. So far this spring only one weak shoot has appeared, which I pinched off."

camellias

Q: We live in southern Connecticut and have read enthusiastically about camellia success in the Washington, D.C., area and in Philadelphia. Has anyone been adventurous northward and successfully grown them above the New York City region? We would like to try if we could be encouraged! G. G. F.

A: Mrs. Kurt M. Vogel of Connecticut reports good success with camellia growing in the Bridgeport area. "The camellias have been growing outdoors for the last few years. They flower profusely in late April. They are planted in a protected spot in the front of the home, facing west, and are fertilized with an acid fertilizer in late March and June-July. After Thanksgiving, they are protected by a burlap windbreak which is not removed until April."

evergreens
burlap winter care

Q: Our home facing east has arborvitae, rhododendron, euonymus, firethorn and azalea in front. Last year we did not burlap any plants and lost two azaleas. To avoid trouble this year which plants should be wrapped and how? Mrs. A. F. P., Livingston, N.J.

A: *Gardeners should not equate winter protection with blanketing plants to keep them warm. Plants are living and breathing and the purpose of any burlap is as a windbreak and should be used as such. Spread burlap to face the wind but keep open to allow plant aeration. None of Mrs. A. F. P.'s plants require protection since all are winter hardy in New Jersey. Azaleas may have been lost because they were marginally hardy. Or lack of water in the fall could have dried them out and caused their demise. Adequate soil moisture plus a thick mulch to preserve it are the best winter protection measure in the fall. Ed.*

plastic wintercare

Q: What is the rule, do you wrap evergreens in plastic or not to protect them for winter? B. M., Brooklyn

A: "No, no," writes Mrs. Beth Freeman, a Long Island gardener. "Evergreens must be free to breathe in winter and the plastic would suffocate them and raise temperatures inside the plastic to an alarming degree. Wind shield evergreens

145

with burlap if necessary or use the newer anti-desiccant sprays to protect them, but do not wrap them.''

propagation

Q: How do I root pine, spruce and rhododendron? G. M. A., Putnam County, N.Y.

A: Y. L. Syzcki of Westchester County writes, ''Needled evergreens are difficult to propagate without ideal conditions and experience. I think it would be much easier for G. M. A. to start with seeds of favorite evergreens and grow them. If ripe seed is kept in a dry cool place, plant it in spring in flats kept in a sheltered area. Rhododendrons are easy to propagate by layering; that is, nick an extra long branch about a foot or so back from the tip and pin the branch down to the ground with a forked stick. Cover with soil and a rock. Next year, sever the new plant.''

propagation

Q: How and when can I root cuttings of some of my evergreens, especially hemlock, azalea and mountain andromeda? J. G., Long Island

A: Writing as a Long Island neighbor, Dinah Foglia says that ''early summer is the time to take evergreen cuttings. Cut shoots four to six inches in length, dip them in #3 or #4 rooting hormone and place in perlite, sand, or half and half mix of perlite and peat. Wet down containers and spray the tops at least twice a day. Or put the container into plastic bags. Azalea and pieris root easily in four to six weeks; hemlock, spruce and other needled evergreens are more difficult. The first winter, store rooted cuttings in a coldframe or cool greenhouse before planting them on their own.''

hedges
pet proof

Q: Is there an attractive cat and dog-proof hedge that I can plant around a rocky portion of my yard where I grow alpines and dwarf evergreens? I love the animals, but the plants, too! T. Y., Pennsylvania

A: Here are a few ideas. H. La Morder, Vermont, suggests Japanese barberry which is available in green, red or golden leaved varieties. Yearly shearing will keep the hedge in trim. George Moore, Connecticut, suggests the low-growing floribunda rose, The Fairy. Celia Polomany, New York, has a better idea. ''Italian cayenne pepper or hot pepper will keep dogs and cats away, without harming them. Place a piece of the pepper, which has an irritating odor, wherever you need to shoo pets away.''

screening hedge

Q: Our property, which is shaded by tall oaks, backs on a state parkway. I would like to plant a natural fence to screen

146

the view of passing cars. What can anyone suggest for a hedge that will have foilage all year, will not require sunlight and will endure automobile fumes? Mrs. E. S.

A: Sol Cohen of New York recommends the upright yews, though slow-growing, they are durable and evergreen.

screening hedge

Q: Any suggestions for a good, narrow screening hedge? I'm tired of privet, we don't have enough water for hemlock and arborvitae just does not appeal. The hedge cannot be too tall, either, about four feet. Mrs. K. G. Y.

A: Mrs. Dinah Folgia of Long Island suggests the upright yews, especially *Taxus media Hicksi*. J. H. V., Mountainside, N.J. suggests *Lonicera nitida*, a form of honeysuckle that responds well to pruning for hedges. It resembles boxwood and is hardy to the Philadelphia region. Richard J. Longleith of Massachusetts suggests euonymus or Japanese holly.

holly
berries

Q: Our holly used for the holiday dinner table has lasted quite well. The berries are still quite red and fresh looking. Has anyone had success planting them? Are there any special clues for success? O. D.

We were told to save the berries from our Christmas holly and plant them outdoors for holly plants for the future. Does this really work and how can you determine if you have male or female holly plants? D. Y. P., Darien, Conn.

A: Here are two approaches. From Professor Carl Withner, Brooklyn College, N.Y. "When holly berries are ripe, the embryos in the seeds are still immature and require generally two years to germinate. Plant out of doors in a sandy, peaty bed with exposure to freezing and thawing. Some seed will grow in two years; others later. The plants should be male and female 50/50 but no one can be sure until they flower after a few years. It was my experience in growing an English holly hedge from seed, that the larger, more vigorous growing plants turned out to be male."

From Thomas H. B. Boothe in New Jersey, "Soak berries about 24 hours, then remove the red outer coats and separate the seeds (they are sectioned like oranges). Mix seed with sand, place in an empty milk carton or glass jar, add a small amount of water to moisten the sand and place in the refrigerator until March. In March, plant out seeds and sand in area where there is direct sun. Wire screening will protect seeds from mice. Germination will take place in one or two years. Transplant seedlings when four leaves show."

Following up on Mr. Boothe's advice about planting holly seed; Robert E. Watts of New York adds his experience as

(**holly** *continued*)

follows: "About 20 years ago we moved to Long Island. After our first Christmas we tossed out our live holly wreaths under azalea bushes near our front door, facing east. About a year later, I noticed a number of tiny seedling coming up in the acid soil heavy with peat moss. By the second year, I had some little English holly plants several inches high. They remained there and after another year, I transplanted the hollies into a coldframe where they grew to a height of several feet. Finally, I transplanted them along the property line in the front lawn where they have grown into a beautiful holly hedge. Since there were no male hollies in the lot, we had to buy a male plant and now we have plenty of berries."

cuttings

Q: We always receive beautiful Oregon holly from friends at Christmas time. Twice I have tried to root it and failed. What are some special tricks I should know to be successful this year? Mrs. G. H., Connecticut

A: Mrs. Belmont Moot of New York has a solution. "My husband made a small coldframe. I put sand in the bottom, then peat moss. I cut the holly about three or four inches long, leaving two leaves and dip the ends in rooting hormone and put them into the coldframe so that the stems penetrate through the peat moss to the sand. I have over 100 hollies of all kinds."

D. D. Johnson of Delaware also had trouble rooting holly cuttings and he suggests shaking berries onto the ground after the holidays. Rake them in and seedlings will appear from time to time.

Henry De Salle, a Long Island reader, says, "Here is a simple way to root holly. Trim off bottom leaves and recut ends with a sharp knife. Dip in rooting hormone. In a sawed-off bottom of a gallon milk carton place a half-half mixture of peat and sand. The cuttings are inserted in it, watered well, covered with a plastic tent made from freezer bags and left out in our attached garage with light from a north window. By spring, the cuttings root. We have several small hollies around the property."

flowers

Q: How do I tell the difference between male and female holly flowers? R. B., Bronx

A: Mrs. E. M. Hopkins of Westchester County writes, "The male flowers have plump yellow anthers which release pollen when the flowers are fully open. Anthers are present in the female flowers but remain undeveloped. The male flowers are usually borne three on a stalk. The female flowers arise

148

singly and have a well-developed pistil (small green knob in the center of the flower)."

grafting

Q: Is it possible to graft a female American holly to a male American holly? The only information I can find is scant and I plan to try with some helpful information. Mrs. C. D. V., Hyde Park, Mass.

A: E. H. B. of New Jersey makes this observation, "As an experiment, such grafting may be attempted employing the customary methods with dormant plant material. Success would depend upon such factors as individual skill in making the union, hardiness of the trees and acceptance of the graft by the female holly. If fertilization of female by male blossoms is the principal object of making the graft, it would be simpler to hang small test tubes filled with water and twigs of male blossoms on the female tree. In the case of grafting or using male blossom sprigs, both male and female trees should blossom simultaneously."

hydrangea
bloom

Q: We have three different clumps of blue hydrangea in different locations with varying conditions of sun and shade. For years we have tried various ways of treating them to get blooms without success. We tried neglect, too. The plants are beautiful; healthy leaf growth but no blooms. We would appreciate some practical suggestions from other gardeners. B. G.

A: Many others asked the same thing. Here are some pointers. Hydrangeas grown for their blue, pink or white flowers belong to the species, Hydrangea macrophylla. To bloom well these plants need well-drained soil with plenty of mois-

149

ture (water in dry periods), and full sun. This is one reason why they do well at the shore. Another, they are not reliably winter hardy and milder seaside temperatures are more suitable.

The flower color is controlled by the acidity of the soil. Addition of aluminum or iron to acid will make blue flowers bluer, and turn pink flowers blue. (White is not affected.) Alkaline soil (lime application) will encourage production of pink flowers. Hydrangeas should be pruned as soon as the flowers fade. Take out all the old flower shoots down to new growth. Thin out weak growth. Flower buds will form at the tips of new shoots formed this year. Never prune in late fall, or in early spring; this destroys flowering wood. Excessive winter cold will, too. Think through these cultural needs, and the answers for "no bloom" may be found. Ed.

Morris Gottlieb of New York offers another idea for people who have had trouble getting their hydrangeas to flower. He writes, "Spread a handful of Epsom salts (magnesium sulfate) around the shrubs in spring, and water it in thoroughly. I have had fabulous luck with this method."

climber

Q: Our climbing hydrangea is vigorous and healthy but does not bloom. This is the third summer for it. Has anyone a clue? Mrs. A. B., Bronx, N.Y.

A: Mrs. J. W. Mersereau, a Cape Cod reader, writes, "I was told when I planted mine that it might be five or six years before the hydrangea bloomed. That proved to be correct. It is now about 10 years old and has grown to the top of the chimney and is covered with blossoms. It does take patience."

standard

Q: How does one grow a standard (tree form) hydrangea? I have tried, without results and would like to know if anyone has succeeded. W. J. B., Kingston, N.Y.

A: "Perhaps our solution will help," writes Mrs. James J. Horstfall of Ohio. "We started several hydrangeas each spring from single whips, but could never winter them over properly as we did not have a greenhouse or cold plant room. We finally bought one from a local nursery and have been delighted ever since. Unless W. J. B. has wintering-over facilities, we suggest purchase might be more rewarding."

**juniper
propagation**

Q: What is the best way to propagate cuttings of juniper and at what time of year? Spring cuttings in sand and peat have not been successful. J. J. M.

150

A: Harvey Freidenhausen of Pennsylvania notes that the timing of taking the cuttings was wrong, not the rooting medium. Juniper cuttings root best when taken in July, after the new growth has started to harden, or they can be taken during the winter months, around the Christmas holidays.

Take short cuttings from the tips of new growth. Dip them in a commercial rooting hormone and place them in damp sand. If they can be kept in a cool room, away from sun, where there is bottom heat, they should root readily. Cover with plastic, keep them constantly moist. Ed.

laurel
bloom

Q: I have a dozen large mountain laurels, very healthy, that have fallen into a cycle of blooming profusely one year and not at all the next. Has anyone else found this and is there anything to be done about it? H. C., East Hampton, Long Island

A: Irene B. Lane, a Connecticut reader, offers a suggestion, "Many years ago, I had the same problem and was told to remove all the faded blooms of mountain laurel and rhododendron. Snap off carefully. I have a mountain laurel that is over 40 years old and it produces massive blooms annually."

transplanting

Q: When is the best time to transplant a laurel which is doing poorly and needs a new site? Mrs. E. H., Long Island

A: Mrs. Edith Raabe, another Long Island gardener, suggests, "April or October is best for transplanting shrubs."

lilac

The following series of questions and answers on lilac bloom are occasionally repetitious, but present a number of different approaches to the problem. Ed.

no bloom

Q: For years my lilacs bloomed. However, for the past four years they have grown rampant, not flowered and developed a white powdery coating on the leaves. Would it be harmful to cut them down? When? Mrs. B. V., New Jersey

A: J. O. Pratt of New York writes that her problem is two-fold. The white powdery coating is mildew which develops in August. Control: Karathane. The overgrown lilac needs hard pruning. In spring, after lilac bloom, cut out the old canes to the ground and leave the younger newer shoots. This can be done gradually over a three-year period or drastically all at once. It may take one or two years for the plants to come back. Addition of lime to the soil helps. Ed.

151

(**lilac** *continued*)
no bloom yet

Q: Three years ago I disposed of my old lilacs that did not bloom prolifically and replaced them with four hybrids with high hopes. Not one of them has bloomed in spite of applications of fertilizer and lime. A solution? Dr. M. K.

A: Carol Manduke of New York notes that it is not unusual for a bush to take three or four years to bloom. She has had favorable results the second year after several applications of superphosphate.

Mrs. E. L. Podenberg of New Jersey adds another tip to Dr. M. K.'s query why lilacs do not bloom. She suggests applications of lime around the lilacs in fall. If the bushes are quite mature, place generous amounts around the perimeter of the roots and they will bloom. "I do this every fall," she says.

sparse bloom

Q: We are concerned about our lilacs. They have grown so tall it is difficult to reach up and remove the seed pods. This year the flowering was quite sparse. I would like to prune them down, but one year our gardener did this to other lilacs and they never bloomed again. When should I prune the lilacs and what can we do to encourage them to bloom? M. C. B.

A: To answer M. C. B.'s question on lilacs, perhaps John Smith's "story" will help. "We bought an old farmhouse in southern Vermont three years ago and clustered around the kitchen door were thick clumps of lilacs. We could hardly get to the door. In early October, we went to it and pruned them very hard. We took out all the old thick wood, and left just the young center canes. Next spring the plants grew a lot of young new shoots. No bloom. We pruned again a bit in summer. This spring the flowers were lovely. We also limed the soil well in fall and applied bonemeal each spring."

top bloom

Q: Can anyone suggest what to do for my French lilacs? I bought them at blooming size three years ago. They bloom each year, but only at the top and they are not making any new growth. They are fed each spring with dehydrated cow manure and later on in the season with an additional water soluble fertilizer. Can anyone help? Mrs. Z. B.

A: Edwin H. Blanchard of New York suggests the following, "Lilacs need full sun; don't allow them to develop seeds and cut off dead blossoms after bloom. Bear in mind that among hundreds of varieties, there are many that are individualistic in their maturity to bloom; some varieties even take a sabbatical leave from bloom every third or fourth year."

Gerald Kilcullen, also of New York, suggests Mrs. Z. B.'s

lilacs may need lime and recommends applying it to the shrubs in spring.

privet rooting

Q: I have tried unsuccessfully to root privet. What is the secret? Mrs. R. M. N., Chambersburg, Pa.

A: Mary Leyland of Long Island has a solution, "simple as ABC. Take a large plastic bag and cover the bottom with a half soil, half sand mixture. Take cuttings from a healthy privet shrub, about 12 or 16 inches long and stick the cut end into the soil in the plastic bag. A good sized bag should hold about 10 cuttings. Add a little water. Seal the plastic bag with a twister and place it on the north side of the house (outside) over winter. By spring, there will be 10 rooted privets."

Mrs. Richard Knight, a New York reader, was successful rooting privet cuttings in the summer months by just poking them into the ground.

pyracantha
berries

Q: All but one of our pyracanthas are located on the south side of the house where they are slightly shaded. Another is on the north side and gets sun in the afternoon. None of the vigorous shrubs has ever produced berries and they are all at least 10 years old. Why? Mrs. E. B.

We have a large, full-flowering pyracantha which produces many beautiful berries. A rooted cutting taken from the base of this plant has grown vigorously for several years, but has never produced berries. I wonder why? Mrs. C. L.

A: To answer the two questions on lack of berries on pyracantha, Dr. Donald Wyman of Massachusetts offers these suggestions. "Like many other members of the Rose Family, pyracanthas can be alternate bloomers, heavy flowers and fruits one year, and few the next. Sometimes plants are heavily fertilized causing vigorous vegetative growth and little formulation of flower buds and fruits for the next year. To correct this, apply no fertilizer and prune heavily immediately after flowering and repeat one or two times later to prevent vigorous vegetative shoots from forming. Also if growth is too vigorous, root prune plants in early spring by shoving a spade into the ground around the plants to cut the roots. Superphosphate, no nitrogen, spaded into the soil in spring might help. Finally, scab, a disease, blackens immature green fruits and often goes unnoticed. Spray with Ferbam when buds break and twice more at 10 day intervals."

pruning

Q: When do I prune my espaliered pyracantha so as not to interfere with the flowers in spring and the berries in fall? L. S., Long Island

153

(**pyracantha**
continued)

A: Dr. Richard P. Keating of New Jersey writes, "Espaliered pyracantha must be pruned at least three times during spring and summer, but there is no problem preserving flowers and berries. Flowers appear on woody side branches, at least one year old and are easily seen in late spring when the first pruning is needed. The older branches without flowers and the soft new growth can be cut away. Prune as often as you like during the summer leaving the branches with the green berries. Michelangelo is reputed to have described his method of sculpturing as simply removal of those parts of the marble block that didn't belong in the finished sculpture. I have a simple method for pruning an espalier. 1. Prune away everything that grows toward the wall. 2. Prune everything that grows more than three inches away from the wall. 3. Prune everything that grows out from the main trunk. 4. Prune everything that crosses in front of another branch."

scab

Q: Our pyracantha berries turn black instead of orange. Has anyone else had this problem and what is the solution? The plant blooms freely and the foliage is lovely. Mrs. T. S., Mount Union, Pa.

A: Walter Westerfeld of Pennsylvania identified the problem as scab. It can be prevented by spraying with ferbam or captan before the buds open, repeat every 10 days until the berries are well formed. He also suggests burning "all black berries from last year."

Joshua Schlanger, Long Island, also identified the problem and recommended the fungicide Benomyl.

rhododendron
bloom

Q: This past winter we purchased an older home. On the north side of the house are several large rhododendrons. This spring there were many buds, but no flowers. Our local garden store tells us that they did not bloom because they were not hybrids. Is this so, or is there something lacking in the soil? Mrs. G. P. C.

A: Dr. Max L. Resnick of Massachusetts offers this help. "While there are many possible causes for failure to set buds, buds which do not bloom are frequently the result of freezing. Not necessarily winter extremes, but early fall or late spring frosts can be harmful. One other thought. It is important to distinguish between flower buds and leaf buds. The flower bud is larger and more bulbous. But in older, larger plants, leaf buds could be mistaken for flower buds."

Rhododendrons are self-fertile, whether a hybrid or not. It is not necessary to have two plants for flowering. Ed.

154

bloom

Q: I have several rhododendrons around my home, some with dense foliage, some with sparse. Over the years, those with sparse foliage have had more blossoms than those with dense foliage. Should I prune those with dense foliage or what? Mrs. E. K.

A: Robert J. Smith of New York suggests to Mrs. E. K. that one reason why her rhododendrons with sparse foliage have more blooms is that they may receive more sunlight. Those with the denser foliage may just be in a shadier locale. "We had a similar problem in our foreyard, and shortly after we had the shade trees thinned (maples) more light came through and the rhododendrons bloomed more fully. We also give them a boost of acid-type fertilizer every spring just as the new growth begins."

cuttings

Q: We have a delightful dwarf rhododendron which we inherited when we bought our new country home. We have tried to root cuttings from it, but have failed. Is there a special trick someone can share? F. R. W., New Jersey

A: Here are two ideas. From J. P. Zollinger of New York, "The readiness of rhododendron to root varies in my experience from 6 weeks to two years. Root in a mixture of half peat and half coarse sand. If only a few cuttings are desired, stick them in a plastic pot, cover with a plastic bag and place in good light on the north side of a building. Or another method is layering."

Dr. Max Resnick of Massachusetts also suggests layering and this is his method, "Bury a low hanging branch in a trench a few inches deep, leaving the tip exposed. Mulch the buried portion well and place a rock over it to hold it in place. A branch of this year's or last year's growth is best. And layering can be done any time of year. A layer made in spring should be well rooted by summer or fall the following year when it is severed from the mother plant. Do not move it for several weeks."

yew yellowing

Q: Several of our yews are dropping yellow needles at a rapid rate although we have watered during dry spells. What is the solution? G. D. D., Scarsdale, N.Y.

A: The black vine weevil is at work. Young grubs feed on roots of yew and adult beetles eat holes in leaf margins of rhododendron. The effective control is the restricted chemical chlordane (50 percent emulsifiable) applied now (June) at the root zone. Follow dilution directions. Repeat again next spring. Ed.

155

trees
from fruits
to nuts

apple
from seed

Q: I have recently eaten some tasty apples and saved the seeds in anticipation that they can be grown into trees. How do I proceed? V. H., New Jersey

A: Mrs. S. Whitney, a Vermont orchardist, writes, "Dry the seeds and plant in soil as you would a house plant. Transplant outside in good drainage when a foot high. This will be a seedling rootstock which is slow to produce—in about 10 years. The fruit produced will be a cross between the apple eaten and the variety that pollinated it. If one prefers to choose a certain variety of apple, the whip (rootstock) can be grafted the following year when it is the size of a pencil."

As Mrs. Whitney pointed out, apple varieties do not come true to seed and bud or graft wood of the desired variety must be grafted onto rootstock. Fruit tree nurseries sell grafted fruit trees in a generous selection of favorite dessert varieties. Ed.

nuisance

Q: Is there a chemical spray that we can use to stop our aged apple trees from bearing? We love the old trees, but not their fruit. Mrs. E. P., Flushing, N.Y.

A: There is no sure way. However, fruit growers have noted some results in thinning with applications of naphthalene acetic acid (NAA) or the related NAB, both plant hormones. (These substances are not readily available at the consumer level.) Another method, Sevin (carbaryl) is frequently used by apple growers to thin fruit, but effectiveness is dependent upon many factors including tree age, variety, pruning, weather, degree of fruit set and other factors.

Warner Thurlow, Cooperative Extension Agent for Middlesex County, N.J., explained that "50 percent wettable powder

Sevin is applied at the rate of two tablespoonfuls per gallon, 14 to 21 days after full bloom. Choose a calm evening or muggy day to avoid spray drift." Note: Though Sevin is rated as a safe pesticide for general home garden use, it is toxic to honey bees. Ed.

Althus E. Forman, New York, offered his solution. "A neighbor, who had the same problem as Mrs. J. P., gave me permission to pick both fallen and hanging apples to my heart's content. The apples were thoroughly washed and trimmed of rotten and wormy areas and put in a large pot with a cupful of water and allowed to boil down, put through a collander and hot packed in quart jars for homemade apple sauce."

scab

Q: Does anyone know an organic solution to apple scab? We do not want to spray chemicals on our tree. Mrs. E. O. K., Manhattan

A: George Slate, a New York State pomologist, writes, "I suggest that she grow Prima and Priscilla apple varieties which are resistant to apple scab."

cherry
fall-blooming

Q: In August our cherry tree lost its foliage due to some sort of malady. Recently (October), buds on the branches bloomed! Why? Will our tree flower and fruit next spring? Mrs. R. B., Scarsdale, N.Y.

A: There could be many reasons for a tree to lose its foliage in summer—insects, fungus, virus. They normally refoliate before the end of the growing season. There is a fall-blooming cherry tree, which Mrs. R. B. may have. If her cherry is a spring flowering variety, those flowers that bloomed in fall will not rebloom next spring. Ed.

crabapple
bloom

Q: Last year our crabapple tree was beautiful with bloom and this year not a blossom. Our neighbor's tree did the same thing. Is there a local problem? G. L., Long Island.

Our crabapple is six years old, but it has flowered only once, the first year. What is wrong? M. J., Connecticut

A: Alex Soave, another Long Island gardener, writes, "According to the Nassau County Cooperative Extension the sparse bloom on crabapples is due to last year's severe outbreak of a fungus disease called apple scab.

Another reason: Many crabapples are alternate bearing varieties, that is they flower in alternate years. According to Wyman's Trees for American Gardens, this quality is true for Almey, Crimson Brilliant, Hopa, Aldenham, Eleyi, Strathmore

157

and a few other varieties. Nurserymen can give guidance on this quality and successive bloom varieties can be chosen to by-pass this void. This may be part of M. J.'s answer. Too much shade could be another. The extended growth made during abundant spring rains may have encouraged flower-bud set for next year. Let's all hope so. Ed.

pruning

Q: I have a flowering crabapple on my terrace. I would like to prune it to grow out rather than up. When and how should I do this? S. B. R., Manhattan

A: J. L., another Manhattan gardener, notes, "Topping would be the best way. Merely cut out the center growing branch of the tree which would force growing strength to the branches. Do it carefully in the spring so as not to ruin the natural branch structure. We top all our evergreens this way to keep them bushy and it should work with the fruit trees."

dogwood
berries

Q: Is it possible to raise dogwood seedlings by planting the berries on our tree? J. P. W., Stroudsburg, Pa.

A: Theodore Fastje, a Westchester County reader, suggests, "I saved berries over the winter and planted them outdoors the next spring. Result: no seedlings. The next year, I took a lesson from nature and planted a handful of seeds on the ground in the rear of my garden and covered them with leaves to protect them from the birds. Next spring, seed-lings."
   Dogwood seed must be planted immediately when ripe or stratified, stored cold in a dormant state, for several months before spring planting. Ed.

no bloom

Q: We have had two Cornus kousa chinensis dogwood for six or seven years and they have never bloomed. They appear to be quite healthy. Can anything be done to force bloom? Mrs. J. J. G., Massachusetts

A: John Tremor of New Jersey suggests "be patient. Our trees did not bloom for eight years and the nurseryman told us they are a bit finicky about getting started. Also, if the trees are growing in shade or wet damp hollows, this could delay bloom."

pruning

Q: When can I prune some low branches from a dogwood. I always have to duck, and one of these days! My amateur tree cutting friends say don't ever prune dogwood, it bleeds! C. J. G., Bay Shore, N. Y.

A: B. Weickert, a Delaware reader, writes, "I had to renew my dogwood because of die-back. I pruned it in the middle of winter and there was no bleeding because the tree was dormant. I plan another pruning this winter."

Though Mr. Weickert was successful pruning his dogwood in winter, trees that bleed (lose sap) after pruning are best pruned in summertime, when there is less sap flow. Among the heavy tree bleeders are birches, maples, walnuts and elms. Ed.

Q: I have had a fig tree in my yard for over 15 years. It always bears figs, but they never ripen. Has anyone a solution? The tree is pruned carefully each year. P. E. J., Bronx, N. Y.

A: The fruit of the fig is actually a fleshy receptacle which has inside male and female flowers; they bloom in the interior of the receptacle. Most fig varieties have a tiny pore in this fleshy receptacle which can be entered by an insect covered with pollen to assure mature fruits and the seeds of the fig. This fertilization is known as caprification since the fig supplying the pollen is called a caprifig. Some varieties require caprification for mature figs; a few do not. A variety requiring caprification: Calimyrna, a type of Smyrna fig. Fig varieties Adriatic, Brown Turkey and Mission do not require caprification. Ed.

Mrs. Richard I. Rudell of Long Island offered some tips on growing figs as follows. "The secret of successful fig growing is water. Roots are shallow. We pruned our three figs this spring and during the summer we set the hose in the center of the trees and let it run for several hours. As the fruits grew to maturity in the early fall, I made certain that the water supply was plentiful and the results have been fantastic. We do not cover or wrap our trees in winter but apply a good layer of dried leaves around their bases to prevent frost heaving. I fertilize with compost, rotted or dried manure in the spring, and in winter when snow is on the ground."

Q: My mother's fig tree is thriving and fruiting in her yard. Now she wants me to have it. Has anyone been successful growing figs in large tubs? I would like to grow it on the deck in back of my home. When should I transplant? Mrs. R. T., New Jersey

A: Mrs. H. P. Blackwood of Connecticut writes, "I have a small fig tree which bears delicious fruit. It is in a redwood tub which I keep on my patio in summer and bring into my plant room in late fall where it stays until the end of May. It requires no special care, but I keep it pruned back so it does not become too large and unwieldy."

Spring transplanting for Mrs. R. T.'s plant is suggested. Ed.

uncovering

Q: How soon do I uncover my fig tree protected for the winter? Our last killing frost is the first week in May but isn't that late for uncovering? F. E. O., New Paltz, N.Y.

A: Mrs. Richard Rudell of Long Island writes, "It's not the killing frost that F. E. O. should worry about but the frost heaving which causes winterkill. The shallow roots suddenly exposed dry out quickly and die. Keep a heavy mulch around the base of the tree and uncover it about the middle or end of April or as soon as the tree starts to leaf out. At the same time, prune back the fig to assure a full and heavy crop."

wintering over

Q: My fig tree has thrived in a pot on the patio. Can I bring it inside as a house plant or should I leave it outdoors and protect it for the winter? Clues anyone? Mrs. R. D. S.

A: Fred C. Lowenfels of New York writes that "fig trees will grow as a container plant in a house, but they usually lose their leaves in winter. It is better to keep them outdoors and protect them well from the cold. If in a garden, it should be protected from field mice; they seem to like the bark."

The fig family, Ficus, has many excellent houseplants, many in tree form. The above refers to the tender species grown for fruit, Ficus carica. Ed.

wintering over

Q: I have two fig trees, one is a red variety, the other white. Since they are too big to hill in the ground for winter, how can I protect them? P. L.

A: Two readers have come to the rescue of P. L. with suggestions for winterizing fig trees. Mrs Gemma Florentine of New York writes, "My husband's mother has kept a fig tree for more than 50 years in south Brooklyn. I successfully planted a cutting from this tree nine years ago in Putnam Valley. Both trees are protected in the following fashion. After the frosts but just before an expected hard freeze, tie the branches of the tree as closely together as possible without cracking them. Wrap the tree in layers of newspapers, tying them around the tree to form a thick quilt. Corrugated paper or other thick paper may be used with the newspaper. After this wrap the entire tree in building or tar paper. Cap this column of wrappings with a plastic bucket or a giant pail so that the rain will not enter from the top. Tie bucket or pail down. Finally mound a good heap of soil about the roots. Fig trees swaddled in this manner are a common sight in south Brooklyn back yards."

And from Morris Colman of New York, "Figs grow only on new wood, so I pollard my tree to four to six inches just before the first frost and swathe it in a bale of salt marsh hay covered by a tarpaulin. I uncover it about May 1. The fig grows full-sized branches by summer and yields hundreds of figs by late fall. This tree is now about 15 years old with a six-inch trunk about four feet high. I keep wire mesh around the lower trunk and scatter moth balls under the salt hay to discourage field mice."

fruit tree
pruning

Q: When is the best time to prune fruit trees, specifically peach, cherry and apple? Do they always need annual pruning? G. H.

A: *In general, fruit tree pruning is done during the late winter months before the buds break. Young trees, not bearing fruit, need training to encourage a strong, well-branched structure. Once the trees begin to bear fruit, then maintenance pruning is needed to keep short fruit bearing laterals developing and prevent crowded inner growth. The whole subject of fruit tree pruning is technical and should be done properly, a discussion beyond the scope of a simple "answer." Library research is recommended or bulletins from Cooperative Extension. Ed.*

spraying

Q: We have a small orchard with apples, peaches and pears and would like to know what the major insect problems are and when we should attack? Last year we lost all crop to bugs and would appreciate some help. G. F. B., Chappaqua, N. Y.

A: *The county seats of most every county in the country have an office of Cooperative Extension, a service arm of each state's agricultural college. They prepare fruit-tree spray schedules for insect and disease control which are available upon request. Or they may be obtained from the Cooperative Extension office at state college. Ed.*

hazel nut

Q: About six years ago, I purchased two hazel nut trees. They have grown nicely, but no nuts. Why? What can I do? S. B. G.

A: *Mrs. Eleanor Perenyi of Connecticut notes that it is necessary to have hazel nuts (filberts) of different varieties—not just two trees—to obtain fruits. (Hazel nuts are self-unfruitful). For example, one plant of Royal and one of Barcelona*

161

will cross pollinate and bear fruit. This is explained in the catalog of J. E. Miller Nurseries, Canandaigua, N.Y. 14424.

magnolia

Q: Three years ago we planted a late blooming magnolia in our New Jersey garden which bloomed magnificently the following spring. But it has not bloomed since. How can we help our magnolia bloom again? Mrs. S. R. E.

A: Mrs. Sadie Smith of New Jersey writes that their tree "behaved that way for a few years until it seemed to take hold and grow. Our local nursery attributed the lack of bloom to two severe winters followed by one early thaw when buds may have been killed by a late frost."

maple

Q: A Japanese red maple tree on my front lawn starts out each spring in a lovely red color. As the summer comes on, it turns completely green. Why? E. R., Long Island

A: Unfortunately, this does happen with certain varieties. Although there are over 80 named varieties available today, not all will retain their original color. Some unreputable sources sell seedlings as particular varieties. The solution is to buy Japanese maples only from reliable nurseries. Many varieties are grafted to guarantee the proper color traits. Ed.

mulberry

Q: I have an "old world" type mulberry tree on my property, very effective for shade and appearance. The tree is enormous, I have been advised not to cut it down. But it bears many white berries starting in July. The berries are a daily mess to clean up. When heat strikes them, they ferment and they clog the gutters. Is there a spray I can use to prevent berries? Mrs. E. M. H.

A: Ernest Christ, extension fruit specialist at Rutgers University, informs us that he knows of nothing that can be sprayed on the mulberry (or wild cherry trees) to prevent the formation of fruits. The hormone sprays that can be used to reduce fruit set on home fruit trees appear to be ineffectual. The alternative treatment would be the sharp axe.

nails in trees

Q: We would like to nail brackets on two of our shade trees to summer our hanging baskets outdoors. Will this harm the tree trunks? Mrs. H. O. N., Manhattan

A: According to Dr. P. P. Pirone, pathologist at the New York Botanical Garden, in the strictest sense, trees should not be bored into as there is always the chance that fungus will enter. However, he noted that labels have been screwed into

162

the garden's trees for numerous years with no damage. He suggested if brackets are put into the trees to hold hanging planters, that screws will give better hold than nails. Also, the screws should be dipped into a fungicide such as copper sulfate, or tree wound dressing before they are inserted in the tree to discourage any fungus entering. An alternative is to hang basket plants from a strong rope looped over a sturdy limb.

peach
borer

Q: Last year, I noted a gummy substance at the ground level around the base of my peach trees which flowered but fruit never matured. What causes this and what do I do about it? E. R. R., Dobbs Ferry, N. Y.

A: E. R. R. has described the work of the peach-tree borer, the tree's most important enemy which also attacks cherry and plum trees. The borer's presence is indicated by the gummy mass and brown frass near the base of the trunk. Inside are the borers which tunnel inside the trunk below and above ground. The borers winter as larvae, pupate and emerge as moths during July and August. For control, Stuart R. Race, extension entomologist at Rutgers University, recommends PDP (para-dichlorobenzene) moth crystals applied to the soil. Remove the grass and weeds from the base of the tree for a distance of one foot. Distribute the crystals in a band one or two inches wide, at least two inches away from the tree trunk. Cover the tree base and crystals with four to six shovelsful of soil and pack the soil with the shovel. Crystals placed against the tree may cause injury. Remove the crystals and the mound of soil from around the trunk after two weeks, otherwise the PDB crystals could injure the tree. For trees 1–2 years old, use one-quarter ounce of crystals; 2–3 years, one-half ounce; 5–6 years, ¾ ounce and one ounce for trees 7 years and older. Dr. Race notes that this treatment is normally recommended during the fall. Emergency measures can be applied during the spring, provided that the soil temperature at the 5-inch depth is at least 60 degrees in late April and early May.

fruit drop

Q: Our miniature peach trees (Bonanza) grow in Connecticut. But in recent years, the fruit has dropped before maturing. Suggestions anyone? G. R. M., Manhattan

A: Peach trees are susceptible to a number of growing problems, particularly rusts, rots, mildews and several forms of blight and leaf spots. Brown rot is a particularly troublesome peach enemy which requires regular spray schedules with

163

fungicides. Spray schedules and correct dosages are available from the local county agricultural agent, located in the county seat, or the Cooperative Extension office at the state's agricultural college. Ed.

pecan

Q: Is there a pecan that can be grown up North? Dr. H. E. McG., Allendale, N.J.

A: George Jones of New Jersey writes, "Yes. There are several varieties of pecans which will mature nuts in a short growing season. Some of the best are Colby, Giles, Major, Peruque and Witte. Since the pollen flowers develop on one-year-old shoots, and nut producing flowers on current season's growth, a cross pollinating variety is usually advised for best nut production. Growing season for the northern trees is a minimum of 150 days."

redwood

Q: I have a 5-year-old California redwood raised from seed. It is about four feet tall, planted outdoors for the first time. Can I leave it outdoors for the winter? Mrs. A. H.

A: Good news comes from Mrs. Lindsay A. Lovejoy of Connecticut, who writes, "We have had a *Sequoia gigantea* living happily in our yard for about 8 or 10 years. It did spend its first three winters on a cool porch where the temperature did not go below 55 degrees. Our tree is about 15 feet tall now."

silk tree ("mimosa")

Q: I have a beautiful mimosa tree that is shedding its leaves and seems to be dying. In fact, the same thing appears to be happening in the entire vicinity. What is causing the trouble? G. G., Rockville Centre, N.Y.

A: First, a name clarification. The trees G. G. referred to are silk trees which are incorrectly called mimosa by many people. (Mimosas are the tropical Acacias with tiny tufted balls of yellow flowers.) Silk trees are members of the genus Albizia, which have fernlike leaves that curl up at night. They have tufted balls of pink flowers in the summer. Silk trees are highly susceptible to wilt, a soil-borne fungus disease which causes leaves to wilt and makes a brown ring in the new growth of the sapwood. Infected trees die in a year or so. To avoid further neighborhood infection, all dead trees should be cut down and burned. Ed.

spruce

Q: A few years ago I planted a blue spruce. The tree is now double its original height and growing well. The new growth

164

has the typical blue coloring but eventually turns yellow-green. Does anyone know the trick to restore the blue color? The soil is acid, shared by hemlock and mountain laurel. F. H., Danbury, Conn.

A: There are several varieties of blue spruce (Picea pungens) available in which the degree of blue coloration varies. The best known are Argentea, Bakeri, Glauca, Moerheim and Pendens, the true Koster blue spruce. This could explain the color variance, or yellow green foliage may indicate a nutrient deficiency, particularly nitrogen. An application of high nitrogen tree fertilizer in early spring may help to correct the coloration. Ed.

stumps

Q: We have chopped down wild cherries and oaks. So they do not resprout, what is the best way of destroying the roots? G. C. W., Manhattan

A: John C. Thomas of Delaware describes a method utilizing a herbicide that has worked "nine out of 10 times" for him. He writes, "Saw the top of the trunk, smooth and level. Cover with a thin slurry of ammonium sulfamate (Ammate) in water. Be sure the slurry wets the entire top. The product is quite soluble in water and only a small amount of water is needed. Adding household detergent will help to wet the top of the stump. Ammonium sulfamate is corrosive to iron and other metals. Any tools should be sponged off immediately. It does not harm glass, stainless steel or most plastics."

Wear gloves to protect hands. Various methods to speed up rotting out of tree stumps have been suggested such as drilling 12- to 14-inch holes and packing them with potassium or ammonium nitrate. The method is usually more work than it's worth. The most practical answer is to have the stump ground out below grade by professional tree men. The larger, well-established companies usually have the equipment. Or, the stump may be dug out and exposed for a foot or more and cut below grade with a chain saw. Then fill in the hole with soil and plant lawn seed or whatever. Ed.

Another idea on what to do with tree stumps from Mrs. George Kish of Connecticut. "We lost about five beautiful trees in the last two or three years. To disguise the tree stumps, we plant around them. An ancient locust stump was covered with soil and portulaca planted there. It reseeds itself and pachysandra fills around. An elm stump has geraniums and lily of the valley, a wild cherry tree has pachysandra with impatiens in the center."

John Haskins of Connecticut suggests, "Burn the stump with charcoal. Commercial preparations didn't work, so I used chips instead of briquets and covered the area with a metal cover to keep the heat in and avoid igniting surrounding trees. I cut the stump low and watched the burning carefully. This whittled the stump to below ground level in about three days. Cost, $5."

Meanwhile, use the stumps with a rack added instead of the family grill for outdoor cooking! Ed.

tree seedlings

Q: Many people have told me that the U.S. government offers 1,000 free tree seedlings to individuals requesting them. To whom do I write? Dr. R. W. G., Long Island.

A: Each state usually maintains a department of conservation–forestry or environmental protection which embraces a program of supplying seedlings to property owners for use in Christmas tree farming or for wildlife habitat/conservation. Minimum size of property is usually stipulated by these agencies and the plants are not allowed to be removed or transplanted once in place (i.e., no ornamental use). The trees, and sometimes shrubs, are seedlings or whips, not free, but sold for nominal charges at minimum orders of 1,000. One-year lead time is needed on orders. For more information contact your state conservation department.

walnut
propagation

Q: We are trying to grow black walnut trees by planting the nuts but so far have not been successful. How does one do it? J. V., New Jersey

A: Myron D. Goggin of New Jersey knows how. He writes, "Remove husks from nuts and dump them immediately in a container of water. Discard any nuts that float as these are often 'blind' and should not be planted. Take a #2 tin can and cut out one end. With a cold chisel, make a small x cut (or plus sign) and push out so the jagged edges stick up. (This will keep out squirrels and other rodents.) Hold the can in your hand with the punched x down and put an inch of soil in the bottom. Deposit the nut and fill the can with soil. Turn the can over so that the punched hole and jagged edges are up. Place the can in this position where the tree is to grow. Submerge about an inch below the ground and cover with earth and mulch with straw about two inches thick. In May or June examine the area and when seedling appears remove some of the mulch and keep weeds and grass away while seedling grows. It is not necessary to remove the can."

166

roots

Q: I have heard that roots of native black walnut trees inhibit the growth of rhododendrons and other ornamentals. Is this true of named varieties? A. B., Edison, N.J.

A: *Black walnut trees produce a toxic chemical known as juglones which is particularly toxic to food plants as well as ornamentals. Ed.*

angles on
edibles

Q: Is it possible to grow artichokes in New England? If so, what varieties, planting and care? H. B.

A: J. B. Dexter, Maine, writes that the true artichoke (*Cynara scolymus*) is a warm weather vegetable grown primarily in the Mediterranean countries and in this country in well-drained, cool land in California where there is sufficient water for irrigation. The Jerusalem artichoke, however, is a different plant related to sneezeweed and the sunflower. It can be grown in the East where it produces starchy, potatolike tubers which are edible.

Just as soon as it's said it can't be done, someone always comes along and says it can. Writing from Canada, Mrs. J. C. Douglas says, "I have grown true artichokes in Sutton, Brome County, Quebec, which is eight miles north of the Vermont border. The artichokes were not particularly good, small and prickly, but the plants were large and thrived. The plant is a perennial and requires a couple of years to establish. The plants had no special winter protection but Sutton does get a lot of snow. In a milder climate, some winter protection may be necessary. I would suggest H. B. procure several varieties of seed and try. He will not achieve the large succulent artichokes that come from California, but he can harvest 'baby' artichokes. Be warned, the plants are quite large, several feet in diameter."

Q: Do you know where I might buy seeds of arugula, the salad green found in many Italian restaurants and markets? F. G. T. III

A: Mrs. Larry Couzens, New York, writes, "Arugula is known in the United States as rucola or rocket, also spelled roquette.

The plant is in the mustard family and generally listed under herbs. The plant should not be confused with the perennial flower rocket sometimes called sweet rocket. Rucola or roquette is listed in many seed catalogs."

Roquette may also be listed as ruqula or erucola. Ed.

asparagus
going to seed

Q: Should I allow my asparagus to go to seed or cut it to the ground? What do I do to assure a good crop next year? D. D., Connecticut

A: Peter N. Baum of New York writes, "Do not cut new plants smaller than the size of a pencil. Stop cutting in June when the growth slows because the exhausted plants need time to replenish. Allow the asparagus to go to seed. The mature plant can be cut after severe frost. Knock the berries off into the soil and add the stalks to the compost heap. In early spring, lime heavily, fertilize and till to a depth of three inches."

transplanting

Q: We have discovered neglected asparagus near our property and we would like to move it to the garden. Is there a special time of year when this should be done? Dr. A. T. N., Mountainville, N.Y.

A: *During the summer months, asparagus puts forth tall ferny growth which renews the roots for next year. This will mature in late summer and can be cut to the ground. At this time the roots or crowns, as they are called, can be dug up carefully for moving. (New beds of asparagus are started in spring with commercially available roots.) The new asparagus bed should be prepared first, digging it deeply and enriching with compost and fertilizer. Set the crowns six inches deep in rows three feet apart, 18 inches between plants. Ed.*

bamboo shoots

Q: I have a large stand of bamboo on my property. Are the bamboo shoots edible, similar to those canned in Japan? Mrs. G. S., Long Island

A: *According to* Wyman's Gardening Encyclopedia, *"There are 700 or more species of bamboo in the world, only 2 of them being native to the United States." After checking with several culinary experts on Oriental cuisine, the answer to Mrs. G. S. is no, because particular species of bamboo are grown for the produce market and imported from the Far East, either fresh or canned. Ed.*

More light on the question is in a letter from William Gripenburg, a New Jersey gardener. "I have a grove of yellow-grove bamboo (*Phyllostachys aureosulcata*) on top of Schooley Mountain, 1,000-foot elevation. In the last two

169

weeks, we put up in the freezer over two quarts of bamboo shoots. The grove is only 20 feet in diameter and I could have taken over 10 quarts."

belgian endive

Q: Has anyone tried to grow Belgian endive with success? M. B.

A: Many replies were received on how to raise Belgian endive. Here is a scheme from F. J. French of New York, "I was successful the first time I tried. Seeds are sown directly in the garden in spring and plants are thinned to stand about 10 inches apart. The plants grow all summer and the roots are dug up after a couple of hard frosts. In digging the roots, get as much of the long tap root as possible. Cut off the tops a half-inch above the crown. Trim roots to the same length, about nine inches, and set them vertically an inch apart in a deep strong box covering them to the crown with garden soil. Water to settle, adding more soil to crown level. Then cover with 5 to 6 inches of coarse sand. Place the box in a cool (55 to 60 degree) cellar in the dark. Heads of endive will appear in a few weeks. Crop, with diminishing supply, continues for months. Water occasionally. My forcing box is 8 × 12 × 17, made of ⅝-inch marine plywood."

carrots
flavor

Q: Each year we try new carrot varieties, but the roots are always bitter and tough. Rumor has it that something can be done to the soil. What is the secret? K. O. P., New City, N.Y.

A: Jerry Simon of Connecticut suggests, "K. O. P. probably has the same clay soil we have. Our carrots were a disappointment until I prepared a special soil for them and thus far it appears to work. Each spring I dig a very deep row to a depth of one foot just for carrots. The soil is set on the side and mixed with one-third sand and one-third rotted compost. The soil is light and fluffy. I wait until mid-May to plant the carrots, never add any fertilizer and keep the row thinned and well mulched. So far so good. The carrots are sweet, straight and bright colored. We prefer two varieties. Royal Chantenay and Nantes Half Long."

small carrots

Q: Can anyone tell me where to find seed of those delectable small carrots served in Europe? Mrs. P. O. T., Wellesley, Mass.

A: There are many dwarf carrots on the market and listed in several seed catalogs. Look for Sucram, Little Finger, Baby Finger, Short 'n Sweet, and Tiny Sweet. Ed.

170

cucumber

Q: My cucumber plants grow well and have had a few first fruits. But now the flowers are dying off. New blossoms develop but only one or two cucumbers. Why? Mrs. P. S., Roslyn Heights

A: Mrs. P. S. may have planted the new all female or gynoecious hybrids which flower and fruit early. Growers mix in sufficient seed quantities of male-varieties to assure fruit development and by now the balance of male-female flowers should have righted itself. Ed.

cucumber and melon ripening

Q: How do I prevent cucumbers and melons from becoming yellow on the bottom without ripening fully? It happens every year. T. Y., Manhattan

A: Terry Kislav of New York suggests 1972's unusually wet season may have been part of the problem. He recommends a good thick mulch of straw, salt hay, grass clippings or the like around the base of all vinelike plants. This keeps the fruits off the soggy ground so they ripen better. Or he suggests using old shingles under the fruits to lift them off the ground if no mulch is possible.

currants

Q: Where can I obtain black currant bushes? J. K. H.

A: Black currant and red currant (Ribes) are alternate hosts to white pine blister rust. For this reason there are strict limitations where fruit plants may be grown. The red currant variety, Viking, is resistant to blister rust, but black currants are considered most dangerous. Black currants cannot be grown in New York State, Massachusetts, West Virginia, Wisconsin and Michigan where there are eradication programs. The U.S. Department of Agriculture will not permit import of black currant if destined for these states. Ed.

dill

Q: Is there more than one kind of dill? Last year our plants (bought as transplants from a nursery) had no flavor. We would like to replace them with better plants but do not want the same poor results this year. Mrs. D. W., Brewster, N.Y.

A: Mrs. Julian Rieser, a Westchester County gardener, offers these suggestions, "Dill should be grown from seed, not transplanted, in a sunny location. Poor, gravelly, well-drained soil is preferred over rich soil which may cause herbs to lose their fragrance and flavor. Cut culinary herbs just before the flowers open, in early morning."

171

fiddleheads

Q: I have seen cans of imported fiddleheads on grocer's shelves. Does this mean all fern fiddleheads are edible, such as those growing in my woodsy plot? M. M. R.

A: Joann Lamb of New York writes that "having grown up in New Brunswick, Canada, I feel I can shed some light" on the edibility of fiddleheads. "Fiddleheads grow in the St. Johns River Valley. They are picked in the spring after the riverwater has receded. Originally the fiddleheads were picked by the Indians and sold to the local green grocers. They are now sold canned and in Canada you can even buy them frozen."

The leaf buds or croziers of ferns that unfurl in the spring are called, in general, fiddleheads. However, the name is sometimes specifically applied to the cinnamon fern which can be found throughout swamps and thickets in the northeastern states. Ed.

To comment on J. L.'s reply on the fiddlehead harvest in the St. John River Valley, John Evans of Connecticut writes that "she missed the point of the original inquiry about edibility. Not all curled up fern fronds are edible fiddleheads as you will find out to your bitter regret if you get the wrong ones."

Mrs. W. W. Ballard of Vermont would like to differ on the species of fern most widely gathered and most commonly canned as fiddlehead greens. She writes that the Ostrich fern is more palatable and digestible. She describes the flavor of freshly pickled fiddleheads, boiled in two waters, as part mushroom, part artichoke and part asparagus.

gooseberries

Q: While visiting in North Devon, England, I enjoyed huge, sweet gooseberries, almost as large as cherry tomatoes. Can they be grown in southern Connecticut, and where can I purchase the plants? E. L. N.

A: Chester Holway of Indiana offers a source. "The Perkins gooseberry introduced in Minnesota 25 years ago has fruit 1½ inches, sweet and good for jam. It is available from Perkins Nursery, Box 128, Crosslake, Minn. 56442."

However, as has been pointed out in these columns before and Mrs. J. G. Bergman, Jr., of New Jersey also reminds E. L. N., there are restrictions for growing Ribes (gooseberries and currants) in some states because the plants are an alternate host to white pine blister rust. Anyone wanting to grow these plants should check state restrictions with his local Cooperative Extension office before proceeding.

herbs

Q: Can someone guide me on a few basic herbs to grow? We will have only a tiny space for herb plants in our new garden and I would like to try a few easy, useful ones for a start. Mrs. T. Y.

A: From Mary C. Rauscher of New York comes some help on beginner herbs. "Easy to grow from seed is the annual sweet basil. There are many varieties—Lettuce Leaf, Dwarf Bush and Lemon. Chives are a perennial necessity, but do not chop off the spears but pick them off at the base. This way the plant is not disfigured. Thyme comes in over 50 varieties."

From Mrs. Adrienne Lind of New York, "Plant one each of the following, salad burnet, chives, rosemary, thyme, sage, basil and parsley. If there is space, include yellow yarrow and lavender. Remember herbs need sun, sweet soil and organic fertilizer."

And an idea for planting herbs in the squares of an old ladder from Mrs. Walter Bregman of New Jersey, who grows chives, garlic, parsley, red basil, green basil, rosemary, lavender, mint, orange mint, lemon balm, ladies mantle and chamomile.

Here is an interesting idea from Laura Kielb of New Jersey, "At the local supplier, I selected several chimney tiles of different but compatible shapes. I measured and marked each tile so that when they were cut, each piece would be a different height. The tiles were arranged upright in an attractive grouping on a concrete slab outside the kitchen door. At the bottom I placed several inches of gravel then filled them with soil and set in herb seedlings. The little herb garden requires almost no care except occasional watering. Herbs grown are thyme, savory, sage, tarragon, chives and parsley, which is planted each year."

horseradish

Q: I have inherited a couple of plants of horse-radish root which grow well in the garden but when pulled up there is scarcely any root. Why? Mrs. P. W., Westchester County, N.Y.

A: Barbara Gold of New York writes, "The problem may be that the horseradish makes its greatest growth during late summer and early fall and harvesting may have been too early. Also, to produce a good horseradish, remove all side roots leaving only those at the bottom of the set. To do this, "lift" the roots twice during the growing season. First, when the largest leaves are 10 inches long; the second, six weeks later. To lift, wear gloves, remove the soil being careful not

173

to disturb the roots at the lower end. Raise the crown end and remove all but the best sprout or crown of leaves. Any small roots that have started from the top are rubbed off, leaving only those at the bottom. Return set to normal position and replace soil.''

late vegetables

Q: We cannot move into our new house until mid-July. Are there any late vegetables we could plant then for an early fall crop before frost? B. O. P., Moorestown, N.J.

A: Robert Zucker, another New Jersey gardener, says there are many quick growing crops that could be tried. ''Even though the weather will be warm, if the soil is well prepared and mulched to keep it moist and the roots cool, leaf lettuce, radish, beets, carrots, late cabbage (if plants are around), beans, and Swiss chard could be planted.''

lentils

Q: Lentil is my favorite soup and I would like to grow lentils. Is this possible and where do I get the seed? M. S., Long Island

A: Hazel Visvadin, a reader who lives in Maine, writes, ''I recently planted a row of lentils from the grocers after culling the broken and unusable seed. Practically all are germinated and producing white flowering plants about a foot tall.''

The lentil is a member of the legume family which requires warm soil and weather. A small plant (18 inches) with thin stems and tendrils, it is not a heavy producer. Pods may hold as few as two or three seeds. Many plants would have to be grown for any large supply. Ed.

lettuce
bolting in heat

Q: With the price of lettuce so high, I would like to keep my leaf lettuce growing as long as possible. Is there any way to stop it from going to seed in the heat? Mrs. J. L. S., Long Island

A: Mrs. Beth Goodman, another Long Island gardener, suggests, ''I keep my leaf lettuce producing for many, many weeks, by cutting rather than pulling the leaves. I cut them off just above the ground level, making sure that enough of the mother plant and the good root system are intact. The plant regrows and produces a second and sometimes a third crop.''

iceberg

Q: For two years I have tried to grow iceberg lettuce on Long Island without reasonable success. The plants grow like Romaine and they never head. What is the answer? L. G., New Hyde Park, N.Y.

174

A: Justine Tenny of New York writes, "Iceberg lettuce will not form a head if the temperature rises to 75 degrees or above. Try planting it in the early spring for harvesting in May or in late August for harvesting in October."

mint

Q: We understand there are several kinds of garden mint. Which is the best one to plant for use in cooking, drinks, etc? G. W., Bronx

A: Mrs. Kay Trepley of New York writes, "There are indeed many kinds of mints and a whole collection can be made of them. The most common grown for kitchen use is spearmint (*Mentha spicata*), but equally popular is peppermint. Some of the more unusual kinds are Bowles (with large leaves), apple, pineapple, orange and curly. Plant them in a bright but moist place and keep the roots confined by a brick or metal edging barrier since they spread readily."

mushrooms
puffball spawn

Q: When we lived in northeastern Massachusetts, we had annual growth of giant puffballs in our backyard. We now live in an area where several varieties of puff balls grow but none of the large type. Where can we get spawn or mature fertile specimens for fall spore planting? K. M. B., Cape Cod, Mass.

A: Margaret Morris of Long Island, who was formerly a field secretary for the New York Mycological Society, writes, "The only mushroom spawn available is for the commercial species, *Agaricus bisporus*. Even if mature fertile specimens of field mushrooms were found, it is unlikely that the con-

175

dition in K. M. B.'s ground would meet their requirements. Fungus spores are present all over and when the conditions are right—nutrient, moisture, temperature and often a particular plant or animal host—they will grow."

'onion' grass

Q: Can onion grass, a spring lawn weed, be eaten? It looks and smells like chives. Mrs. A. L., Manhattan

A: Miss Rosalie Friend of New York writes, "It certainly can. I substitute it for chives in recipes and I like it as an addition to tossed salads or in soups."

parsley

Q: Every year I plant parsley and lose most of the plants from root rot. When I pick parsley, the entire plant pulls up. Has anyone solved this problem? H. I. S. B., White Plains, N. Y.

A: John Latimer of New Jersey suggests, "Parsley should be picked by pinching the stem with your fingernail and be sure not to jerk up or pull the plant. The root rot is probably caused by excessive moisture or standing water around the plants. By adding composted vegetable matter and sand to the garden soil, and making sure the water drains off properly, the problem should be solved."

peppers

Q: I like sweet red peppers but for the past three years, I have had crop failures. The pepper plants grow fine and produce large green fruits, but just as they start to turn red they rot and become watery. Can anyone suggest a cause and cure? F. R. Z.

A: Mrs. Robert Bettmann of New York suggests that he may be planting late-season varieties. She suggests the early season varieties such as Canape or Vinedale which ripen in 62 days and are started indoors in early spring.

176

pumpkin seeds

Q: How do you get the green pumpkin seeds out of the white shell? I have opened a few with my fingernail but it is tedious and unrewarding. H. T. R., Manhattan

A: Here are a few ideas. From Dr. J. G. Diener of Long Island, "A convenient method which should take a few moments to master is to gently bite the point of the seed while held vertically. This will split open the shell point and two more bites farther down the shell will complete the task."

From Kay Vining of Maryland, "With a sharp paring knife, cut off the raised edge of the seed on one side. Then the white husk can be pried open easily."

Although not an immediate solution, there is hope for the future. The U.S. Department of Agriculture has released a new pumpkin variety called Lady Godiva which has naked or hull-less seeds. Ed.

purslane

Q: I am interested in obtaining a vegetable called postelein grown mainly in North Holland. It resembles tall clover and tastes sweet and delightful, and is sold in the Dutch market places by the pound. Does anyone know what it is and where I can buy the seed? M. L. C., Yorktown Heights, N. Y.

A: Rachel de Leeuw identified it. She writes, "The Dutch vegetable postelein is the same as our garden weed purslane. Our grandmothers ate it and call it pussley. It comes up here among the beans and in my rock garden. Like its cousin, portulaca, it flourishes in dry sunny places."

To cook, treat as spinach. Ed.

raspberries
pruning

Q: I'm puzzled about pruning my raspberries. I have the two-crop variety, September, which fruited in June and is beginning to ripen fruit now (August). When and how do I prune it? I want to be sure of having fruiting wood next summer. G. D.

A: Inga Holm and Lily Mattesky of New Jersey write, "In late summer after first crop has been picked, cut the fruit-bearing canes at ground level and burn. Thin new canes where too thick. New canes grow tall and bear in fall and until frost. Leave these intact over the winter. After danger of frost is past in spring, cut these new canes off to a height of two and one-half to three feet, depending on how high you are prepared to pick the early fruit."

rhubarb

Q: How do I maintain rhubarb in the garden? Mrs. H. M., Long Island

177

A: Margaret Sein of New York writes, "Rhubarb needs plenty of manure and moisture. When planting the roots, manure should be placed in the planting hole. After planting place well-rotted manure around the plant. In spring, after the new shoots appear, again place weathered manure around the plants. In dry weather, water well and keep weeds away from the plants."

saffron

Q: I have read that saffron is made from crocus flowers. Is there any way that I could make it myself? M. S.

A: Stephen Troner of Wisconsin writes, "Saffron is composed of the dried stigmas of the autumn flowering or saffron crocus (*Crocus sativus*). The corms are available from most bulb growers. The flower stigmas (pollen bearers) are cut off with the finger nail as soon as the flowers open and then dried in the sun or in a warm oven. M. S. should be aware of the fact that it takes 5,000 plants to produce .01 ounces of saffron."

shallots

Q: For the past two years we have grown shallots successfully but their flavor has been sharp and almost bitter. Does anyone know why and have a solution? H. G., Connecticut

A: *Shallots grow best in a soil that has been enriched with compost or humus to make it light and well-drained. Heavy clay soils produce poor results. Ed.*

spinach

Q: What is the best way to grow spinach? Last year the seedlings hardly grew and many just sent up stalks and flowers. Mrs. G. F.

A: Mary Lynn Vickers of Connecticut has a solution. "This is the first year I have grown spinach and it has been quite prolific. I think cool weather is the most important factor. Here are some pointers: soak the seeds overnight before planting; plant early, April 1 in the New Haven area, for example, and cultivate a little cottonseed meal in the soil before sowing for nitrogen."

squash
bugs

Q: My zucchini plants have done beautifully this year, but for the past three summers I have had to kill hordes of squash bugs. What can I do to ward them off either now or next summer? Miss S. K., Ellenville, N. Y.

A: Tom Thurlow, a Putnam County gardener, writes, "Trap the squash bugs under boards placed on the soil. They hide under them at night and stay there until early morning. Just

lift up the board and scrape off the bugs and destroy. I keep watch over my plants and as soon as I see any signs of bugs, I kill every one I see, and pick and burn leaves with the egg clusters. The eggs are easy to find as they are bright red. If the bugs do get out of control, there is a botanical dust called sabadilla which can be used, but I have found by keeping watch on the plants, I have never had to use it."

vine borer rot

Q: What is it that kills my summer squash plants every year? The plants grow healthy and produce a few fruits. Then a mushy rot appears in the main stem and the plants slowly die. I have never found a worm or insect. Have tried dusting seed with a fungicide and have tried insecticides. It happens every year. L. H. D.

A: Dr. Doris G. White of New Jersey, a squash geneticist, writes, "The problem sounds like the squash vine borer. The female moth lays eggs in June and the inch-long larvae hatch into the stem, near the base of the vine, achieving full size in 4 weeks. As larvae grow, orange excrement is pushed out of the holes in stems or fruit. Control is difficult. One per cent rotenone is dusted to stems and plant bases at 10-day intervals. Nicotine sulfate spray is also helpful. Insecticidal treatment depends on early and repeated applications because once larvae reach inside the stem, insecticides will not kill them."

And another idea from Mrs. William A. Ridge of Rhode Island. "If L. H. D. will take a sharp knife and slit the squash stem up several inches, he will find several large juicy white grub creatures who must be pulled out and promptly dispatched to eternity. The organic preventive for these is to form a ring of wood ashes around the hill at planting time. To save the vines after removing the grubs, mound dirt around the plant to cover the 'incision'."

179

strawberry
french

Q: Can anyone tell me where to buy the plants of the tiny French strawberry, fraises de bois? J. K. L., Darien, Conn.

A: *The sweet strawberry of the woods can be obtained from White Flower Farm, Litchfield, Conn. 06759 or from The Guild of Strawberry Banke, Inc., State Street, Portsmouth, N.H. 03801. Seed of the alpine strawberry, quite similar, is available from Park and Burpee. Ed.*

tarragon

Q: On two occasions in the past five years we have bought tarragon plants and set them out. In each case, the plant while looking exactly like the tarragon I know, has been nearly tasteless and odorless and useless as an herb fresh or dried. Are there different kinds of tarragon? Or could the heavy alkalinity of our New Mexico soil and water affect the plants? Rev. B. P. F.

A: Mrs. William T. Golden of New York writes, "True French tarragon is *Artemisia dracunculus* and what you want for flavoring. The French call it 'estragon'. This tarragon needs full sun, good soil drainage and good fertile ground. It will withstand temperatures of 30 degrees. Cut it back in the fall to within a few inches of the ground. This species does not set viable seed and must be propagated by root divisions or cuttings. Seed catalogs do list a 'Russian' tarragon, but it has no culinary flavor."

thyme

Q: Some help on thyme, please! Which one is grown for flavoring, and which one is grown as a mat between flagstones on the terrace? S. S., New Jersey

A: Deborah C. Dilitz of New York straightens him out as follows. "Culinary thyme or English thyme is *Thymus vulgaris*, a hardy perennial growing upright. Creeping thyme (*T. serpyllum*), also called Mother of Thyme, is very hardy and grows only two inches high but spreads into dense mats in sun or partial shade. This one is perfect for a flagstone terrace."

tomatoes
beefsteak split and rot

Q: For the past nine years I planted all kinds of tomatoes without any trouble. This year, I decided to try beefsteak tomatoes. What is causing the beefsteak tomatoes to split as they ripen? S. G.

What has gone wrong with the majority of my tomatoes? I have 18 plants. All grew well and bore a considerable amount of tomatoes. But as the tomatoes ripen, the entire lower half becomes rotted. The plants have been watered and fertilized. What is the trouble? G. C. M.

A: We consulted Dr. Carl Clayberg, Associate Geneticist, specializing in tomatoes, at the Connecticut Experiment Station. The beefsteak problem he explained is one of too much water (rainy August) at a time when the late-season varieties were ripening. The tomato flesh swells faster than the skin can expand, so the skin splits. The rotting is called blossom end rot, a problem resulting from calcium deficiency and lack of water. Some tomato varieties are particularly sensitive. The solution is proper soil pH (not too acid soil) and amply moist soil during the growing season. Mulching in summer helps, provided the plants are watered well in droughts. If the trouble persists in several summers, try different varieties. Ed.

curiosity

Q: I saved seeds from small cherry tomatoes and planted them. This year I have large tomatoes growing on the vines. What happened? S. K. W., Rego Park, L. I.

A: Peggy Houke-Castaldo of New Hampshire offers this explanation. "Vegetable and flower seeds are often the results of careful crossbreeding to bring out desirable characteristics. The seeds produced by these hybrids would be second generation (F_2) and the results will produce fruits reflecting the qualities of the two hybrid parents."

do not ripen

Q: My tomato plants are loaded with green fruit—and have been for several weeks. They are not ripening. The same thing happened last year! Does anyone know the answer? Mrs. C. G. H., Westport, Conn.

A: George Maybill, another Connecticut reader, suggests, "Next year Mrs. C. G. H. should plant early and midseason tomato varieties which will ripen sooner than the late varieties which she probably is growing. Ripening is delayed if tomato plants are not pruned of suckers; excess foliage hides the fruit. Overfeeding will also delay ripening. But, we are always glad for some green tomatoes in September as they make marvelous relish!"

rot

Q: The bottom leaves of my tomatoes have started to turn brown. And as the small fruits form, black spots develop on the bottom, spread and soon rot. Is there anything I can do? Mrs. C. L., Saddle Brook, N. J.

A: The problem is two-fold. Evidently Mrs. C. L. did not plant disease resistant tomato varieties. The vegetable is susceptible to two soil-borne fungus diseases—verticillium and ferticillium wilts. Many fine disease resistant varieties are avail-

181

able and should be selected. The "rot" is called blossom-end rot and is caused by a combination of calcium deficiency in the soil and drought. Lime tomato soils well before planting and water deeply in dry weather and mulch heavily. Ed.

seedlings

Q: I planted tomato seed indoors in some garden dirt put in a clay pot. The seeds sprouted but when they were about an inch high, they fell over and died. They were in sunlight but no drafts. What happened? Mrs. E. K., New Jersey

A: Mrs. Joseph Gratucci of Connecticut writes, "The seedlings were knocked out by damping off disease, a soil-borne fungus that strikes seedlings. The prevention is to start seeds in a sterile growing medium such as perlite, vermiculite or sphagnum moss. Commercial packaged seed starting mixtures are available and so is sterilized soil."

worms

Q: For the past eight years I have grown tomato plants and have never had any diffficulty with tomato worms. This year I have already found five worms. What is the solution? L. S., Long Island

A: Ann Bodine of New Jersey has some thoughts, "I have four or five tomato worms each summer but since I use no sprays, I just pick them off. This year before I could get around to picking off the worms, the tiny white egglike cocoons of the braconid wasp, a parasite of the hornworm, appeared and now most of the worms are dead. If L. S. is patient, maybe the natural parasite will establish itself in his garden, too."

vegetables as ornamentals

Q: Can anyone suggest attractive vegetables that can be grown in front of the house with flowers or in place of them? G. S., Laurelton, N. Y.

A: J. LaRue of Connecticut notes, "We grow Romaine lettuce in various spots around our garden and find it attractive as a border and rock garden plant."

Margo J. Handschue of Long Island suggests rhubarb chard as a lovely border plant with delightful maroon color. Another attractive plant is eggplant, or tomatoes can be made attractive with lattice."

Larry Litvak of Rhode Island suggests ornamental kale.

watercress

Q: We are interested in growing watercress either in the home or garden and know very little about it. Can someone give us an idea on how to start and grow plants? Dr. H. F. D.

A: Mrs. Algernon D. Black of New York answers, "Watercress

182

needs fresh, preferably running water. After numerous failures, I have lush beds achieved by begging a few rooted shoots from a neighbor and by sowing seeds direct in a stream. I formed a little protective dam with stones. However, in turn I would like to know if plants should be thinned and how commercial growers attain such large leaves."

Here is another idea from Jane McBeath of New York. "Buy a bunch of watercress at the grocers; set it in a bowl of water in a light but not sunny window. In a few weeks many roots will form. Put a little soil in the bottom of a deep 4-inch bird bath and plant the watercress. Keep the bird bath full of water and you will have a constant supply of watercress."

cooking, curing, drying, and storing

cooking
candied violets

Q: This spring several friends and I are interested in candying some violets. How do we go about it? Mrs. W. S. A., Long Island

A: Mrs. Louise Drexler of Massachusetts writes, "The violets should be picked early on a sunny day to aid drying. Detach flower heads from stem and sepals. Beat egg white into foam, then dip each violet into it until well coated and then roll flower in granulated sugar. Dry on wax paper. Another method: Boil a cup of sugar in a half cup of water until the mixture becomes threadlike when poured from a spoon. Coat violets in syrup and dry after which the sugar crystallizes, making the petals firm. For added violet taste, extract of violet (from pharmacy) is mixed with the egg white or boiled sugar. Also blue food coloring may be added to heighten color."

flowers in a salad

Q: Last week we were served a salad with nasturtium leaves and marigold petals. This is such a fascinating idea, does anyone know of recipes or books on flowers as food? Mrs. G. H. L., Manhasset, N. Y.

A: Jean Marra, a Westchester County reader, lists the following books on the subject, *The Forgotten Art of Flower Cookery* by Leona Woodring Smith (Harper): *Flower Cookery* by Mary MacNicol (Collier Books); *Cooking with Flowers* by Zack Hanle (Price, Stern, Sloan).

geranium leaves

Q: Can I use the scented leaves of my geraniums for cooking? Mrs. T. G., Manhattan

184

A: "Yes," says Donald Clark of Connecticut, "if the geranium is a rose geranium. The leaves can be used to line the bottom of a loaf pan in which a pound cake is baked. Remove leaves after baking, leaving the cake with a delicate flavor. They can also be placed in jelly jars before homemade apple jelly is added to provide a delicate rose flavor."

grape leaves

Q: Can I use the leaves from my grapevine for cooking and/or freezing? Mrs. J. M. G., New York

A: Mrs. Peter Scott of New York writes, "Wash the leaves and stack them in uniform piles—small, medium and large—of 30 leaves. Fold them lengthwise, stem to tip, tie around the middle with string. Boil two quarts of water and ½ cup of salt. Boil the bundles for a minute. Place them tightly packed in sterilized canning jars. Add the hot salted water to the top of the jars and seal. They are ready after a week, but will keep indefinitely. You may also use a few leaves at a time; just return the unused ones to the brine."

herbs fresh/dried

Q: Is there a rule of thumb to use herbs correctly for flavoring? I understand the dried are more potent than the fresh. Do you use half as much dried as fresh or what is the rule? Clues please. Mrs. J. D. D., Manhattan

A: Jeanne Lindaman of Pennsylvania writes, "It is generally agreed that ¼ teaspoon of dried herbs equals one teaspoon of fresh. However, some herbs are more potent than others. Any beginner in herb cookery should experiment with all herbs to determine which accent is preferred. Less is best in the beginning."

185

Q: I have been researching American Indian cooking and many recipes include juniper berries. Do they refer to a particular species or can I use berries from any juniper? Mrs. T. Y., Brooklyn

A: *The common juniper was probably the species most widely available to Indians but most any juniper berry should do. The berries are dried after picking and stored in jars with tight covers. Use them sparingly in recipes as the aromatic flavor is strong. Crush or grind berries to bring it out. The flavor goes well with meats, game, ham and stuffings, or in basting liquors. Ed.*

Q: Is the Golden Needle used dried in Chinese cooking a tiger lily or a daylily? Mrs. T. P. H., Philadelphia, Pa.

A: Dr. Allen Lacy of New Jersey writes, "The daylily used in Chinese cooking is derived from daylily (*Hemerocallis*) usually but not always *H. fulva*. This is the tawny daylily naturalized on American roadsides, not the tiger lily (*Lilium tigrinum*). In China fresh daylily buds are dried and sold as a cash crop. Picked early in the morning just before they open, they are dried on a mat in the hot sun and called Chin-chentsai. In American Chinese groceries, Golden Needles are known by their Cantonese name of Gum-jum or Gum-tsoy. This food is used in soups, salads, and meat dishes especially with pork and chicken."

Q: Is it possible to make capers from garden nasturtiums and if so how is it done? Mrs. E. H. C., New Hampshire

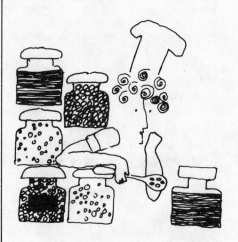

A: Here is a recipe from Mrs. Patricia Donohue of Pennsylvania. "This seventeenth century recipe appeared in the garden section of the *The London Observer* about 20 years ago. Gather a pint of nasturtium seeds soon after the flowers have fallen. Soak them in salt water for three days, changing the water twice. Empty and wipe dry on a cloth. Put them into jars in layers with tarragon leaves and grated horseradish. Boil half a pint of white vinegar for 10 minutes with a tablespoon of salt, a small shallot, *not a scallion*, a teaspoon of peppercorns and a dash of nutmeg. Strain the liquid and when cold cover the seeds and seal the jars. We keep these indefinitely in the refrigerator and consider them much better than capers."

vanilla beans

Q: How can I grow vanilla beans for baking? C. S. G., Manhattan

A: Joe Simmons of Pennsylvania writes, "Vanilla is a member of the orchid family. The common commercial species *Vanilla planiflora* is a climber and under favorable growing conditions can become quite large and must be supported and wound back on itself. Like most orchids, it is not patticularly attractive when not in bloom and the vanilla flower has a short life. Flowers must be hand pollinated for fruit. I highly recommend a good gourmet shop as an alternate source of beans."

Vanilla is a large vigorous climbing orchid suited mainly for greenhouse culture and not likely to bear fruit in captivity. Ed.

curing
walnuts

Q: How should black walnuts be cured after gathering so the nut meats do not shrivel or mold? R. E. S., Long Island

A: Here are two methods. From Mrs. Norman L. Smith of New York, "Remove green pulpy hull. Use plastic gloves and pound or step on them as the hull stains. Dry the black hard shelled nut near the heating unit or in the sun. If mold develops, it will not damage nut inside. When dry, crack and remove inside nuts. Store in closed mason jars in the refrigerator. Burn discards in the fireplace."

From Dr. J. D. Kernodle of Missouri, "Step on walnuts to remove soft hull. Pick up nuts with a tong or waterproof gloves to avoid staining hands and throw into a large tub of water. Wash well and flush with garden hose. Drain. Place in a wide mesh container (½-inch wire mesh) to protect securely from squirrels and leave nuts outside all winter. For use, crack shells, remove nuts and keep meat in the deep freeze or they will become rancid. The most important thing is to keep the walnuts cold or frozen before and after the nut meat is removed."

drying
autumn leaves

Q: I would appreciate learning the method of drying autumn leaves so they do not curl and crumble. Mrs. N. G.

A: Mrs. W. Lawrence of New York writes, "Smash cut ends of boughs or twigs with hammer. Immerse end in solution of 4 ounces of glycerine and 1 quart of water. Keep soaking and let stand until leaves feel tacky, about one week. Then arrange."

autumn leaves

Q: I'm interested in doing some collage work with dried autumn leaves. Are there some special clues anyone has to dry the leaves perfectly so they will retain the color? Is one glue more satisfactory than another? Miss F. D., Manhattan

A: Jean Kaminski of Long Island says, "A good way to preserve leaves is to press them between two sheets of wax paper with a hot iron. This will coat the leaves on both sides with wax so they won't dry out and also preserves the colors. The pressing should be done on a heavy brown paper bag to absorb the excess wax."

Another Long Island reader, Mrs. John T. Groves, concurs, and adds, "A white glue is used to adhere the leaves to the background." She also suggests another method, "Press the leaves between smooth blotters on the pages of a telephone book with heavy weights on top. Leave for two weeks. Using acrylic polymer available in art stores, one part to two parts water, apply one coat to background with a brush. Place leaves in desired design and immediately go over the leaves with additional solution. Give a second coat when dry. Lovely nature collages may be made by this method, pressing flowers and leaves as they become available from spring on."

basil

Q: How soon do I start drying basil leaves for use indoors in winter? Mrs. R. N. M., Connecticut

A: Here are three ideas. From Mrs. Lawrence Clum of Long Island, "I find it much easier to freeze basil. Wash the leaves, dry them and place on a cookie sheet to freeze. Store in a container in the freezer and use in salads and for tomato dishes."

From Mrs. Alice M. Stempel of Ohio, "Like many herbs, sweet basil should be cut for drying before blooms appear. When the plant is tall enough, cut stems four or five inches long. Tie a string around the bunch, rinse in cool water, shake and hang up to dry. After a few weeks the leaves will be brittle and dry. Separate the leaves from the stems, working on a sheet of wax paper. Store in a small, air-tight jar. The plants will branch out again."

From Mrs. Federico-Martin of New York, "Don't dry basil. Make an attar of basil in olive oil in the blender. Rinse basil and allow water to dry off. Pour olive oil in the blender and add the leaves while running the motor at chopping speed. Add salt to help preserve the puree, and garlic, if you like. Use mixture by the spoonful in soups and gravies or in salads. Keep basil covered with oil and refrigerated."

basil

Q: I like to dry sweet basil for winter, but lately I have had trouble with the leaves turning brown. I dry it in a warm, dry attic. Is there some trick I am missing? Mrs. J. S., Long Island

A: Here are three rescuers' ideas. From Mrs. John Billings of New York, "I dry my windowsill basil by washing and thoroughly drying the basil by hanging it in a brown paper bag, open end down. Aim the stem ends toward the bottom end of the open bag, cluster stem ends and tie together with a rubber band so that the basil stems are hanging toward the open top of the bag. Secure near the rubber band with a thumb tack to a high ceiling beam or fasten to a hanger and hang in a cool airy location. To test for dryness put a few leaves in a tightly closed jar; check for condensation."

Mrs. James Wheeler of Virginia dries basil on a cake rack in a very slow oven (250 degrees). When thoroughly dry, she crushes the leaves and stores them in dark glass jars kept in a cupboard.

From Mrs. Jeanne Lindaman of Pennsylvania, "Don't dry basil; freeze it. Wash and pat leaves between paper towels. Lay them on cookie sheets, put in freezer until frozen. When dry, put them in plastic freezer containers. Take out leaves as you need them. Or buy a package of basil seeds, sow them in a flower pot and snip off what you need."

chinese lanterns

Q: Last year we planted Chinese lantern in our garden. They grew well, but when I dried them the main stem was too weak to hold the lanterns and the lanterns shriveled up. How can I have better results this year? Mrs. L. S.

A: Mrs. Edith Kao of New York cuts her plants near the ground when the lanterns turn orange. Then she ties the stems in a bunch and hangs them upside down. When dry, she strips off the leaves and arranges the lanterns in a vase.

189

Q: How do you dry or freeze-dry chives? Mrs. A. C., Long Island

A: Karen Young of New York writes, "Chives should be frozen. They lose a great deal of flavor when dried. To freeze them, snip the desired amount, wash them gently, pat dry with a paper towel. Place them in an air-tight, frozen-food container and place in the freezer."

currants

Q: Our currant bushes are prolific bearers and I use them for jams and jellies. But now I would like to dry them for plum puddings and Dundee cake. Does anyone know how? Mrs. C. H. L., Fair Lawn, N.J.

A: Stuart C. Dobson of Westchester County writes, "Currant bushes are of the genus Ribes, related to gooseberry. The dried currant used for baking is the raisin of a dwarf seedless grape from Corinth, hence the name currant. The confusion dates back to sixteenth century England."

flowers

Q: What types of flowers are best for drying? Is there a simple method of drying that can be done in most homes? Mrs. J. S.

A: Here are two replies. From Mrs. Warren Naugler of Connecticut, "The best flowers for drying easily are wild flowers such as goldenrod, butterfly weed, Queen Anne's lace, etc. Garden flowers to dry are hydrangea, strawflowers and statice. Strip the leaves from the stems, tie the flowers in bunches of one type and hang them upside down in the attic. They dry in about a week."

And from Miss Margaret Caskey in New Jersey, "Though many people recommend corn-meal and borax mixed for drying flowers, I have had good results with silica gel. Flowers are broken off with 1½ to 2-inch stems and laid upside down in a tin box with a tight cover. Sift a layer of the silica-gel over the flowers to cover and tape the can shut for a week or so. Success has been achieved with Queen Anne's lace, daisies, black-eyed susans, single French marigolds, cornflowers and wild chicory. I also dry weeds throughout the summer; timothy, wild geranium, wild bergamot, wild Chinese lantern. Try spraying dried plant material with a clear plastic. It minimizes shedding."

Unscented hair spray can also be used to guard against shedding with fair results. Ed.

gourds

Q: How do you dry gourds without their molding, rotting or deteriorating? I am growing the large kind from which bird-

190

houses will be made and have tried various drying methods and failed. Has anyone solved this? Mrs. W. R., Pittstown, N.J.

A: Mrs. Muriel Finneran of Long Island forwarded the following information. "Pick the gourds after several light frosts and dry in the attic. After several months, they will turn to light brown and be ready for use when the seeds inside rattle. Cut an opening 1¼-inch in diameter on the side about five inches from the bottom. Hang with the entrance facing south and away from prevailing winds."

Mrs. Joseph H. Orr, Sr., Altoona, Pa., offered another method with "extremely good results. Do not pick gourds until stems are very dry and ready to break. Take indoors and place over a radiator or where there is warmth. Each day, wipe with a cloth saturated with alcohol. It may take several months until the gourds are dry. Seeds will rattle when gourd is shaken. Then cut hole for birdhouse and shake out seeds."

Mrs. D. D. D., Bennington, Vt., writes, "Cut holes two inches wide but high enough to keep baby birds from falling out. Three small holes bored at the bottom of the gourds allow for drainage. Paint them, preferably white."

Mrs. Harald Bergen of Connecticut writes, "There is no special trick to drying gourds but the gourds must be thoroughly ripe before picking, otherwise they rot. The stem where the gourds are attached to the vine will shrivel, turn brown, when fruits are ripe. Cut gourds off with a sharp knife, never pull, and allow a few inches of stem to remain on each. Wash them well and dry to get off any mud and grime. Dry fruits in an open, airy sheltered place, for a week or so. Shellac or wax to make them shine."

hydrangea

Q: We have tried several suggested methods for drying hydrangea, without success. Does anyone know how to dry and/or preserve the blue and pink snowballs? Mrs. M. O. McC., Sausalito, Calif.

A: Here are two ideas. Mrs. Elyse Underberg, a Long Island reader, says, "I have never had a problem drying hydrangea. I cut the stems on a cool day, remove all the leaves and place them in a vase to dry. I have never experienced any difficulty. The flower color does tend to fade a bit, but the dried flowers take on very interesting colors. The pink seems to dry the best and will last all winter as a floral display."

And from a New Jersey reader, C. Jane Boning, "The most successful drying is with a silica gel product, using care as the powder is poured to preserve the shape of the bloom.

191

(drying *continued***)**

Drying in this manner, I have preserved the color for a three-year period. Blossoms dried with silica gel must be packaged during the summer because they will reabsorb moisture during this period."

lavender

Q: There must be a way to dry lavender and retain the fragrance. I have tried but find the scent quickly disappears. Has anyone a special secret? Mrs. I. S., Gloversville, N.Y.

A: Mrs. Bruce Randall, a New Hampshire reader, suggests, "Perhaps Mrs. I. S. is not growing the most fragrant plants. There are about 30 species of lavender with many varieties and hybrids. The most fragrant are *Lavendula officinalis* from which several selections have been made and nurseries specializing in herbs list them. Lavender should be picked in the morning before the heat of the day just as the flowers are fully open. I check my plants every morning and cut a few stems each day. I hang them to dry and in a few days, the flower heads can be rubbed off the stalks to use in sachets and potpourri."

locust pods

See Locust pods, page 102.

mushroom

Q: Can anyone tell me how to dry fresh mushrooms? They have a superlative flavor. T. G., Pennsylvania

A: Kathleen D. Scott, a New York reader, writes, "It is very simple and worthwhile. Use a narrow-eyed needle and strong thread. Sew fresh mushrooms into a chain, pushing the needle in through the bottom of the stem and out through the top of the crown. Tie a toothpick or matchstick in the end of the thread (as they dry, the holes will enlarge). Hang the string of mushrooms in a warm dry place. Drying takes about two weeks. When dried, put the mushrooms in a jar or wrap in cellophane. To reconstitute, whole or crumpled, pour boiling water to cover and let sit for 15 minutes."

rose petals

Q: Are some rose petals better for drying than others? Neighbors dry their rose petals at the same time I do for potpourri, but their mixture is always more colorful. Why? Mrs. G. T., New Jersey

A: Mrs. Kenneth David, another New Jersey gardener, offers these suggestions. "It may be that Mrs. G. T. is picking her roses for drying at the wrong time of day. I always cut my roses early in the morning before the sun is high and while the foliage is damp with dew. Choose the finest roses,

192

fully developed. Some of my favorites are the most fragrant hybrid teas: Crimson Glory, dark red; Charlotte Armstrong, pink; Mister Lincoln, red; Sutter's Gold, yellow; Tiffany, pink; and Tropicana, red-orange. Next break apart the roses and spread them on an old window screen supported on two chairs. (I use the dining room which faces east, is airy and cool.) Shuffle through the petals gently each morning with an old spatula until the petals are crisp, like cereal. Then store in an air-tight jar until enough petals are gathered to mix the potpourri."

strawberries

Q: Has anyone ever heard of a method of drying strawberries? Mrs. W. L.

A: Kim Kimble of New York says that she does not know a practical way of drying strawberries at home, but they are done commercially for back packing and hiking. The fruits are frozen and dehydrated in a vacuum.

strawflower

Q: I have been fortunate enough to raise strawflowers in my garden this year, but now I am at a loss to know how to dry them. Does anyone know? Dr. H. L. R., Delaware

A: Mrs. Evelyn Wenber of Long Island suggests, "Harvest the strawflowers when they are ⅓ to ½ open. They will open more fully as they dry. Strip all leaves off the stem and bunch the flowers to hang upside down on a line or wire coat hanger to dry. Do not expose them to direct sunlight."

strawflower wiring

Q: I have successfully grown and dried strawflowers, but I am having difficulty trying to put wires into the tiny blooms without crushing them. How should it be done and is there a special kind of wire? Mrs. C. W. C., New Jersey

A: Miss M. McPhee of Ohio recommends, "Soak dried strawflowers in lukewarm water for 20 minutes. Remove from water and drain a half hour. Push florist wire, sold in coils, through flower from the back, form a small hook and pull back into flower. With this method I have been able to wire very small flowers and even buds. When dry, all flowers and buds will revert to original appearance."

sunflower seeds

Q: My daughter grew sunflowers this summer, but now the blue jays are pecking out the seeds. How do we dry and harvest the seeds for eating ourselves? Mrs. N. K., New Jersey

A: Mrs. Judy McGinn of Pennsylvania suggests, "When birds peck seeds, they are ready for drying. Cut off the flower heads, leaving a foot of stalk attached to the head. Hang

193

them upside down to dry. When dry, rub two flower heads together over newspaper or a box to remove seeds. Hull seeds to eat them. Store in air tight jars."

Dr. M. C. Moross of New York suggests, "After drying, bake the ripe seeds in a moderate oven (200 to 250 degrees) for about five minutes. They're delicious!"

storing
Jerusalem artichoke

Q: How can I store my Jerusalem artichokes after they are dug so they do not shrink and dry out? Mrs. E. L. J., Quogue, N. Y.

A: Here are several ideas. From C. Suzanne Blatz of New Hampshire, "They are best left in the ground and dug as needed. A hay mulch put over the area now would probably permit Mrs. E. L. J. to dig tubers all winter."

From George Degener, another Long Island reader, "Do not wash Jerusalem artichokes before storing. Take them out of the ground, put them in a box or basket and cover with dry sand. Place in a cool, dry place. Mine keep for months this way."

And from Thomas Mozell, a New Jersey reader, "For outside storage, I use a supermarket lettuce crate and fill it with leaves or seaweed and disperse the artichokes through-out. If they freeze, I thaw them out before use. Or wash them thoroughly and put in a plastic vegetable bag and store in the refrigerator."

tomatoes

Q: Our tomato plants are still full of green fruits. Frost is just around the corner, and we want to save the tomatoes. What clues can anyone offer on good storage methods? G. G. C.

A: Here are three suggestions for G. G. C.'s question on storing green tomatoes. From Christine Burton of New York, "When I lived in the mountains, we always had an early frost. To save the tomatoes, we would dig up the whole tomato plants with the green fruits on them and hang them upside down in a woodshed. The tomatoes kept ripening gradually. Lacking a woodshed, a cool basement would do."

From Mrs. William Ramsey of New York, "For years I have been ripening green tomatoes by wrapping them separately in a half-sheet of newspaper. I then place them in a box and put it in the bottom of a closet. Check them frequently and they ripen gradually."

From Harold Lindemann of New Jersey, "The simple but successful way is to lay the green tomatoes on newspapers in the basement. Cover them with newspaper. There is no need to wrap them. Every day or so lift up the newspaper and pick out the ripe ones. Some years I have had ripe tomatoes until Christmas."

vegetables in the ground

Q: This spring when checking my garden, I found I had overlooked a leek from the previous year. It survived the winter and proved to be tasty. Are there any other vegetables that can be wintered in the ground for spring harvest? How do I do it? R. B. P., Westport, Conn.

A: Here are two ideas. Mrs. Anna Zollinger, a New York state reader, suggests, "Leeks. Put a thick mulch of leaves around the plants before the ground freezes. Dig and use them all winter and in spring, before they flower." She also suggests keeping over Brussels sprouts, parsley, kale and DeCicco broccoli.

Fred Lowenfels, a Westchester County reader, adds, "I have eaten carrots up to April and beets but the most gratifying are parsnips. Cover the rows with a foot of leaves or pine needles and take up what is needed each week. Be sure to mark the ends of each row with a stick to know where to dig! For winter keeping plant parsnips in spring, but beets and carrots in July or August."

Carol Delaney of New York recommends hilling over the plants with straw, several inches thick. "This will prevent the ground from freezing hard, and harvest can be delayed until December if the weather is not unusually cold."

treating pine cones

Q: When I was a boy we burned cones dipped in chemicals to add colors to the fireplace. My five-year-old son likes the idea, but what chemicals are used and how? J. R. R., Connecticut

A: Many readers came to his rescue. Their answers were best summed up by a letter from Mrs. John A. McKenna of Delaware. "This is our recipe: copper sulphate, blue; calcium chloride, orange; lithium chloride, purple; strontium chloride, red; potassium chloride, lavender; copper chloride, green. Wear rubber gloves and work outside or in a well ventilated place. Dissolve a pound of chemical in each gallon of water in a plastic bucket, not any kind of metal. If the water is warm, the chemicals dissolve better. Let the cones soak several hours, then spread out to dry. Old cones absorb more chemical solution; the new ones are sappy. And please remind J. R. R. to supervise his 5-year-old while using the chemicals."

other hints and what have you

acid–alkaline

Q: Our house is fronted with some large rhododendrons and azaleas. We would like to introduce some sunny hypericums and potentillas for summer bloom color but these plants require alkaline soil while the evergreens require acid soil. How can we accomplish our goal? J. L. R., New Rochelle, N. Y.

A: J. L. R. is trying to accomplish a very difficult thing by trying to grow acid soil and alkaline soil plants on the same property. Nature just doesn't work that way, according to Dr. J. B. de G., Cambridge, Mass. Plants with similar environmental needs should be selected for the best results. Trying to mix plants of differing requirements, so basic as soil, can lead to problems. Most of the soils in the Northeast are predominantly slightly acid, a plus for gardeners because the loveliest ornamentals prefer slightly acid soil.

cemetery plantings

Q: Has anyone found a solution for attractive plants for a family gravesite? The maintenance is deplorable and we would like to know of something that will be attractive yet survive without much care. Mrs. T. Y., Trenton, N. J.

A: Here are two suggestions. From Mrs. Florence Just, a Long Island reader, "A sedum called live-forever is a hardy plant that requires little care and will survive lack of moisture and attention. In the fall, lovely lavender flowers appear."

And from a New Jersey reader, Mrs. Joseph Brown, "Myrtle will grow year-round but must be fertilized periodically. I have also planted narcissus and snowdrop bulbs and the myrtle acts as a protective cover for them."

196

ivy

Q: Can anyone suggest a sturdy ivy that will thrive from season to season on a gravesite? We have had no success with plants tried and replanting is costly. Miss M. K., Brooklyn, N. Y.

A: Mrs. D. Dexter Davis of Vermont suggests "Instead of planting ivy, why not try the small-leaved euonymus, *E. fortunei minimus,* which is hardy in Vermont and a graceful vine."

children's summer garden

Q: We are renting a seaside cottage for July and August. Are there any vegetables or flowers our children (7 and 9) could grow in the short period? Mrs. G. L. M., Manhattan

A: *The ideal would be to find a garden center that still has available some annual seedlings that could be transplanted to the garden for a quick display. That late in the year, the selection dwindles. A few vegetables such as leaf lettuce and radish could be started from seed. If there are any cherry tomato seedlings available at garden centers, these could be grown as well. Ed.*

christmas tree

Q: What should I do with my Christmas tree after the holidays? It seems sad to toss it on the dump heap. Ideas, anyone? M. N.

A: *We suggest three practical uses for the cut tree. Poke it in the ground outdoors and trim it with tidbits for birds such as peanut-suet balls, strung popcorn, orange-halfs filled with sunflower seed, etc. Or, trim off the branches and use them for mulch over perennial borders and as "fencing" around tender evergreens. Or, many municipalities have tree recycle days when trees can be taken to the town's mechanical chipping equipment to be chopped and bagged for mulch in the garden. Ed.*

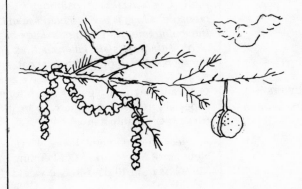

197

coldframe

Q: Our new house has a coldframe built by the previous owner. How soon will it be safe for us to plant vegetables in it for early harvest? H. L. P., Hartford, Conn.

A: Virginia Terris, a Long Island gardener, writes, "Judging from my experience, a coldframe is an all-year supplier of food. Lettuce has been plentiful throughout the cold months. I put it in in October and have been picking it all winter. It is heading now (February)."

creosote
on railroad ties

Q: Do we have to treat old railroad ties before using them to terrace a slope? We would like to plant along their edges. Mrs. K. W. M., New Jersey

A: Old railroad ties should not be a problem as the creosote preservative has weathered. If there is any doubt, the ties could be painted with a primer-sealer available in paint stores, but it should not be necessary. Ed.

on telephone pole

Q: I planted silver lace vine to camouflage a telephone pole. However, the creosote on the pole is proving caustic to the plant and the tips have dried up. Is there anything I can do to the pole to prevent this, or should I give up? Mrs. M. K. P., Connecticut

A: S. A. Whitlow of New York suggests that she cover the telephone pole with chicken wire to a height suitable for vine growing, 16 to 20 feet. Use pointed tacks or a staple gun to fasten it loosely to encircle the post. He suggests growing morning glories or nasturtiums.

toxicity

Q: Two years ago I built a coldframe and made the mistake of painting it with creosote. How long do I have to wait before the toxicity of creosote to plants wears off? Is there anything I can do now to neutralize it? S. G.

A: S. G.'s mistake of painting a wooden coldframe with creosote, which is toxic to plants, can be rectified by painting the coldframe with either a latex-based stain killer or an alcohol thinned stain killer such as Enamelac or B. I. N. If the stain seeps through the first coat, apply a second coat. Ed.

cut flowers

Q: I can't keep cut flowers much longer than a day or two, especially roses. I put them in fresh water. Is there some trick? J. G., Manhattan

A: He received many ideas. Here are some. From Julie Neumar of New York, "On keeping roses, mist them daily. Mine last from 10 days to two weeks."

Esther Kluss of New York referred to a magazine article which recommended a pinch of salt in the water or the use of liquid chlorine bleach which disinfects the water and keeps it sweet. A similar suggestion from Myra M. Patner of Maryland mentions using, "½ water with ½ Seven-Up soda plus one to two tablespoonfuls of laundry bleach. The soda supplies sugar and the bleach disinfects."

Daryl Altman of New York suggests, "The trick is to recut stems at an angle with a sharp knife and put the flowers in hot tap water for a half-hour. Then pour out the hot water and put in fresh cold water. Recut stems daily."

Eric B. Schecter also of New York, "smashes his flower stems a bit and adds dishwashing detergent." Other ideas were to keep them in the refrigerator at night or to add charcoal to the water.

double lilacs

Q: In anticipation of May bloom, how do you keep French double lilacs from wilting when cut? No problem with the singles. R. B., Westchester County, N.Y.

A: Another Westchester County reader comes to the rescue. Mrs. Elliot Seward writes, "I found out the hard way. First remove most of the green leaves from each stem. Then smash the bottom of the stem with a hammer and immerse immediately in a pail of water (temperature doesn't matter). A period in a dark, cool place will also help."

forcing branches

Q: Has anyone had good success forcing dogwood? I would appreciate some clues. H. G. L.

A: Mrs. Gerald W. Johnson of Maryland has some help. "The process is the same as for forcing forsythia. Bring the dogwood branches indoors when the buds begin to swell. Put them in water and set them in a sunny window. Dogwood buds take a little more time to open. The flowers are miniatures, an exquisite pale-pink tan, suggesting an Oriental scroll painting."

identifying plants

Q: We are new homeowners and have many unusual shrubs and trees on the grounds. We know some plants, but these are foreign to us. Is there anywhere we can turn to have the plants identified so we can care for them properly? Our house is in northern Westchester. Mr. and Mrs. D. K. E.

A: To help Mr. and Mrs. D. K. E. to identify the plants on their property here are two excellent suggestions. Dr. Howard S. Irwin, executive director of the New York Botanical Garden, writes, "The New York Botanical Garden,

199

Bronx Park, N.Y. 10458, operates a plant identification office, staffed by professional botanists, which not only provides plant identification services but also offers horticultural tips and advice. Instructions for submitting plant material by mail can be obtained by writing the garden."

Mrs. John Stanton of New York suggests a helpful book published by Syracuse University Press. It is a ring-bound paper edition entitled, *Trees, Shrubs and Vines, A Pictorial Guide to the Ornamental Woody Plants of the Northern United States Exclusive of Conifers* by Dr. Arthur T. Viertel. Available from Syracuse University Press, Syracuse, N.Y. 13210.

importing plants

Q: We are going to spend part of January in the Caribbean and would like to bring back some of the unusual plants we find there. What are the Federal regulations for importing plants? R. T., Manhattan

A: *Gardeners must have a permit to bring live plant material into the U.S.A. from foreign sources. Permit applicants should describe the plants in question by their scientific name, if at all possible. Travelers originating from the U.S. Virgin Islands, Puerto Rico and Hawaii can import plants, without a permit, if they are free of sand, soil or earth. Failure to comply with these quarantine regulations results in loss of the plant material or delay. For permit applications, contact: Plant Importation Office, Permit Section, United States Department of Agriculture, 209 River Street, Hoboken, N.J. 07030; phone 201-433-4510, ext. 301. Ed.*

landscape architects

Q: We live in a large old house, Tudor style, and would like to bring a sense of solitude to the landscape and have a professional submit a plan to us. Can you tell us how to locate a good landscape architect who will help us with our hopes? Mrs. C. K.

A: *Mrs. C. K.'s question on how to locate a landscape architect brought to the surface a common problem with homeowners. Here are two approaches. For the refurbishing, updating or remodeling of a landscape planting, the most practical solution is a visit to a local, well established nursery which has a landscape designer on the staff. A new plan and planting arrangements can be worked out in this way. Or, if a particularly pleasing planting in the neighborhood suggests a scheme for your own plans, inquiries might be made as to the designer. A professional, licensed landscape architect, on the other hand, is the person to call upon when a new home is being placed on a site, or a large scale property plan is to be worked out. Usually the architect can suggest a landscape architect or a local office of the American Society of Landscape Architects may be available for assistance. Ed.*

light at night

Q: My back yard is illuminated from dusk to dawn with spot lights. What influence does this have on plant growth? Dr. H. B.

A: To answer Dr. H. B.'s query on the effect of night lighting on plant growth, here is an answer from Home and Garden Bulletin No. 188, *Growing Ornamentals in Urban Gardens,* available for 15 cents from Superintendent of Documents, U.S. Government Printing Office, Washington, D.C. 20402. "Several kinds of lamps may be used for lighting gardens at night, including ordinary incandescent lamps, incandescent flood lamps, mercury lamps and high-pressure sodium lamps. . . . Incandescent lamps of all kinds will alter plant growth if they are used too many hours each day.

"If you use incandescent lamps, light your plants only in the early evening. If you keep the light on later than 9:30 to 10 P.M., the extra light will cause the plants to grow and flower later in the season. Serious cold damage may result when plants continue to grow into the fall.

"Ordinary mercury lamps and high pressure sodium lamps are extremely efficient light sources and they do not cause plants to grow and flower longer than the regular season. . . . High-pressure sodium lamps appear amber to the eye and do not attract insects.

"Both mercury and high-pressure sodium lamps require special installation. They cannot be used in ordinary incandescent light fixtures."

moon phases

Q: Is there any substance to the theory expounded in the *Farmer's Almanac* that the moon has a significant effect on plants and that crops should be planted in accordance with certain phases of the moon? R. T. A.

A: "R. T. A. may be referring only to that small part of lunar astrology found in almanacs which advises to sow seeds or plant in the waxing phase (new to full) of the moon. If a person wants to believe in this particular nonsense, he can easily do so since half the time the moon waxes and half the time it wanes. By relating to the phases of the moon, an appropriately rationalized theory can always be verified." Dr. Louis Winkler, Pennsylvania State University

The Old Farmer's Almanac *publishes the nodes of the moon on its calendar pages. According to the Almanac, "Many farmers plant for more rapid growth during the ascending node (of the moon); and cut brush, prune, etc., during the descending node when things don't grow as well." Ed.*

moving to Florida

Q: We have recently purchased a home in Fort Lauderdale and would like to take some northern plants there to feel at home—rhododendrons, azaleas, any you might suggest. Mrs. J. D. S., Jackson Heights

A: Mrs. G. E. Kendall of Florida discourages such a measure and writes, "No northern plants will 'feel at home' in Florida. Northern plants need a spell of coldness. Besides who needs northern plants? As a gardner who moved from Westchester County six years ago, for every plant growing in the North, there is a tropical plant to match that may be even more beautiful. When you retire to Florida don't look back at Long Island. Look ahead to your future in a tropical land where palms sway and the sun beams almost every day."

oil soak

Q: A pipe feeding oil into our house burst and the oil spilled into the ground. It killed the grass and flowers. Now what do we do? P. A. M., Brooklyn

A: M. L. B. Hill of Massachusetts had a similar problem. He suggests, "Wait two years for complete damage to develop for insurance claims. Remove oil-soaked soil below two feet, replace and you should be able to grow plants again."

seed
harvesting

Q: Although I know it is not recommended, just out of pure curiosity, how would I obtain seeds from my own vegetable garden? And what about flower seeds? Mrs. D. H. B., Jr., Huntington, N.Y.

A: *As the questioner points out, saving back-yard vegetable and flower seed is not recommended as so many of the modern varieties are hybrids and self-infertile. Because of their complicated parentage they may revert to the parent type. However, for those who want to experiment, simply allow several plants to bolt or go to seed, that is send up a flower stalk and it will form its own seed. To save seed of beans, melons, tomatoes, etc.,allow the fruit to ripen fully on the vine (beyond eating ripeness) to mature the seed inside. Ed.*

Jack C. Rossetter of Illinois says, "She can save the seeds of annuals known to seed themselves such as larkspur, dianthus, violas, portulaca, daisies and hollyhocks, zinnias, dahlias, morning glories and four o'clocks. Bury a few cherry tomatoes and they'll produce early and well next year."

left over

Q: We left all our leftover vegetable seed in our unwinterized country house. Will the cold temperatures kill the seed or can I use them again? Is keeping seed for the following season a good idea anyway? Mrs. B. K., Manhattan

A: M. J. Mosse of Connecticut writes that there is a discussion of seed longevity in *Wyman's Gardening Encyclopedia*. Dr. Wyman states that "many annual flower seeds keep their viability 2 or 3 years . . . and vegetable seed up to 10 years." The key is proper storage . . . and much depends on the individual seed.

James Aldrich of New York writes, "Recommended conditions for seed storage are cool dry places, covered but not sealed. Ideally, temperatures should be 23–41 degrees. To see if kept-over seeds are viable, test them. Take a portion of them and place them in a moist paper towel or between two damp blotters. Keep moist in a shady place to prevent their drying out. If a high percentage germinates, they are good to use."

slime mold on a brick patio

Q: During the summer months, the bricks on our densely shaded outdoor terrace acquire a slippery coating of a slime mold. Is there a way to correct this without staining the bricks? Mrs. L. A. R., Rhode Island

A: Mrs. George W. Schiele of Connecticut suggests " a solution of Lo-Bax and water. Lo-Bax is a sanitizer, algicide, etc., sold in paint and hardware stores. It should be applied with a stiff scrubbing brush and then rinsed thoroughly."

The product is a granular dry form of chlorine and should be used with care and flushed well. Ed.

soil testing

Q: I am planning my first organic vegetable garden and I would like to have my soil tested. Where do I send the sample? Ms J. W., New York

A: *Local offices of Cooperative Extension will test soil samples for home gardeners. Offices are located in the county seats and listed in the telephone book, usually under county agencies. Fee for soil tests is usually $2. It will report the soil pH (degree of acidity or alkalinity). Soil samples should* be taken from assorted areas in the garden to a depth of four to six inches. Mix well and send a half-pint sampling in a plastic bag, protected in a cardboard box or book-mailer. Ed.

sprays—home-made

Q: I have heard of using cayenne pepper and garlic powder as insect repellent sprays for vegetable gardens. Can anyone tell me how to use these sprays and how to mix them? Mrs. C. T.

A: Ty Tyler says, "Here in San Diego, the pest problem is a big one. Being organically oriented, I won't use pesticides and have tried infinite concoctions to repel bugs. My best results have been garlic and cayenne pepper used as a spray. I run a couple of fresh garlic cloves through the blender and add about an ounce of cayenne pepper. This is added to an equal amount of water, strained and sprayed on the plants. I use it once or twice a week to control bugs, worms, spiders, aphids, mites and pets."

water
how much?

Q: I read that vegetable gardens need an inch of rain (or water) a week. Not having a rain gauge, how do I calculate how many hours I leave the sprinkler on the garden to achieve that one inch? Miss A. E. C., Crestwood, N. Y.

A: Floyd Parliman, a New York state gardener, writes, "Use a straight sided can (such as a coffee can), set it upright in the middle of the sprinkler area. See how long it takes for one inch of water to collect in the container, which would be the equivalent of one inch of rain."

rain

Q: Forty years ago my grandfather would not water his garden with anything but rainwater which he collected in wooden barrels. Aside from water conservation, are there any merits to this? D. H.

A: William H. Hall of Delaware says that there are. "Electrical lightning in the atmosphere fixes nitrogen in the water vapor present. This nitrogen is brought to earth as rainwater. Therefore rainwater contains more nitrogen than groundwater used for irrigation and is superior for raising plants."

Dr. W. P. L. McBride of Vermont concurs. "For several years my wife has watered her indoor plants with melted snow water warmed to room temperature. Any gardener will tell you that the vegetable leaves are always greener after a warm rain than they are when watered with tap water or spring water."

204

Q: Our Connecticut property has a well, and water supply for the garden is limited. Our brook is a potential source but it means lifting the water about 30 feet with hose lines 400 feet long to the yard. Does anyone have any suggestions for an inexpensive pumping system? Dr. E. M. C.

A: Several helpful answers were received. Here are a few of them. Mrs. Walter Bregman of Connecticut writes, "We had a nearly identical situation which we solved with a self-priming centrifugal pump from Sears, which we placed beside our backyard pool. The pump was hooked up to a basement switch and we ran enough lengths of garden hose under shubbery to bring the water supply to a convenient spot in front of the house. This system provides enough pressure to use two lawn sprinklers at one time."

And a neighbor in Connecticut writes, "We had struggled for more than 50 years with country water supplies and the ideal solution is a hydraulic ram. I now lift more than a gallon a minute 75 feet through a ¾-inch plastic pipe, almost 1,000 feet long. Once the ram is started in spring, it works day and night until frost."

window box
planting

Q: Now that it is seed ordering time, I would like some help on what to grow successfully in two window boxes that are heavily shaded by oak trees except for about an hour's sun a day. B. B. N.

A: From Dr. Wallace Lipton of New York, "Fuchsia would be ideal. A small number of inexpensive plants bought in the spring, both upright and trailing kinds. In late winter I cut my plants down to three inches and root the prunings in water and save them for the next year."

From Mrs. H. H. Foster of Connecticut, "Tuberous-rooted begonias are very showy if the location is not too windy; wax begonias interplanted with variegated vinca or small-leaved ivy or dwarf impatiens."

And from Robert Birds of New Jersey, "I have found coleus and impatiens do very well. A wide variety of colors are available."

soil

Q: I have been using the same soil mixture for planter boxes every year adding peat moss, cow manure and compost. The past few years my petunias were stunted and my marigolds didn't perform. What is the solution? Mrs. H. L. P., Brooklyn

A: Ray Tackett of Pennsylvania writes, "The condition of her plants suggests that a fungus has established itself in her planter boxes. Farm manures and compost are often sources of fungi and it is wise to sterilize such material before using. Replacement of the soil may not do the job, since fungi live on in the wood planter boxes. Wooden boxes can be treated with formaldehyde, one pint commercial formalin to fifty pints of water is satisfactory. Soak the planter for 24 hours, cover and keep outdoors because of the toxic fumes.''

in winter

Q: What can anyone suggest for brightening up window boxes and planters during the winter months? We have several around our home and they always look so drab from November to early spring when the bulbs bloom. J. J. K.

A: Many ideas came in to help J. J. K. with decorating window boxes in winter. From Mrs. M. E. Schultz of New Jersey, ''I tacked a wooden board across the window box outside my kitchen window and to it tacked some green indoor–outdoor rug. I placed a large piece of driftwood on the rug and made it secure. Around it were attached several evergreen boughs. All winter long I placed bird food in and around the boughs. At first the birds hesitated to feed, but gradually they came and went as they pleased.''

From Mrs. Ann O'Neill of New Jersey, ''Fill the boxes with evergreen boughs which are always available around Christmas time. Try to get them in place before the ground freezes.''

From Mrs. Robert Gillespie, Washington, D.C., ''My answer for the past three years is inexpensive artificial boxwood. We have a small garden scene from the living room through French doors, and as soon as frost kills the impatiens, I 'plant' the boxwood hedge. The artificial material can be washed, dried and stored for the next year.''

And from F. V. Wedekind of New York, ''Plant heather in them. It is colorful all winter and needs no watering once it has settled in the box.''

index

Transplantation. *See also under individual
    plants*
  of annuals, 120–121
  of bulbs, 124
Tree roses, 138
Tree stumps, 165–166
Trees. *See also under individual names of*
  in city garden, 51
  indoors, 67
  ivy on, 115
  nails in, 162–163
  seedlings for, 166
  wintering over of, 53
Tulips
  and animal pests, 82, 91
  blossom rot, 139–140
  forcing, 42

Vanilla beans, 187
Vegetable gardens (Vegetables). *See also
    under individual names of*
  black plastic mulch in, 96
  for children, 197
  fertilizers for. *See* Fertilizers
  indoors, 42–44
  iron in, 101
  late, 174
  mulches for. *See* Mulch
  as ornamentals, 182
  for weekend gardener, 51
  wintered in ground, 195
Venus fly trap, 44, 55
Vine borer, 179
Vines, on city terrace, 51
Vermiculite, 136
Violets
  candied, 184
  as weeds, 93, 111

Walnuts
  curing of, 187–188
  propagation of, 166
Water garden, for children, 55–56
Watercress, 182–183
Watering (water). *See also under individual
    plants*
  amount required, 204

  in decorative container, 67–68
  for herbs, 29
  from rain, 204
  from stream, 205
  while away, 51, 68
Wax plant, 57–58
Weed killers, 86, 111
Weeds
  bindweed, 83–84
  between bricks, 92
  in driveways, 92–93
  in groundcovers, 118–119
  nettle, 85
  onion and garlic grass, 85
  ponds, 86
  violets as, 93
  in zoysia lawn, 112
Wheat hulls, 136
White fly, 12, 93–94
Wild flowers, 140
Wilt, of silk tree, 164
Window boxes
  planting of, 205
  in winter, 206
Windy areas, mulch in, 102–103
Winter care. *See also under individual plants*
  of evergreens, 145–146
Wisteria, 141–142
Wood, termites in, 92
Wood ashes, as soil additive, 63, 106
Wood rose, from seed, 45
Woodchucks, 80–81

Yellow jackets, 94–95
Yellowing
  on fronds of ferns, 21–22
  of pachysandra, 118
  of yew, 155
Yew tree, 155

Zebra plant, care of, 45–46
Zineb, 28, 132
Zinnia, 120
Zoysia lawn, 111, 112
Zucchini, and squash bugs, 178–179
Zygocactus (Christmas cactus), 12

HB9E